6.50

Recollections

Colette

RECOLLECTIONS

Includes

Journey for Myself

and

The Evening Star

*Translations from the French and Prefaces
by David Le Vay*

B
COLETTE

COLLIER BOOKS
MACMILLAN PUBLISHING COMPANY
NEW YORK

Macmillan Publishing Company
866 Third Avenue, New York, N.Y. 10022

Library of Congress Cataloging-in-Publication Data
Colette, 1873–1954.
Recollections: includes Journey for myself and The evening star.
Translations of: Le voyage égoïste and L'étoile vesper.
1. Colette, 1873–1954—Biography. 2. Colette, 1873–
1954—Translations, English. 3. Authors, French—20th
century—Biography. I. Colette, 1873–1954. Etoile
vesper. English. 1986. II. Title.
PQ2605.028Z4713   1986   848'.91209 [B]   86-13686
ISBN 0-02-013360-X

Macmillan books are available at special discounts
for bulk purchases for sales promotions, premiums,
fund-raising, or educational use. For details, contact:
Special Sales Director
Macmillan Publishing Company
866 Third Avenue
New York, New York 10022

10 9 8 7 6 5 4 3 2 1

Printed in the United States of America

Contents

Journey for Myself

Preface

The first four essays in this volume—*Sunday*, *I'm Hot*, *Respite* and *Invalid*—originally appeared in *La Chambre Éclairée*. They were first collected for publication, together with a number of other essays from the same and other sources and entitled *Le Voyage Égoïste*, under the signature of Colette Willy in a *de luxe* edition illustrated by coloured lithographs issued by Éditions d'Art Édouard Pelletan in 1922.

In 1928 Ferenczi, using the same title, published the four essays named above and included a group of fashion articles written by Colette for *Vogue* between 1925 and 1927; the latter were accorded the subtitle *Quatre Saisons*.

At about the same time a dozen of these later essays of Colette were privately published by Philippe Ortiz for his friends in a volume also entitled *Quatre Saisons*. But the rest of this volume included the last group of essays, the *Aventures Quotidiennes*, which did not appear in any generally published version until their inclusion in the *Oeuvres Complètes* of the Le Fleuron edition of 1949, from which they are now translated for the first time.

The publishers of the present volume wish to express their gratitude to Monsieur Maurice Goudeket for his help in making available for translation some of this material.

Journey for Myself

Sunday

What's the matter with you? Don't bother to answer 'Nothing', bravely screwing up your features; the next moment the corners of your mouth fall again, your eyelids droop over your eyes, and your chin is really regrettable. *I* know what's the matter with you.

Your trouble is that it's Sunday, and raining. If you were a woman you'd burst into tears because it's raining and it's Sunday, but you're a man and you daren't. You lend an ear to the sound of the fine rain—the trickling sound of thirsty sand—despite yourself you contemplate the glistening street and the mournful closed shops, and you take a grip on your poor masculine nerves, you hum a little tune, light a cigarette which you forget and which goes out in your dangling fingers. . . .

I'd really rather wait till you've had enough and come to me for help. . . . You think that's malicious? No, it's just that I'm so fond of your childish way of stretching out your arms to me and dropping your head on my shoulder as if you were giving it to me for keeps. But it's raining so gloomily and it's so Sundayish today that, even before you ask, I make the three magic passes: draw the curtains, light the lamp, and arrange on the divan, among your favourite cushions, my shoulder, hollowed for your cheek, and my arm ready to encircle your neck.

Is it nice like this? Not yet? Lie quiet then, wait for our shared animal warmth to penetrate the cushions. Slowly the silk loses its chill under my cheek, under my back, your head gradually sinks on my shoulder and your whole body becomes heavy and limp beside me and spreads out as if you were melting. . . .

Don't say anything: I can hear your great shuddering sighs better than words. . . . You hold your breath, you're afraid your sigh may end in tears. Ah, if only you dared. . . .

There, I've thrown my blue scarf over the lamp; across the stems of a tall bunch of chrysanthemums you can barely see the firelight dancing; stay there in the shadow, forget that I'm your lover, forget how old you are and even that I'm a woman, relish the humiliation and the pleasure—because it's a desolate November Sunday, because it's cold and raining heavily—of once more becoming a nervous child who returns irresistibly and innocently to female warmth, undemanding save for the living shelter and the still caress of two encircling arms.

Stay there. You're back in the cradle; you want a magic song or story ... I don't know any stories. And I shan't invent the happy story of a fairy princess who loves a magician-prince, even for you. For there's no place for love in the heart you have now, in your orphan's heart.

I don't know any stories. .... Isn't it enough if I whisper in your ear? Give me your hand, grasp mine firmly; it will take you back, without stirring, to those humble Sundays I used to love so much. Here we are, hand in hand, getting smaller and smaller, on the steel-blue road glinting with metallic flints—it's a road in my own part of the world. ...

I lead you quietly, as you're only a nice Parisian child, and as we walk I look at your white hand in my small brown paw, dry with cold and reddened to the finger-tips. My little peasant's hand, it looks like one of the leaves that linger in the hedgerow, lit up by autumn. ...

The steel-coloured road bends here, so sharply that we stop in surprise at an unexpected village. .... My God, I lead you religiously towards my old home, you small, well-mannered, un-astonished child, and all you can say while I tremble on my regained threshold is: 'It's only an old house ...'

Come in. Let me explain. First, you can tell it's Sunday by the smell of the chocolate that dilates your nostrils, sweetens the throat deliciously. .... See, when you wake up and breathe the warm smell of boiling chocolate, you know it's Sunday. You know that at ten o'clock there will be cracked pink cups on the table, and flaky girdle-cakes—here, see, in the dining-room—and that it's all right to go without the big midday meal. ... Why? I couldn't say. ... That's how it was when I was a child.

Don't cast up your eyes so timidly at the dark ceiling. Everything in this house takes care of you. It has so many wonderful things! This blue Chinese vase, for instance, and this deep window recess where the falling curtain hides me completely. ...

You say nothing? Oh! little boy, I show you a magic vase whose belly mutters with imprisoned dreams, the enchanted grotto where I immure myself with my favourite ghosts, and you stay unmoved, disappointed, your hand doesn't even tremble in mine? After that I hardly risk taking you into my bedroom, where the mirror is draped with grey lacework, more delicate than a veil of hair, spun by a great spider that's come in from the garden, sensitive to the cold.

It watches from the middle of its web and I don't want you to be frightened of it. Lean over the mirror; our two children's faces, yours pale, mine scarlet, smile through the double lattice. . . . Don't stop by the commonplace little white bed, rather by the wooden judas-window that pierces the wall; it's there the straying cat enters at dawn—she flops on my bed, cold, white and light like an armful of snow, and goes to sleep on my feet. . . .

You still don't smile, my sophisticated little friend. But I've kept the garden to win you over. As soon as I open the worn door, as soon as the two rickety steps have given under our feet, can't you scent a fragrance of soil, of walnut leaves, of chrysanthemums and smoke? You sniff like an untrained dog, you shiver. . . . The sour smell of a garden in November, the gripping Sunday silence of the woods, abandoned by the woodcutter and his cart, the sodden forest path where a strand of mist moves languidly, all this is ours till evening if you wish, as it's Sunday.

But perhaps you prefer my last, my most haunted domain—the ancient hayloft, vaulted like a church. Inhale with me the floating dust of the old embalmed hay that tickles like a fine snuff. Our sudden sneezes will stir up a whole crowd of silvery rats, of thin, half-wild cats; bats will fly for a moment in the ray of blue daylight that transfixes the velvet shadow from roof to floor. . . . Now you'll have to grasp my hand and hide your head, glossy and black as a well-groomed kitten—under my long hair. . . .

Can you still hear me? No, you're asleep. I'd like to keep your heavy head on my arm and listen to you sleeping. But I'm a little jealous. Because it seems to me, seeing you unconscious there with your eyes closed, that you've stayed back there, in my very old country garden, and that your hand is still clinging to the rough little hand of a child who looks like me. . . .

9

I'm Hot

Don't touch me. I'm hot!... Keep away from me! But don't just stand there in the doorway, you're blocking, you're stealing from me the slight breeze that struggles from window to door like a clumsy, imprisoned bird....

I'm hot... I can't sleep. I contemplate the dark atmosphere of my sealed-up room, where a golden rake with equal teeth moves and slowly, slowly combs the smooth lawn of the carpet. When the striped shadow of the shutters reaches my bed, I'll get up—perhaps ... till then I'm hot.

I'm hot. The heat engulfs me like an illness, like a passion. It's enough to fill every hour of the day and night. I can't talk of anything else; I complain of it passionately, and meekly, this pitiless caress. See! That's what's given me this glaring mark on my chin and has slapped my face, and I can't rid my hands of the gauntlets, the colour of brown bread, that it's drawn on my skin. And this fistful of golden specks, all on fire, that have sanded my face, it's that, it's that again....

No, don't go down into the garden, you bother me. The gravel will crunch under your feet, I'll think you're crushing a bed of cinders. Quiet! I can hear the fountain playing feebly—it's going to run dry—and the panting of the dog stretched on the hot stone. Don't move! I've been waiting since morning under the limp aristolochia leaves, hanging like hides, for the first breath of wind to stir. Oh, I'm hot! Ah! Listen, there's the silky noise, like a fan opening and closing, of a pigeon flying round the house!

I can't stand any longer this thin, crumpled sheet that was so grateful to my bare heels earlier. But at the end of my room there's a mirror, all blue with shadow, ruffled with reflections....

How tempting and cold the water is!

Imagine you're seeing yourself in it, the water of the lakes where I come from! They slumber in summertime, warm here, made icy there by the upsurge of a deep spring. They are opaque and bluish, with treacherous inhabitants; the water-snake there twines round the long stalks of the water-lilies and the arrow-heads. . . . They smell of reeds, of musky mud, green hemp. . . . Bring me their coolness, their fever-cradling mists, so that I shiver. I'm so hot. . . .

Or else give me—but you won't—just a small piece of ice in the hollow of my ear and another there on my arm, in the bend of the elbow. . . . You don't want to? You let me ask in vain, you're so tiresome. . . .

Do take a look and see if the daylight is beginning to change colour, if the dazzling stripes of the shutters are becoming blue underneath, orange-hued above. Look out at the garden, tell me about the heat the way one talks of a catastrophe!

Do you think the chestnut-tree is going to die? It holds up its frizzled leaves to the sky, the colour of mottled marble. . . . And nothing can save the roses, caught in the flame before they've opened. . . . Roses . . . dewy roses, swollen with the night rain, chill to the touch. . . .

Oh, come away from the window! Deceive my languor with tales of flowers bowed under the rain! Deceive yourself, tell me of the storm yonder, with bulging violet back, of the rising wind that rears up against the house, rustling the vine and the wistaria, tell of the first heavy drops slanting in through the open window! I'll drink them from my hands, taste in them the dust of distant roads, the pall of low cloud that bursts over the town. . . .

Do you recall the last storm, the bitter water that weighed down the beautiful marigolds, the sugared rain dripping from the honey-suckle, the silver-spangled fronded fennel from which we sucked a flavour of fine absinthe in a thousand droplets! . . .

More, more, I'm so hot! Remind me of the quicksilver that quivers in the hollow of the nasturtiums after a shower and on the downy mint. . . . Picture the dew, the high breeze that bows the tree-tops but doesn't brush my hair. . . . Picture the pond, sur-rounded by mosquitoes and dancing tree-frogs. . . . Oh, how I'd like to hold the cool belly of a little frog in either hand! . . . I'm hot, if you only knew it. . . . Go on talking. . . .

Go on talking, cure my fever! Evoke autumn for me, give me, prematurely, the chill grape that's picked at dawn, and the last strawberries of October, ripe on one side only. . . . Yes, I'd like to crush in my dry hands a bunch of grapes forgotten on the vine, a little wrinkled by the frost. . . . Couldn't you call up two fine dogs with very cold noses? You see, I'm really ill, I'm wandering.

Don't leave me! Sit down and read me the story that begins: 'The princess was born in a country where the snow always covers the ground, and her palace was made of ice and frost. . . .' Of frost, d'you hear, of frost! . . . When I repeat that sparkling word, I feel that I'm biting into a ball of crunchy snow, a fine winter-apple made by my own hands. . . . Ah, I'm hot! . . . I'm hot, but . . . something stirs in the air. . . . Is it only that golden wasp? Does it herald the end of this long day? I abandon myself to you. Call down on me clouds, evening, sleep. Your fingers at the nape of my neck untangle the damp disorder of my hair. . . . Bend over me, fan my nostrils with your breath, squeeze over my teeth the sour juice of the currant you're biting. . . .

I've almost stopped grumbling, though you wouldn't know if it's because I'm relaxed. . . . Don't go away if I fall asleep; I'll pretend not to know when you kiss my wrists and arms, cooler now, beaded like the necks of the brown water-coolers. . . .

Respite

'Did they tell you that while you were away I led a lonely exis-tence, unsociable and faithful, apparently waiting impatiently? . . . Don't believe it. I'm neither lonely nor faithful. And it's not you I'm waiting for.

'Don't get upset! Read this letter right through to the end. I enjoy taunting you when you're far away, when you can't do anything to me, only clench your fists and break a vase. . . . I enjoy taunting you without any risk, seeing you—separated by distance—quite small, angry and harmless. . . . You're the watch-dog and I'm the cat in the tree. . . .

'I'm not waiting for you. Did they say that I threw open my

window at sunrise, longing for the day when you'd stride down the path, chasing your long shadow before you up to my balcony? They were lying. If I have left my bed, pale and still dazed by sleep, it's not the sound of your step that beckoned me. . . . How beautiful it is, the light, empty avenue! My gaze encounters no obstruction from dead branch or straw, and the blue stripe of your shadow no longer moves over the clear sand, patterned only by the birds' small claws.

'I was only awaiting . . . that moment, the start of the day, my own, the one I share with no one. I let you take hold there just long enough to welcome you, to seize your coolness, the dew of your path across the meadows, and close the shutters on us. . . . Now the dawn is mine alone, and I alone enjoy it, rosy and be-dewed, like an untouched fruit despised by others. It's for that I abandon my sleep, and my dream that's now and then of you. . . . You see. Barely awake, I leave you in order to betray you. . . .

'Did they also tell you that around noon I went down, bare-footed, to the sea? They were watching, weren't they? They've praised me to you for my sullen solitude and the still, aimless pro-cession of my footsteps on the beach; they've pitied my bowed face, suddenly watchful, turned towards . . . towards what? Towards whom? Oh! If you could have only heard! I was laughing, laughing as you've never heard me laugh! It's because there, on the wave-smoothed beach, there's no longer the slightest trace of your games, your gambolling, your youthful violence, your cries no longer sound in the wind, and your swimmer's prowess no longer shatters the harmonious curve of the wave that rises, bends, rolls up like a transparent green leaf, and breaks at my feet. . . .

'Waiting for you, looking for you? Not here, where nothing remembers you. The sea rocks no boat, the gull that was fishing, clasping a wave and flapping its wings, has flown away. The reddish, lion-shaped rock stretches, violet, under the water attack-ing it. Is it possible that you once spurned that lion under your bare heel? The sand that crackles as it dries, like heated silk, did you ever trample it, forage in it, did it soak up odour and sea-salt from you? I say all this to myself as I walk on the beach at noon and shake my head incredulously. But sometimes I turn round and look about me like children who frighten themselves with made-up stories—no, no, you're not there—I've been afraid. I suddenly thought I might find you there, looking as if you wanted to steal my thoughts . . . I was afraid.

'There's nothing—only the smooth beach that crackles as if under an invisible flame, only splinters of shells that pierce the sand, fly up to prick one's nose, fall down again and hem the seashore with a thousand broken, glinting stitches. . . . It's only midday. I haven't finished with you, absent one! I run towards the shadowy room where the blue daylight is reflected in the polished table, in the brown paunch of the sideboard; its coolness smells of the wine-cellar and the fruit store-room, thanks to the cider that froths in the jug and a handful of cherries in the fold of a cabbage-leaf. . . .

'Only one place is laid. The other side of the table, opposite me, glimmers like a pool. You know, I shan't put the rose there that you used to find every morning, limp on your plate. I'll pin it to my blouse, high up near the shoulder, so that I need only turn my head slightly to brush it with my lips. . . . How big the window is! You used to half-screen it from me and I never saw, till now, the mauve, almost white, underside of the drooping clematis flowers. . . .

'I hum quite quietly, quite quietly, just to myself. . . . The biggest strawberry, the blackest cherry, it's not in your mouth but in mine that they melt so deliciously. . . . You used to covet them so much that I gave them to you, not out of tenderness, but from a sort of shocked good manners. . . .

'The whole afternoon lies before me like a sloping terrace, all radiant above and plunging down below into the indistinct, lake-coloured evening. It's the time—perhaps they've told you—when I seclude myself. Faithful seclusion, eh? The sad, voluptuous meditation of a solitary sweetheart?. . . What do you know about it? Can you know the names I give the illusions I cherish, my thronging advisers, can you be sure that my dream bears your features?. . . Don't trust me! Don't trust me, you who've caught me unawares, crying and laughing, you whom I betray every moment, you whom I kiss saying, very softly, "Stranger". . . .

'Until the evening I betray you. But when it's night I'll rendezvous with you and the full moon will find me beneath the tree where the nightingale was so frenzied, so drunk from singing, that he did not hear our footfalls or our sighs or our mingled words. . . . No single day of mine is like the day before, but a night of full moon is divinely like any other night of full moon. . . .

'Does your spirit fly through space, across sea and mountain, to the rendezvous I've made with you, under the tree? I'll be there as I've promised, unsteady as my head, thrown back, seeks vainly for the arm that once supported it. . . . I call you—because I know you won't come. Behind my closed eyelids I conjure with your image, soften the colour of your glance, the sound of your voice, I shape your hair to my liking, refine your mouth, and I refashion you—discerning, playful, indulgent, tender—I change you, correct you. . . .

'I change you . . . gradually and completely, even to the name you bear. . . . And then I depart, furtive and embarrassed, on tiptoe, as if, having joined you under the tree's shadow, I left with a stranger. . . .'

Invalid

As on every morning a slender lilac wand, an erect pillar of light, cleaves the darkness of the room. It stands out sharply against the ornate, sombre background of my dream, a dream of gardens with dense verdure, foliage as blue as that in tapestries, gardens that murmur languidly under a warm breeze. . . . I close my eyes again, in the hope of reconciling, beyond the luminous shaft, the two sumptuous panels of my dream. A pain, centred exactly at my eyebrows, brings me quite awake. But the stormy rustling of the blue foliage lingers in my ears.

I reach for the lamp, which blossoms from the shadow like a rosy gourd, trailing behind it the dry tendrils of silken threads. . . .

The painful throbbing persists behind my eyebrows. I swallow painfully; something like a rough arbutus berry sticks in my throat, I clench my fists and hide my nails to avoid the touch of the sheets. Cold, hot—shivering. . . . Ill? Yes. Decidedly yes. Not very ill—just enough. I put out the light and the luminous shaft, an icy blue that cools my fever, reappears between the curtains. It's six o'clock.

Ill. . . . Oh yes, ill at last! A little influenza, perhaps? I shut my eyes once more and wait for the day to begin as if it were my birthday. A whole long day of weakness, semi-sleep, of humoured cravings and pampered feeding! As it is, I want the fragrance of lemon-flavoured eau-de-Cologne around my bed—and when I'm hungry there will also be the odours of warm vanillaed milk and roast apples frosted with sugar. . . .

Must I wait for the household to wake up? Or shall I ring to make them hurry, startled, with slippers slapping on the stairs, with exclamations of 'My God!' and 'It was only to be expected, there's flu about. . . .' Better to wait, spying the growing daylight, the carpet that pales and brightens like a pool. . . . Vaguely I hear vehicles passing, the tinkling of the bottles hanging from the milkman's fingers. . . . The diapason of a bass drum sounded gently and regularly, muffles my ears and shuts out the noises of the street; it's the monotonous, pleasant ground swell of my fever. Far from trying to forget it, I encourage it, I study it, I fit into its rhythm the simple tunes and songs of my childhood. . . . Ah, now, borne on music towards the gardens abandoned by my dreams, I glimpse again that dense blue foliage. . . .

'. . . What? What d'you want? I'm sleeping. . . . Yes, you can see I'm ill. Yes, yes, really ill! No, I don't want anything, except for you not to burst suddenly into my room. . . . And don't touch the curtains—oh, how insensitive well people are! Have you done with opening and closing them, waving great flags of light that chill the whole room?

'Just give me . . . a glass of iced water. I want just a plain glass, a goblet free of flaw or ornament, thin, grateful to the lips and tongue, filled with sparkling water that seems a little blue because of the silver dish—I'm thirsty. . . .

'No? You refuse? Ah, burning with fever, what do I want with

your infusion smelling of boiled linen and dead flowers? Clear
out, all of you! I loathe you! No one's to hug me with their cold
noses, no one's to touch me with the blunt chapped hands of an
early-risen governess. . . .

'Go away! I'll enjoy the perverse frail pleasure of being ill more
when I'm by myself. I feel so superior to you all today! Sensitive
sore eyes, longing for soft lights and muted reflections—delicate
ears, moving under my hair, disturbed by any sound—a skin
capable of detecting any flaw in the linen clothing it—and a
miraculous sense of smell that evokes at will, in this room, the
scent of orange-flowers or bruised bananas, or the overripe musk-
melon that splits to spread its blood-stained juice.

'I feel that there, behind the door, you must be a little jealous,
you who can't conjure, as I do, with the November sun that falls
gently on the roof down there, at the bottom of the garden, with
the branch bent by each breeze, each time dipping the tips of its
mildewed leaves in a bright ray. . . . It springs back and now it's
pink. . . . Violet, pink . . . pink, violet . . . violet-blue, like the
foliage of my dream . . . they're not so far away, those blue leaves,
their marine murmur fills my ears; shall I have time enough to
dwell in their shade?

'. . . Who's there? What's the matter? I was asleep. . . . Why do
you leave me alone? How long have you left me here, too weak
to call out? Come here, help me. . . . Oh! You don't care for me
a bit. . . . But who left this bunch of violets by my face while I was
asleep? Give them here, so I can touch them. . . . How fresh and
cool and grateful on the lips! . . . Yes, I know, the pavement was
dry and blue, my dogs ran in front of you in the path in the Bois,
they stirred up a squall of leaves . . . I'm jealous. . . . Don't look at
me; I wish I were small enough to cry unashamedly. I don't want
to be ill any more. I'll be good; I'll drink the bitter draught, the
infusion too. Isn't it yet time to light the lamp? Don't bother to
lie, I shall hear well enough when the children run shouting out
of school, and the clogs of the bread-woman who comes at five
o'clock. . . .

'Tell me, would you stay with me so faithfully, indulgent and
scolding, if I were ill for a long, long time? Or if I suddenly grew
old, imprisoned as old people are? It makes one shudder to think

of it. . . . It makes one shudder. . . . Why do you think it's fever that makes me shudder? I shudder because it's the evil hour, the twilight hour*. . . . Quick! Light the lamp so that its glow scares off the phantom dog, the ghostly wolf. . . .

'See, I don't shiver any more now that it's shining, enormous, round and pink like a colocynth with ornate skin. . . . What a beautiful fruit, and from what a fabulous garden! It still clings to its torn-off tendrils, trailing over the table, and perhaps, if I close my eyes. . . . Wait, yes, I can see the branch that bears the fruit and the tree beyond the branch, the blue tree, at last, at last! And all that dark garden, beaten down by the hot wind, rustling with water and leaves, the dream-garden I shall always thirst for, after tonight. . . .'

* *L'heure entre chien et loup.*

Four Seasons

Christmas Presents

More productive of worry than gratification, these two words shine like a shimmering frost-flower over a dark doorway that's about to open. Let's face it, we who give but no longer receive, we parents and old friends, are in the grip of an annual anxiety. And with good reason. The least demanding of our wards, the youngest of our children, may confine their requests to a bicycle! Ours is a terrible era. The lisping babe covets a cine-camera. 'You know, I'm still waiting for my five horsepower,' confides the first communicant. 'What do you want for your New Year gift?' a godfather asked his eight-year-old godchild. She turned towards him the frank blue eyes that seemed just to be discovering the world and answered simply : 'A bedroom, mine's worn out.'

I know of parents who sigh with discomfiture when their offspring demand a fur-coat at the age of ten, a car at twelve, and a string of small pearls at fifteen. They cross-examine each other in detail to discover the causes of this precocious maturity that resembles a perversion. 'In our day. . . .'

I nod my head out of politeness. But I know nothing of 'their' day, nor they of mine. I know that, for me, 'New Year's Day' was not taken to mean presents, excursions, shops, insincere good wishes and empty pockets. . . .

Empty they virtually were, the hands and pockets of those who showered me, nevertheless, with favours and every kind of gift. But they achieved miracles within their means. Before daybreak, a red streak across the snow, on 1st January, the hundred pounds of bread, baked for the poor, were already warming the tiled kitchen of the house where I was born, and the hundred ten-centime pieces clinked in a basket. A pound of bread, a ten-centime piece, and the poor folk of yesteryear went on their way, grateful and unpretentious, calling me by my childhood nickname. Standing gravely upright in my sabots, I distributed the hewn bread, the big pennies; on my hands I could smell the appetizing odour of the fresh loaves; and surreptitiously I licked the wheat-flour from beneath the braided belly of a twelve-pound loaf. In my recollections the smell of new bread is closely linked with the sound of cock-crow beneath the red streak of dawn in the depths of winter and the drumstick variations of the towncrier on my father's doorstep. How keenly I still feel it in my heart, this memory of an icy holiday with no gifts other than a few sweets, some silver-wrapped tangerines, a book. . . . The night before, the traditional cake sauced with a flaming sauce of rum and apricot, served around ten o'clock, and a cup of pale, fragrant China tea had ushered in the evening's vigil. A crackling, leaping fire, a few books, the sighs of sleeping dogs, sparse words—whence did the hearts of me and mine derive their joy? And how transmit that sober happiness, that darkly glowing happiness, to our children of today? Who has made them so grasping and sophisticated? Modern life, this harsh era, and we ourselves. . . . Ourselves, because our guilt dates from that first neglect, the first shame that followed and declared within us: 'Just when your child most needed your presence, your advice, your understanding help, you compensated for your failure with a gift, when what was needed was yourself. . . . And then you did it all over again. . . .'

It's the fashion to feel a cheap superiority over the younger generations, to shake one's head and declare: 'When we were the age of these children we were content with trifles, always the same cake, always the same little tree, a simple statement of sentiments and good wishes, always the same. . . .'

Ah yes, always the same. Who changed it for us? From sentiment and economy of effort, the child fears anything that may disturb an exact recollection, a picture whose every detail is fondly preserved by his implacable memory. Did I not seek with an expert tongue in the annual cake, speckled with raisins, the exact flavour of the previous year's cake? Did I not summon to aid my gustatory faculties the unchanging colours of carpet and lampshade, the howling of the east wind under the door, the smell of a fine new book, the grain of its binding a little sticky?

The joy of the five senses! On these delights, that might be called pagan, a domestic religion is founded, and the spirit warms itself at the smallest flame, if the small flame endures. Parents, around your faces—which don't age for them—arrange at Christmas for your still tottering children a setting that time will barely alter. No matter if it lacks ostentation. For the lights of the feast will become ritual, and the flowers or the holly, and also—a little —those words that will evoke Christmas during the rest of the year or the midnight vigil of New Year's Eve. It's only the old who find the invisible, irrevocable passage of time so poignant. A child's emotion, when one re-creates for him a picture from his brief past, does not depend on surprise or wonder. He cherishes what he already knows, prefers what he knows, and chants it within himself to the rhythm of a spontaneous poetry.

Enough, I'd say, of careful diplomacy and circumspect approach to surprise those of our little ones who display the current mode—bored, contemptuous of simple offerings. It's hopeless to try to please them by stuffing them. An effort at restraint, a return to a more refined conception of the annual holidays, is a noble exercise. And we penitent instructors should not overlook the fact that such a sentimental exercise, like every exercise, trains instructor as much as pupil.

Visits

Visits, terror of my childhood, uneasy burden of my life as a young woman! Wedding visits, postprandial visits, visits of condolence and congratulation, New Year's Day visits especially! . . . Do the number of hours I've devoted to you surpass the forty-day life-span of a long-lived butterfly? I think not. I can't believe that such a brief purgatory could compensate for all my sins.

In children the desire and the need for sociability should be fostered. Where could I have acquired this need, this desire? A happy childhood is a bad preparation for human contacts, and mine was fully engaged with fond relatives, somewhat eccentric, rich in personality and a grim sensibility. The shrill bell at the

threshold of the house where I was born used to herald the inva-
sion—the Visit!—and dispersed even the cats. My brothers scattered like Chouans,* intimately acquainted with the escape-route
and its rustic hiding-places, and I followed them. My mother
would shout 'Little savages!', spying in us, with secret approba-
tion, her own inborn wildness. . . . She never realized that the
jungle no longer exists for the children of men and that—before
pleasure, across all grief, above private dramas and work—there
looms the rite, religion and duty of the Visit. I learned this late.
I learned it at an age when there no longer burned within me any
regimented faith. How could it endure, my patience in visiting
two Aunt Marys, several aged relatives named Henrietta, and
those families, allied and alike to one another, who dragged me
here and there beset with a kind of feeble vertigo produced by
fear, fatigue and an empty stomach?

New Year's Day in Paris is not often blessed with good weather.
The rain mixed with snow, a thaw more penetrating than the
frost, a sudden shower of fine snowflakes soon glazed with thin
ice, all added to the mournfulness of the holiday. And as a very
young newly-wed I dared not break with the conventions of
in-laws whose combined kindliness and high moral tone seemed
to my youthful vigour and zest for life like a strait-jacket that
incites to suicide. The whole deadly day I proceeded from visit to
visit with the anguished soul of a prisoner. Along a path blazed
by dry cakes, cups of tea and black-clothed women, I encountered
seasoned sisters-in-law, cousins scattered over Paris from the
Passage des Eaux to the Grand-Montrouge, nieces studded with
chilblains, and uncles by marriage—elderly brothers, invariably
confused by me when one of them died. . . . I also encountered
civilized dejected children, used to the unprotesting sacrifice of
their free day, their afternoon's devouring reading, stoic children
who would give up their seat in a bus or their place in Paradise
with the same stiff, submissive expression. I wasn't taken in by
their passivity. A schoolboy who is unhappy or teased at school
bequeaths to the man he becomes his scholastic phobias, the re-
gressive dreams that wake him at night, that most tragic of

* Rebel Breton Royalists of 1793.

examinees' dreams—the nightmare imposition. Even at that time, twenty years ago, I should have liked to apply to those ill-employed adolescents the wise counsel of a marquise to her grandson : 'Make only those mistakes that you really enjoy'; I should have liked to say to them : 'Perform only those duties that are meaningful. In so doing find the desire and firm intention to visit your friends when mutual affection impels you. There's no grace or sincerity about today. There's not even a holly-sprig or mistletoe-berry, pagan ornaments of Christmas, or the spirit-sprinkled yule log. . . . It's devoid of everything, even the sharp lasting cold, fleecy with snow, the cold—if I may so describe it—that keeps one warm and excites laughter, sliding and sport, the heavy white backcloth that enhances the yellow of the orange, the pink of children's cheeks and satin handbags, that makes the beggar's coarse, extended, mittened hand more welcome. Your greeting, spiteful and embarrassed, no longer moves from door to door with a gay clatter of clogs; it lies in ambush, waiting to be paid its toll. . . . The truth is, my poor children, it's a miserable day that stinks of cash and has lost its good odour of friendship. . . .'

Those children of yesteryear never heard what I preached *in petto*. Today my twelve-year-old daughter radiates an untrammelled worldly sociability, and she it is who informs me that human beings are never so stubborn as when it comes to imagined duty. But, in fact, I know how much the determination of reformers is worth when the reforms they advocate stigmatize the puerility of our manners and customs. I've known this ever since a cousin of mine left a visiting-card bearing the engraved words :

RAPHAEL LANDOY

Vice-President of the League against the Use of Visiting-Cards

25

Tomorrow's Springtime

In January the saffron rose climbs the uprights of the Monégasque pergolas, assaults the Nice palm-tree, lifts itself to the light, turns its face to the sun and unfolds, in an instant, a corolla of incomparable amber flesh colour and perfumed disorder. . . . 'There you are,' says this hardy harbinger. 'That's the pink Paris will be wearing . . . four months from now!'

From December on the first white dresses, blossoming beside the green lawns of the Riviera, display a certain arrogance. 'Look at this waist, as long as a rainy day, this embryonic panel that's an excuse for a skirt, this tube of material minus any curve or belt, this brimless hat that protects neither the complexion nor the eyes —that's what Paris will go crazy over when the spring comes. We may be white, here. But Paris will see us multicoloured. We are like the "mock-ups" that the model-makers and costume designers of the great Revues deliver "in blank"—and no mistake—to the whims of the colourists. But the whole springtide of fashion is already within us. White as a sleeping virgin, we await only the earth's awakening to assume the colours of the bud, the yellow daisy, the blue gentian and the flushed wild rose.'

I watch them pass, these white cocoons of linen, supple silk, spotless wool and simple cashmere, and I sigh. A new fashion year is about to begin, fatal again for those women whom Nature has provided with unambiguous contours. It's true that the species is becoming rare. But it has a hard time of it—as I know only too well. Alas, I could never—as did a fashionable woman in a restaurant who had stained her snowy dress with a drop of gravy —run to the washroom and return triumphant and immaculate —at least in front, for she had simply turned her dress back to front. . . .

Yes, spring pronounces that the fashion will be flat and short. A spring for women to stand poised like a slim lamp-post at the angle of a building, to start up from a lawn like a fountain, to lean against a balustrade like a pillar less bulging than the others.

Walking, golf and tennis—you will be more in vogue than ever; we shall see our Dianas always fleet and never seated, and for good reason. For, if they should sit down, their short, tight, sweet, miserable little skirts will ride up beyond what is permissible, exposing stockings to which inflexible whim has given the exact shade of the dolls we used to make out of bran. Let them sit down —and behold them, I won't say embarrassed, but sometimes embarrassing. However, most of them are devoid of ulterior motive, used to their partial nudity, as untroubled as our half-naked children, and they lower neither the hem of their skirts nor their eyelashes. Once a woman would show her leg because the leg was pretty—she might conceal it for similar reasons. Today the leg is a neutral prolongation and completion of the shape of the garment; beneath twelve inches of visible skirt the *couturier* demands twelve inches of visible leg, no more, no less; he doesn't ask you women for your opinion and it doesn't matter much if these last twelve inches are sticks, spindles or pillars, or if they are mounted on boats, does' feet, or dull slices of bread and butter.

Short, flat, geometric, rectangular, the female garment is based on patterns that derive from parallelograms, and 1925 is not going to witness the return of the fashion for flowing curves, jutting breasts and lascivious hips. An adventurous designer has imported into France half a dozen American mannequins who are surely not going to settle matters for you, you sturdy French ponies, strapping Latins inured to fatigue, resistant to disease. This squad of archangels, in a chaste flight unimpeded by the flesh, will reorientate fashion towards an increasingly slender line, clothes increasingly simplified in the making, cut with a single scissor-slash from magnificent material.

The time can't be far off when the *haute couture*, having created a kind of luxurious indigence, will be dismayed by its work. It favours anyone capable of cutting out from two lengths of material a double rectangle pierced by two sleeves, on which the embroiderer, the weaver, not to mention the colourist, will subsequently exert themselves. Whenever *couture* has created a design so strict, so like a uniform that only colour, ornament and consistency can add distinguishing features, it has rashly abandoned an important part of its prerogatives. A certain excess of

Colette

refinement, proceeding by elimination, exposes the creation to a danger that the properly jealous designer must always dread—facility.

Farewell to the Snow

The first curtain of cypress erect against the rising sun, the first Mediterranean bay buried like an axe-head between two hillsides, the first orange-tree and the first rose—in the train that brought us from Paris the evening before we concede them the easy conquest of our heart. But the winter sun now has a rival—the clean enduring snow, bluely reflecting the circumambient azure.

I haven't been acquainted with it very long. I still don't know how to make use of it as well as the multicoloured children, gliding on their winged feet or upright on the firm but yielding sledge, who play on its flanks and traverse its violet crevasses. I could gauge its power from the first gulps of air that carried a glacial taste of peppermint to the very depths of my lungs. The snow a country? The snow a climate? No, a planet. There the conqueror's lust is stayed in dream. Only on the snow nowadays can the races meet in full sociability. Its tranquil chaos welcomes the stranger, who can abandon there his spleen, his chauvinism, his advancing years. For it conceals the earth, that earth whose living texture a man cannot touch, whose odour he cannot breathe, without again becoming a savage and temperamental pioneer.

Only on the snow can both sexagenarian and child squat on the same small sledges and abandon themselves to the slopes. They feel alike and exchange smiles. They don't envy the bobsleigh, that clamorous meteor that skims devouring the air between its double spray of pulverized ice. Space and giddy incline are the realm of the toboggan also. Its drivers handle two reins which the little runnered sledge can well dispense with. But before every

28

driver of an enchanted sledge there marches a phantom charger, and the two ends of the sledge-rope most certainly girdle the neck and bridle the mouth of a mare of transparent frost speeding at thirty miles an hour. My faëry-mare knew perfectly well that she was pulling a passenger addicted to worldly pleasures. She slewed round to a halt that deposited me on the very threshold of a chalet where red herrings were curing in pine-smoke, where cheese, mixed with alcohol and boiling wine, wept heavy, succulent tears on the toast. A pale insidious white wine conveyed to my palate the very temperature of the ice-pail where the glass jug nestled; and the domestic poetry and lyricism engendered by appetite steamed from the sizzling stewpot and in the blue breaths of us well-fed mountaineers.

O simple, precarious, eternal realm of snow! You turn a man into a gay child, intent and devoted to his playful leisure. You have created this indulgence—the duty to amuse oneself, the right to live in a body which, from every hour devoted to you, enhances in perfection, pulsing with new strength at every fall. You see your disciples leaving their hotel at morning twilight, the time when the speeding dawn leaves the foot of the mountain slumbering in violet shadow but carves on its face an orange hue of heavy, incandescent metal slashing across the blue. They depart, with their long, tapering wooden blades across one shoulder, their double stick in hand. They are as grave and quiet as if they were all ten years old.

The previous day they'd chosen today's objective, some arbitrary invisible point—a mountain peak or perhaps a chalet hidden under its snow-furred porch. Here or there, what matter? Here or there, so long as it's at the cost of rhythmic exertion, mental and physical exercise, so long as they reach a peak of mental and physical exaltation, so long as, standing somewhere very high against the dark blue that burdens the peaks, constrained to open arms and heart to embrace their Eden, they attain an inexpressible happiness. They return at noon, steaming with joy and healthy sweat, their small, deep-blue shadow crouching at their feet. Or perhaps they do not return till evening, laggard and silent, and their silence seems full of poetry because they are beyond thought. O snow, they are your satiated lovers! They have possessed you alone since daybreak, and you have satisfied them. They have seen the mountain diminish under their tread, the scenery expand. Halted, they sat on a fold of your virginal garment, turning from side to side as the sun burned their shoulders. Hollow and light-headed with hunger, they rummaged in their pockets and ate facing the sun, careful to gather the scraps. Then they bound their blades to their feet and began their flights above the little valleys. As they leaped they saw the concave expanse fall away, return, to be distanced once again. . . . Their falls powdered them with snow; they plunged head-first into the spangled craters where the sun cast the seven colours of the rainbow.

They have rivalled each other in audacity and speed. They have not pursued or slaughtered harmless game. They gave no thought to the love of women or their neighbour's good. For you require your devotees to be chaste, O snow, and you purify them. At night they sleep the long sleep of children and are faithful to you even in dreams. They behold you in their dreams and fly even better than the day before. Your silence enters unimpeded through their big open window and nothing stirs in your realm, which the wind cannot reach, except the pulsating gleam of the stars. They sleep, forgetting for a few hours the dedication they owe you, and it's you, greedy for their company, who sometimes descends in showers, moves hesitating about their slumber, and empties on their bedspread a melting tribute of snowflakes, immaculate jewels that dissolve like the content of a dream at the first hint of day.

Models

Two men, five men, ten, twenty . . . I stopped counting them. They attend this ritual of *couture* more eagerly than any boule-vard parade. They profess to 'adore' these processions of dresses and pretty girls, of materials whose ever-diminishing coverage calls for ever-increasing magnificence. They loudly proclaim their liking for those vestimentary rites that every recognized designer organizes with theatrical or religious pomp. Monsieur accompanies Madame to these shows and Madame tilts her chin as if to imply : 'Yes, yes, it's just that he wants a close look at the models!' In which she's often wrong. For Monsieur is capable of one or two pure sentiments, among them the appreciation of colour, movement, form and, especially, novelty. Men at the *couturier's* have long discarded the embarrassment of big boys caught playing marbles, the awkwardness of castaways thrown up by storm on the Isle of Women. Only men derive a total pleasure, unmarred by covetousness, from the parade of models. While his companion, secretly frantic, broken-heartedly renounces a little 'creation' at six thousand francs, the man beams, observes, takes note of X's low waistline and Z's draperies as he might absorb the characteristics of a school of painting. He can appreciate an *ensemble* better than a woman. He can assess the model quite objectively, better than the woman. While the female spectator is feverishly murmuring to herself 'I'd like that one, and that one, and that dress there', the male quietly admires the copper hair and milky pallor of the red-headed model, set in a bronze sheath more revealing than any swimsuit. He realizes that the absinthe- and moonlight-coloured tunic could not be separated, without losing its value, from the young blonde with a greyhound's dignity of carriage, coiffed with long hair unblemished by steel or scissors. He knows what a grave responsibility rests on the girl his wife calls 'that creature' between her teeth; and he would be distressed if anyone who desired the dress wanted to take it away as the designer conceived it, across the shoulders of the dazzling young woman whose voice he hasn't even heard.

In short, a man now feels at home wherever feminine adornment is arranged and displayed, and current snobbishness finds him at his ease there; for there, as the models parade, he can meet the artist fashion favours, the woman of the world and her novelist, the parliamentarian and his Egeria. The model glides from one group to the next, a long gleaming shuttle weaving her web. The model, a disturbing colleague, is the end-point of a concerted effort that everyone now recognizes. The public appreciates the part played by the weaver, the designer, the cutter, the sales-woman, the *couturier* who directs them all; but, as far as the model is concerned, it is more reserved, it ponders—admiring or suspicious. Among all the modernized aspects of the most luxurious of industries, the model, a vestige of voluptuous barbarianism, is like some plunder-laden prey. She is the object of unbridled regard, a living bait, the passive realization of an ideal. Her ambiguous profession makes her ambiguous. Even her sex is ver-bally uncertain. People say : 'This model is charming';* and her job is to excite covetousness, a demoralizing mission that distances her from both *patron* and ordinary workers. Isn't that enough to justify and excuse the model's strange capriciousness? No other female occupation contains such potent impulses to moral dis-integration as this one, applying as it does the outward signs of riches to a poor and beautiful girl.

'Patience,' you say, 'everything will change; the advancement of the model is in train. We designers, we'll turn the model into a loyal colleague, properly and punctually salaried, able to live decently on her grace and beauty. . . .'

Gentlemen designers, I'd like to believe you. But if I'm not mistaken, you're hardly there yet. Granted, you pay up to forty thousand francs a year for the quivering shoulder, the noble neck, the regal carriage of those who, more than any other female creatures, exalt the products of your genius. All right. You claim to give your model not only an adequate honorarium but the esteem and trust you bestow, for instance, on your leading sales-lady. You don't want to see your slim, elegant Diana swooning and yawning in your salon after who knows what nocturnal esca-pades. There speaks an honest man with an understanding heart. But beauty is one thing and bureaucracy another. Beauty is meant for admiration, and you fit her out to increase this admiration. On matters of love and war you say to Beauty : 'This is your domain, you're not to go any farther. Use this salon, this gallery, for your deer-park. Walk, come back, turn round, come back again. Though half-naked, you're not to admit to feeling cold until the time when, leaving your audience, you find yourself alone and

---

* I.e. *ce mannequin.*

shivering. You must understand that this year we want you rid of all superfluous flesh, as tough as any gymnast. But you're not to indulge in any sport, so eat as little as possible and don't spoil yourself buying roast chestnuts at the street-corner. . . .'

Visionaries! Do you really want your arrogantly beautiful models, imprisoned in your luxury, awash with coffee, deprived of the manual work that steadies the heartbeat and regulates thought, to acquire the souls of accountants? But that's not the end of your problems, though your effort is a praiseworthy one. You may recruit and guard your wayward model, hoping for ultimate success, hoping that the lure of gain and a liking for tranquil independence will provide you with beautiful young women of unruffled countenance and placid temperament.

Nevertheless, you will induce in her over an undetermined period the neurasthenia, the nervous yawning, the tearful outbursts and unforeseen fatigue, the brief acclaim singling her out for tribute, the graceful trampling underfoot, like natal soil, of matchless luxury—you will foster all this in her that you tolerate, that you excuse, that you respect, in her favoured brother—the artist.

Elegance, Economy

Was it the same one? Or perhaps another, and another, and yet another? 'Not quite the same nor yet quite different. . . .' I'm referring to the young woman in black satin and pink stockings who contravened both hygiene and commonsense this winter, you know the lady I mean. . . .

February and March have poured on Paris the blackest rain that ever fell from a grey sky, snow the colder because it melts, hail crackling underfoot like a broken necklace. In March, on some miserable afternoons, you can see the drayhorses halt with lowered heads under the half-liquid, half-frozen downpours, taxi-drivers run for the nearest bar, delivery boys under open porches turn into statues of polished oilskin. You can see the hesitant bus, the blinded, pondering tram. You can see the place de l'Opéra, the boulevard and the rue de la Paix deserted, gleaming, bombarded by the wrath from on high. . . .

It was in this weather, in such times of meteorological disturbance, that I saw her, the woman in a marocain or black satin coat, shod with three small patent-leather straps, legs clad in silk the hue of urticaria or a bilious attack. Swathed in badger, but with feet nearly bare, she went her hardened way, chin jutting, stomach out, and backside tucked in.

She encountered—too rarely—her antagonist, the woman in a black macintosh, a waterproof raincoat or fisherman's sou'wester. The latter strode along, sturdy on stout soles, feet warm in ribbed woollen stockings. One day I recognized my friend Valentine, sheltering and shivering beneath the Roman archway of a *porte cochère*. She was paddling in the general quagmire, waiting for it to clear up. I accosted her to tell her off, to call her to account for her unsuitable get-up. She replied, with the acerbity attendant on an incipient laryngitis: 'My dear, do you really think, with material and fashions costing what they do, that I can afford thirty-six outfits to suit every change of weather?'

For women have retained several military expressions from the war, they say 'outfit' where they used to say 'costume'. My friend Valentine was content with the figure thirty-six. Less definite, more exaggerated than a hundred thousand, she brandished it under my nose like a shield with her miserable little conical umbrella, this thirty-six. But I wanted to conduct a serious inquiry and I insisted on knowing whether, in a feminine budget, economy need banish elegance, that supreme elegance that consists of wearing the right garment at the right time, in the right place and circumstances. My friend Valentine's shudder, like a chicken under a downpour, showed that I'd put my finger on the spot where indiscretion ends and sacrilege begins. One may always tease a woman, even unkindly, about her short matt hair, her scraggy schoolgirl neck, her shoulder-blades like those of a starved chicken, her too-short dress, her slop-pail hat, her Kanaka jewellery. But one can only venture with extreme caution, using rubber gloves and a miner's lamp, into the domain where a woman, constrained to use her own initiative, has chosen badly instead of well.

Pressed on another occasion to explain why she had opted all winter for an all-purpose outfit of a coat-dress of black satin with a collar and facings of lynx, superimposed—dare I add—on dishrag stockings and sieves of shoes, my friend Valentine ungraciously admitted : 'You see, this not only saves me the expense of a woollen costume, the silk coat over a satin or georgette dress make a "number" that can cope with any daily emergency, lunch out, even dinner, dancing or a theatre.... Why, only the other day....'

I didn't hear much of what followed. I was clinging to a truth, a feminine truth, somewhat condensed and cloudy, but a truth nonetheless. 'That can cope with any emergency. . . .' Since the first rape, Woman, afraid of nothing, has not forgotten to watch out for emergencies. And yet she is lazy, and laziness often distracts her from a healthily vigilant coquetry. You think her changeable, diverse? Hardly, for what is her dream? To be dressed and got up, as she says, 'once and for all'. When she had her hair cut short she thought she'd wake up in the morning with her hair done once and for all. But the coiffeur, lord of the curls, pruner of the neck, with the copyright of a certain twist of hair by the ear, was alert; and I know many a freed woman who already groans : 'Oh, it's too much . . . I shall have to get it cut every fortnight . . . and that curl behind my ear won't stay put. . . .'

Decked and groomed at ten o'clock like prize horses, how many women approach their second *toilette* before dinner with any eagerness? How many of you are nonchalantly content with a 'paint-job' performed in a restaurant cloakroom? Powder and rouge in clouds, a stroke of the comb, a brushing of hands and nails. . . . And then one undoes the coat-dress that still shows— but let's not inspect it too closely—a few splashes of sandy mud from the Bois to reveal a flat, gold-spangled tunic, embroidered in a hundred colours, and one feels ready for a good night out.

It's you I meet so often in the mornings, by the lakes, you apostles of economic elegance. You walk quickly, noses buried in fur of badger, pijicki, mink even, for the wind is sharp and the water splashes and your pink stockings aren't much to be proud of. But I know that you conceal another pair of pink stockings in your bag and that, under the black satin or nigger velvet, there's a butterfly-wing tunic, low-necked and sleeveless.

Spring is here. If it's fine you'll be able, around eleven, to put on your bright sandals and flowered dress—under what new uniform coat?—the dress in which you'll dine tonight, you elegant ones who expect me to call you thrifty. Thrifty? Pah!...Lazy....

Excursions

You called on me this afternoon, my young friend. And you said, as you sent your little brimless felt hat flying with a flick, as a clown does his wig when he comes to bow to his audience : 'I'll pick you up tomorrow morning! Be ready at seven and leave things to me. We'll lunch at B...at midday on the dot. We'll have a snack at C...at four. And may my tongue be covered with ulcers if half past seven doesn't find us at D..., elbows on the table, with an aperitif!'

Your arm pointed through the open window to your smart eleven horsepower alongside the pavement, coachwork in expensive wood, nickelled prow, stern inlaid with mahogany and rosewood. I know from experience that this outstretched arm holds the steering-wheel firmly and that this hand, freckled and hardened since the spring, could not possibly, from timidity or rashness, contravene any paragraph of the highway code. All the same, I shan't obey the gesture of this hand. It's not with you I'll travel, my young friend. You'll wrinkle up your small unpowdered nose and reply : 'You *are* difficult!' Well, you've hit on the right word, I *am* difficult. You're perfect on a trip, but I want both more and less than perfection, something other than your inexorable timetables, which put to shame the ambitions of a railway system.

You are a young woman of twenty-six or twenty-eight. It's the misfortune and the good luck of women of your generation to have experienced everything at your age, even suffering. War made you wise, love saw you tremble. Modern education has also taught you to travel, if by travelling is meant covering long distances, and at sixteen you were able, unembarrassed, to settle hotel bills single-handed, tips included. The disdain of the *blasé*, the omniscience of the rich, these were your lot from your first communion. You don't hesitate, you don't dawdle. When you're seated at the steering-wheel you yield with dignity the right of way both to monster cars and to those buzzing insects of the road, a sort of terrible harvest-bug, small and generally scarlet, wingless creatures, whose passage strikes terror. You brush certain small vehicles with your wing in order to teach them to have respect for a straight line. And you decipher maps with such a virtuoso air that I always expect, as you unfold the thousand-square hectares' sheet, to hear you vocalize the *cavatina* 'Paris-Biarritz' or the scale of the hills and slopes of Nîmes-Le Havre.

You know the villages, their resources and their pitfalls. You are not imposed on by the 'hostelry', furnished in the ancient style, for the salad is no better served in an old chipped Rouen *jardinière*, or the fruit salad in a warming-pan deflected from its proper usage. You are, I repeat, perfect; I shan't travel with you. I've too many defects, let alone that of no longer being your age. The ribbon of the road, the woods and fields that flank it, no longer appeal to me when they are half-obliterated by speed. And I know that, in our epoch, there is only one luxury—to be dilatory, only one aristocracy—leisure. So leave without me and speed the summer long, impassive and undazzled, at a 'good' average of eighty. For my part, I'll go away and I wager that you won't join me. You are like the greyhound, Lola, who couldn't run with the little bulldogs because in three bounds she had reached the horizon and was searching everywhere for the winded bulldogs she had passed without seeing. Space is yours; leave me what is more beautiful: the woods of scattered pines, the stream turning and twisting in the trough of its valley, the pink foxgloves ranged between the domes of the charcoal furnaces, the brown bread taken from the oven as I pass, with its smell that excites hunger and sleep; the sandpit with purple heather, the lake guessed at behind the hedges—or was it perhaps a field of blue-flowered flax?—the paddocks planted with hemp, drowsy with the flight of butterflies . . . and much more beside, even more irresistible. All this is mine, together with the rural silence, varied and accessible, that you can't hear; for nothing halts you on the road as you plunge through the smoke of the bakehouse fire and transfix the butterflies' flight, you who told me that day when I wanted to sleep on the moving velvet of a sandpit : 'Don't be childish !'

Soon, one of the very smallest motor-cars will be taking me away. Do you want to place yourself at my disposal for my kind of trip? Don't worry about me, I beg you. Yes, I'll have a can of petrol in the boot, and four new sparking-plugs. But, most important, I'll have a thick rug, some Gruyère cheese, some duck *pâté*, fat roast pork in its own jelly, fruit, a flask of good wine, some hot coffee. So provisioned, I shall travel fifty or five hundred kilometres from Paris. I've learned from experience that the summer nights are short and mild, and that the red streak heralding the dawn tinges the sky with a light so severe as to wring the heart. But it's a moment so pure that one savours in it the joy of thinking of nothing and no one, except childhood. Even should you pass, at daybreak, on the road you would go on your way ignorant that I had slept there at the edge of the wood in the most sumptuous solitude, that I'd just awoken under the sad dawn, moistened with a niggardly dew that is dried up, drop by drop, by the black fan of the pines.

Captive Gardens

Two months ago my neighbour was jealous of my yellow laburnum and then of my wistaria, vigorous even in its youth, that throws from wall to lime-tree, from lime to the climbing roses, its snake-like shoots dripping with mauve clusters and heavy with perfume. But at the same time I cast an envious look at his double-flowering cherries; and, with July here, how to compete with his geraniums? At full noon their red velvet achieves an indescribable violet, mysteriously evoked by the vertical light. . . . Patience! He'll see my purple sage in October and November, my neighbour will.

And, without having to wait, he can always catch sight of those ambitious crossed poles that I dignify with the title 'rose-pergola', the heavy clumps of roses, capsized like drunken heads. I have left for my other neighbour the shade flowers, the clematis as blue as it is violet, the lilies of the valley, the begonias made blowzy by an hour's sunshine. An old garden nearby nurtures a giant mallow to which the rest of the plant kingdom has been sacrificed; ancient and untiring, it bears a dazzle of blossoms, pink when they open, mauve as they fade. A little farther away flames the red hawthorn, glory of the Breton spring, and a bushy vine, arranged like a mosaic on the facade of a small mansion, appeases with its vertical lawns the rustic taste of an inhabitant of Auteuil whose land has only the width and breadth of an orange-box. Friendly rivalry that summons old folk and well-conducted children to the threshold of these captive gardens, brandishing of rakes and hoes, clashing of curved beaks of secateurs, truck-garden odour of manure and mown grass, how much longer can you save Paris from the mournful cubism, the rectangular shadow of apartment blocks? Every month in the 16th *arrondissement* sees the felling of an avenue of limes, a thicket of spindle-trees, an old-fashioned arbour rounded to the measure of the crinoline.

On my outer boulevard, drowned in foliage, there has risen in six months a block of flats with the shape and self-importance of a glaring new tooth. A charming low dwelling, content for a hundred years to flourish in the middle of its garden like a sitting hen on its nest of straw, has now—flanked by seven new storeys— lost for ever its right to the sun, its scarab-coloured mornings, its fiery grave sunsets. It stays mute and frozen like an extinct planet, clad in its own mourning.

Our captive gardens can be saved now only by foreign money. A millionaire from far away may chance to become infatuated with a begardened mansion in an old district. Then he purchases it and improves it. He says : 'I'd like two or three others like this', in his grand conception; or else explains : 'It's for tennis.' But let us do him the justice to admit that at times he placards his dislike of tennis and his enthusiasm for everything to do with France's past. It's thanks to him that, on some extensively cleared and regally enlarged piece of land, there confront each other Gothic village churches assembled stone by stone like jigsaw puzzles, Basque terraces, a faithfully scaled-down Norman orchard, court-yards of little low funereal box-trees from the Midi and some Breton thatched cottage, not to mention an antique theatre. A collection made in rather puerile taste but which touches us pro-vincials, shrinking prisoners of Paris, we who tremble at the fall of a lilac or the lopping of a chestnut, who inhabit the shore of a tide of building that nibbles at and encroaches on the Bois, who fervently defend our narrow allotment of greenery. What still remains, deserves to be sung in a melancholy key. Boylesve recalls a garden destroyed. Abel Hermant, though still in possession, already mourns the stately unfolding of the spring under his balcony, two steps from the Madeleine.

The Duchess of Sforza grows her Morère strawberries between the pillars of a balcony in the avenue Henri-Martin, and Philippe Berthelot can see the cherries ripen on his grafted trees in the boulevard du Montparnasse. Behold, at the quai Saint-Michel, the garden raised on a roof ! On the quai Malaquais, Albert Flament guards his souvenirs of Florence within four walls, in the midst of a cool and charming courtyard where rounded cypresses and box-trees are rooted in a mosaic setting. In the rue Jacob, Gour-mont's 'Amazon'* fails to make the dried-up plot blossom, un-visited by the sun. But the fine anaemic grass that grows there in the shade is welcome to the nocturnal cat, and the screech-owl perches, in literary style, on a dead tree draped with a rag of ivy. . . . It doesn't need much of a vine on a wall to comfort a glance that goes from white paper to window, from window to white paper. . . .

* Rémy de Gourmont (1858–1915), symbolist essayist and critic. His *Letters to the Amazon* were addressed to the American Natalie Clifford Barney, a friend of his last years.

An open doorway, in a seemingly no-account street, one day revealed to me a kind of deep provincial paradise, adorned with ancient weeping ash-trees, magnolias, stone vases, sleeping cats, and even apple-trees in cordons, planted in palisade around the lawn. . . . Apple-trees in cordons. . . . O you bucolic Parisians, decked in May with lilies of the valley, gatherers of lilac, you who go into ecstasies over a tuft of grass or a snowdrop, aren't you the guardians of Paris's remaining rural secrets? Apple-trees in cordons. . . .

Holidays

The hot weather, the mid-year three months' flowering, is theirs at last. For six months family negotiations have revolved around some near-inaccessible oasis. Dates, budgetary manipulations, vehicular planning, all have converged on holidays. Our children have suffered the resentment of schooldays in June, the tiresome overall with its sleeve sticking to the small damp arm; they have braced their failing young spirits in the general afternoon somnolence—all the desires and intentions of ten parents are subjugated to the 'little one's holiday' as a just reward.

Children of Paris, even those of you whom maternal solicitude exiles from Paris to the care of suburban schools, you've long deserved your annual reward.

June has passed, with its roses and strawberries. Bagatelle has blazed, its every rose-bush afire. Every empty nest testifies to a thousand flights. Children, you raised your heads to sniff the breeze like jaded colts when July brought through the open windows of your prisons the call of the resin-exuding pines and the shaven lawns.

It's a hard, uncaring rule that keeps children and adolescents seated studiously before note-pad or a textbook at 30 degrees centigrade. . . .

Now our children are free. See them, in the river or on some seashore's eroded strand, naked or as near as makes no difference. Their elegance is in that bloom like the blushing cheek of a nectarine, that fine dry knee, that shoulder endowed with a sudden feminine smoothness since last year. The shoulder-strap of last year's old swimsuit stretches and breaks, the edge of the short trunks is taut against the muscles produced by twelve months of growth.

My astonished daughter regards her last year's slough; the young snake stifles in the skin that it had abandoned on the Breton sands, that other August. 'In 1924 I came up to here,' she says, placing the flat of her hand under her chin. She feels some pride at this, and a little embarrassment. 'Oh, I can't get through the gap in the fence any more,' she announces. A tear even swells on the fresh, lash-guarded margin of her fine eyelids: 'Oh, my little blue sweater! . . .' 'But you can get another one.' 'Yes . . . but it won't be my little blue sweater any more! . . .'

Must she, at twelve, impelled by growth like all that's shooting up, must she already experience the sorrows of growing older, lament for the time she no longer possesses?

I don't like to see her sentimental, moved by a memory, vulnerable to a sound, a colour, a scent inhaled, that she recognizes. Doesn't she still know how to assail fiercely the rocks, how to watch for the flotsam of wrecks and snatch it from the waves? It's one thing for a child to screw up her eyes and announce, like a herald, in a shrill voice: 'The steamer from Granville! The two o'clock plane! A curlew, Mama, a curlew!' It's quite another to stay idly silent, with mouth half-open and bemused eye. Premature reverie is disquieting for observers. How can one not be anxious? The eyelashes flicker feebly over the dazed pupils; but this countenance, so soon visited by so much grace, reveals no ecstasy to greet the immense marine light. A formidable quietude, a boundless expectancy. Alas! She has dropped her unwanted toys at her feet.

Presently I'll take her to Saint-Malo; along the way we'll rediscover, she and I, the holidays of childhood, the handful of sweets proffered by the village grocer, the new-laid egg from the nearest farm, the bowl of milk, the peach firm under its velvet skin, all those gifts, all the homage paid to the arrogant little barefooted queen.

In town again, my daughter will still despise the children playing on the beach '*en chapeau*' and the small girls dressed as young damsels. 'Can't they dress like boys, like everyone else?' But she doesn't fail to display a new and strange mechanical knowledge as she studies the cars that pass on the Sillon. 'When *I* drive. . . . How wretched to see a fine X. . . chassis with such coachwork! I can't imagine what they can have been thinking of!' And to turn to me, astounded, over the young garage fledgling I've managed to hatch out. . . .

As before, the dressmaker will throw some striped rag over her shoulder. But I'll wait in vain for the circus-urchin gesture with which she was wont to tie a strip of cotton round her forehead, unless she proudly drapes it round her bare bronzed thigh. Just now she arranges herself like a model, tucks in her backside, juts out a hip and murmurs : 'Let's try it with the waist a bit higher. . . .' She looks for a mirror, no longer for a bandeau of bright shreds. And, leaving the *pâtisserie*, she's both gauche and graceful, collides with a table, raises an eyebrow, bites her lip, blushes at last like a dark rose, all because a young man steps aside to open the door for her, saying : 'After you, Mademoiselle. . . .'

Grape Harvesters

'Where will you go this September?' my friend Valentine asked me in May. I feel slightly guilty whenever she questions me. She asks questions easily and expertly. She disturbs me with her knowledge of the future, immediate or remote. She fixes a point in the future and there one is, at spa, Saint-Moritz or Rome. Six months before the event she announces : 'On the afternoon of 14th January I shall be having tea at Caux.'

'September? September, hmm. . . . Let's see, it's high tide at full moon. . . . I shan't budge from here because of the fishing, because the equinoctial gale will be superb. . . .'

My friend Valentine shrugs her thin, even somewhat scrawny, shoulders. Her whole body is possessed by a sour youthfulness, as if devastated by unending adolescence. Seen from behind in the street she seems, like so many women nowadays, to be ten or twelve years old. Face to face she seems weary of having acted the little girl so long. So what? What will be, will be. So, in May, she shrugged her shoulders, draped in transparent organdie.

See her now, after a most cultivated Parisian summer. She has 'done' the decorative arts, dined on the *quais*, kept open house till 1st August, lunched in the gardens of the 17th *arrondissement*. She doesn't pay me a visit, she drops in while passing. A small white hat, a dress of white, black and green—what's she looking round for, her umbrella? No, her motoring coat. It's been left outside, on the road, in the car, the car that's out of sight; it's smart to drop in on a friend *en passant*, four hundred kilometres from Paris, as if one had walked all the way. . . . At the bottom of the meadow the sea, with courteous tongue, moistens the iron foliage and fiery flowers of the cardoons. But my friend Valentine doesn't notice the sea, or the beach, or the summer-stripped headland, brown and yellow as a deer; she's thinking of grape-harvesting. For two or three years now the grape harvest has been as assiduously cultivated as cashmere. Between my friend Valentine and the calm milky sea there interposes, incongruously, a picture of grape-harvesting endowed with an arbitrary charm, and I pity this young woman constrained by Fashion to endless anticipation. Thus it is that in winter's frosts the *couturier* must deal with crêpe and embroidered wild flowers, drape swathes of fur in the dog-days. . . .

'You'll be going to harvest, then, Valentine?'

'Of course, my dear.'

'Is it the first time?'

She blushes.

'Yes . . . that is . . . I was to have harvested last year on the estate of my friends X. . . , and two years ago, even at . . .'

'Don't make excuses. And what sort of harvesting get-up do you envisage?'

'Violet-purple cretonne printed with yellow grapes,' retorts my friend straight off.

'Hat?'

'Yellow. A violet ribbon tied under the chin.'

'Shoes?'

'Plaited. In yellow and white kid.'

'Scissors?'

'Like a stork's beak. I found some ravishing ones at Strasbourg.'

Can't I catch her out? She's even thought of scissors! I'm amazed to find that her ignorance of natural things stands her in almost as good stead as consummate experience—except in actual practice. She characterizes the season by the material, sport by the equipment, female beauty by jewellery. She interprets the language of symbols like a romantic sweetheart, in fact. . . . But I shan't tell her so, it would certainly hurt her feelings.

'You know, Valentine, you can do without scissors if you like.'

My friend's plucked eyebrows rose in astonishment and disappeared under the little chalk-white hat.

'Do without! When I've an antique steel chain to hang them from my belt!'

'. . . It's up to you,' I say. 'You see, the stalk of each bunch at an inch or two from the parent stock is swollen like a snake that hasn't yet digested its meal. If you press with your nail on this barely visible swelling it breaks like glass, and the bunch falls into the basket held out by your other hand. It's a little peasant trick I'm teaching you, Valentine, so that you can fill your basket faster. . . . That's how I used to manage, in 1917. . . .'

To be sure, the rest was none of her business. Those wartime harvests belong only to my memories. Red earth baked by long sunny days, a broiling September moistened with dew at dawn, unexpected bunches beneath the fig-trees smelling of fresh milk. . . . That year the sky distilled a flawless blue from pink dawn to pinker evening. Never were there so many peaches on the peach-trees, screening, when ripe, the vines; never were there so many yellow plums and greengages mingled with the vine-tendrils. So many kingfishers gleaming over the river, so many bees in harmonious aureoles around the limes, so many shrilling swallows piercing the clouds of midges. . . . So much animal joy and unresponsive vegetable luxuriance at our silent harvestings. . . .

Women's hands, children's hands turned back the foliage, handled and cut the warm grapes. There was not a man to be seen between the parallel rows of vines. The males spared by the war were those under seventeen or over fifty; these carried with bowed back, from vine to vats, the wooden containers that weigh, full, half a quintal or more.

Towards noon a young woman emerged from the vines, ran on to the path, sat down in the shade of a fig-tree, and picked up a child fastened in swaddling clothes. Her milk was urgent and while she freed and woke the nurseling I saw mingled drops of milk and tears falling on the child from the mute and solitary harvester.

Fur and Feather

The year has started well for huntsmen. A premature abundance of game, and by no means of the smallest, set the hardy trackers of Paris afoot from August onward. The 16th *arrondissement* held the record for a time with its leopard, and its kill in the boulevard Lannes. But furred and feathered creatures were brought down, in emulation, on every side. Two foxes, one of which installed itself in the preserves of the Opéra, an 'unknown' bird resembling 'a large turkey-cock with flattened beak', another bird, equally devoid of pedigree, black, immense, that inspired terror—but why?—in flying away, a lion cub, a magnificent release of exotic birds beneath the glass roof of the gare du Nord. . . . I give up. The fauna of Paris, these recent months, defy the imagination.

Among others, what is one to make of the hornbill and the white-throated laughing thrush? Never fear, the laughing thrush heralded in September, flew timidly enough and meant its tormentors no harm.

The 16th *arrondissement*, my own, does not fail to offer the student several interesting examples of European fauna. One night I found by the gate of my small garden a pretty white cow that I might easily have captured. I know now that the nocturnal white cow allows one to approach, accepts water in a bucket and salt from an outstretched hand. The twilight ewe possesses the same peculiarities, as observed by me in a ewe recumbent by the side of the outer boulevard. Perhaps these remarks may serve for a treatise on Parisian venery. A panther from the Chad, captured with the aid of Philippe Berthelot in a staff-room at the Foreign Office, brightened my stay for a time. But I implore you to believe that I would not countenance the inexcusable negligence of a menagerie proprietor who allowed it to slouch about on the pavement, or in the weighing-in enclosure at Auteuil, or among my neighbours' flower-beds and rose-gardens. Its beautiful coat, its golden-amber eyes, its confident deerlike grace and gentle friendly call, these I would cherish, aware that the urban scalp-hunters are in earnest and that all is fair for them on the warpath: the Browning, the halberd, the tomahawk, the slingshot, and asphyxiating gases.

They needn't count on me, these decimators of partridges, pond-frogs and hornbills, to inform them when, and in what part of the Bois, I spy—without any evil intent—a small mysterious animal that warms itself, autumn and spring, in the length of a ray of sunlight that slants across a path. I confirm that it is chestnut, smooth-coated, shorter and chunkier than the common marten, lacking the dash of a squirrel. My bitches know it, it flees from prudence rather than fear and disappears into a lair burrowed in the very slope of the old fortifications. It is always alone, and old perhaps. Its life is a wretched little life. . . . But perhaps I've said too much already. Perhaps, in my imprudence, I may have brought about a militarily organized *battue* in the copses of Auteuil.

As I write there take place the pursuit, wounding and killing of the plump partridge, noisier in full flight than an aeroplane, the unreflecting quail, the pheasant that ornaments the trees it roosts in. The hare's heart beats fit to burst, even the night brings no respite for the smallest trembling game. The fashion journals promote a hundred different outfits for huntresses, with an illustration alongside the text showing that the huntress of 1925 is no improvement on that of 1924. Without bust or buttocks she stands heronlike, yet endowed with an interminable bosom. If I am to believe these facile designers, the huntress is shod with dainty pumps or high boots in soft leather. She is armed with a carbine as long as a boat-hook, a powder-puff, a cigarette, and a wrist-watch that points, no doubt, to the last hour of the nearest marksman. She is patterned with great checks, like a bathroom, or wears an old warrior's stripes. Beneath her masculine cravat she wears a blouse of white *crêpe de Chine*, ensuring—God willing—that the game can spy her from afar. Well, well, if I can believe the facile designers, the huntress on foot is a brave little creature who wouldn't harm a dove, even with a rifle.

But as for the woman who goes in for big-game hunting, I maintain the most malevolent silence on the subject. May the powerful dry foot of the stag, slain among the tears it has shed, may the small delicate hoof of the roe-deer, brought in with gaping throat and dangling neck like a murdered child, return at night to trouble her dreams for ever—it is all she deserves.

A friend of mine, a literary young man with plenty of talent, had been used to hunting from infancy, and with all the rage of a bloodthirsty child. He hunts no longer. I evinced my surprise and asked the reason for this sensible behaviour. He hesitated only a moment before telling me this: 'I was shooting partridges last year in Brittany. I wounded one, which still fluttered and hid behind a bush; but I had marked it well and felt sure of getting hold of it. I reached the bush, pulled up against a low fence, and encountered a little grey-bearded man on the farther side. The old gentleman was holding my wounded partridge in his hands, caressing its beating wing and its frantic little head. I told him that . . . that I had shot the partridge in the open field, that it had originally fallen on the stubble, that . . . well, that was all there was to be said! He continued to caress the partridge and seemed not to understand me. Finally he raised his head and asked me in the most moderate tones : "Sir, have you ever thought that one day, in this world or another, you might be the game in your turn?" I tell you, it affected me so strangely, that little phrase, that ever since I've lost all inclination to hunt. . . .'

Fads and Fashions

Jewellery in Peril

The year will end uneasily. How many women are pondering as they fiddle with the 'idle capital' on their fingers. Never have they felt so directly menaced. And yet silk costs as much as woven hair, raw yarn doesn't lag behind silk, the smallest piece of kid-leather, shaped more or less like a foot, costs three hundred francs. And pears and apples desert the modest table, already abandoned by the leg of mutton, and women—even those who survive on toast and a cup of tea—have already voiced their loud, ravenous clamour. . . .

But the threat of a particular tax finds them dumb, full of rancour and scheming. They are not going to be had so easily. The dramatic *dénouement* is their familiar element. You'll see, these apparently imprudent ones will give men one more surprise. Already, one who is garlanded, sleeping and waking, with a row of incomparable and inseparable pearls, a necklace she fondles and kisses, already this fetishist loses fervour, speaks of her necklace with a waning passion. 'You know, it would cost me something like thirty thousand francs a year for the pleasure of keeping a necklace of this value. . . . Thirty thousand francs! The rent of a good apartment. . . . The price of a small property! Do you understand. . . ?' We understand. We go further and understand clearly that woman, surprising creature who blends poet, starling and perfect lawyer, doesn't want to pay more than once for her pleasures and won't agree to pay rent for her luxuries.

Perhaps in every woman there is a businessman. This has, rather unkindly, been stated more than once already. Happy or unhappy, this businessman, engaged with dress, art, life, even science, seems to be roused by certain sounds—of coin, of safe deposits, of prattled figures; he dreams with ear pricked like a war-horse when the breeze brings bursts of martial music. . . . The words 'a tax on idle capital' arouse woman from a frivolous dream. Where she was prodigal she has turned rapacious, once scatter-brained she is defiant and calculating. . . .

Fine jewels, family heirlooms, birthday gewgaws and New Year surprises, already you are weighed, your value calculated, your limpid clarity attracts a legatee's glances. The same proud mouth that once announced 'They're worth so much!' now murmurs: 'They'll cost me so much.'

I suppose that this misfortune will see the triumphant renaissance of the once so pretentious, so-called 'artistic' jewellery, to the profit of exoticism. Already the heavy necklace of Peking glass finds favour. It is blue, green or yellow, translucent or veiled with milky flecks. The rounded beads, save when shaped like nasturtium seeds they imitate the Oriental emerald, delight us with their periwinkle blue. Their compressed substance seems moist; they play happily on the brown skin where each bead trails behind it, in place of shadow, a little spot of bluish light.

I know a Chinese necklace of green glass, long and heavy as a slave's chain, that burdens as well as adorns a charming neck. It is as green as a frog, as blatantly green as royal jade. Czechoslovak glassware cannot match these refined barbarities, also fashioned in thick circlets round the arm, tinkling like bronze cow-bells. The vogue for Chinese necklaces and bracelets has only just begun and we are barely acquainted with those whose crystalline substance conceals—competing with the overesteemed 'sulphurs'—a little pink and green snake, a twist of gold powder. . . . It's not that they're beautiful, but that they come from afar. And then they are all, like the necklaces, the constructs of sphere and circumference, and this eternal simplicity is no negligible magic. If the pearl had been created studded with facets, it would be able to laugh at this famous tax. A cut rock crystal appeals to us less than a perfect sphere, smooth to the touch, transparent, impenetrable, that mirrors every terrestrial image on its surface, fantastically distorts them and turns them into sorcery. . . .

No tax threatens the necklaces, all blue, Chinese, that tinkle from my neck to my knees. Other worlds, virgin and multicoloured, roll in a casket that I can open without fear of tax demands. These spheres have their history.

After the war our children searched in vain—and still search—for glass marbles. To satisfy my daughter, one day I wrote to the master of Fire and Glass, the creator of the marvellous Fountain, to Lalique in fact, and asked him : 'What has become of our children's glass marbles?' Lalique offered no explanation. A few weeks later I received a hundred marbles from Lalique—pink, red, opalescent, blue as the flame that saw their birth, green as grapes, as waves, as silvered absinthe.

But—and here you see the extent of childish deprivation and maternal selfishness—it was I who kept the precious 'taws' in a casket and my daughter Bel-Gazou still hasn't got her glass marbles.

Too Short

Too short, gentlemen, too short. I write 'gentlemen' since few women make it their profession to dress women. They are in a minority, a minority of rare quality that readily gains acceptance, but a minority. An habitual shamelessness leads women to prefer a salesman to retail the sheer stockings, the mesh of which, stretched over a man's hand—'See how very flattering to the thigh this stocking is, Madame'—reveals all its delicacy. It seems that a masculine arm is the best measure for Valenciennes lace and for ribbon. . . . We speak of the embroiderer, the cutter, the milliner, the hosier, as masculine. We say 'the *couturier*', using the male gender, even when the *couturier* walks on two feet shod with brocade and paste jewellery and adorns her swanlike neck with two million francs' worth of pearls. . . . Well, *Couturier*, great *Couturier*, trousered or skirted, I tell you to your face : this year again, it's too short.

All very well for the walking costume, so named by antithesis, since its skirt hobbles the legs, pulls the knees together, wears out the stockings and hinders walking. Shortened, it gives the stationary woman a pretty little alert air which she loses as soon as she begins to walk—but what need to begin walking? The elegant 'walking costume' does not ambulate. If we want to get about, on foot or on horseback, climb a mountain or traverse a marsh, it won't be you, *Couturier*, that we'll consult, but specialists that you despise, the technicians of the waterproof raincoat, the puttee, the ski-boot and the Saumur riding-breeches. *Your* walking outfit covers four hundred yards between midday and one o'clock and that's quite enough for the delicate stitched kid-leather that your accomplice, the expert in footwear, calls his *matinée* shoes. So cut it at knee-level if you like, or higher still. But this year you have shortened both the afternoon and the evening gown. A scissor-slash of some importance, after which the exertions of the embroiderer, the ingenuity and luxury of the weaver, go un-rewarded. It's in vain that you hang on your clients' backs a loose panel, billowed up by the least movement; in vain that you dust an already silvered veil with seven hundred thousand little stars; in vain that you 'cheat', attaching a *lamé*, pleated, embroidered, fringed train that sweeps the carpet, slender guy-rope of a tunic suspended sixteen inches higher. . . . It's in vain that you scatter suns, rockets, palms, fountains, roses over the flat stomach, the illusory backside and steppe-like bosom of the Peri of 1924; your evening gown, your full-dress rig-out resemble some abortive project, a novel minus a *dénouement*, an ostrich that has moulted, an idyll without poetry. Too many feet, too many feet, and not enough material!

I am told, O great *Couturier*, that you easily lose your temper and that your first word will be to tell me to mind my own busi-ness. That's just because you're not accustomed to criticism. Your art—which has a turnover of as many millions as the cinema—is content, with singular modesty, with 'communiqués' and provides an income for those two second-rate bards, the public relations officer and the official reporter. But no one treats your work, as it so often deserves, like a fine painting, like an enamel, a new novel, a stage play, like a ceramic. . . .

Whose fault is this? Up to now your petty tyranny has admitted only paid hirelings. You deserve less 'fixing' and more considera-tion, you surely deserve that I should give myself the pleasure of coming to you, seeing what you create, saying what I think of it and going away again—in my nice little dress that hasn't your trademark.

In one month I have already seen two hundred dresses on parade. At the opening of a new season this is an instructive as well as amusing parade. I learned there this year's way of carrying one's stomach which, though flat, retains a shieldlike arrogance and sways forward and back, backwards and forwards. Where is the Spanish or Martinique hip-rolling of the models of 1914? All very well to talk of hips, we don't bulge at the sides any more! It was there I learned that 'the waistline is rising'. I'll say it's rising, as far as the navel, and doesn't hesitate to descend much lower, much, much lower. Then again, the length of the back is startling, if I can call this flat parallelogram, with a skirt fit for a little girl of ten hanging at the end, a back. 'Three inches of legs and right on to the back.' Oh, that back! Thirty inches of back, without pleat or fold. Smile, Mr Embroiderer, this is where you can let yourself go. Embroider, on this vertiginous back, pagodas, fruit, Arabic numerals, rural scenes, Pompeian friezes and automobiles. But your smile is sickly, Embroiderer. And with reason. The Weaver, who is a genius, has got it into his head that he can manage without you and he weaves marvellously. In relief, in depth, silky, ribbed, variegated, pale as the shadow of smoke, vigorous as the summer foliage in an avenue, he executes his arabesques on every material and defies you. Get cracking, Embroiderer, and improvise, you too.

Two hundred dresses! O great *Couturier*, you've shown me them in every shade. They bear charming names—you're not short of affectation, great *Couturier*, nor of a sense of the ridiculous, or phrases. Blessings on you this year for bringing blue back into fashion. The long-banished blue reappears, interposed between violet and purple, and the eye bathes in it happily, suddenly aware that happiness is incomplete without the savour of blue. Black competes with the entire rainbow, calling to its aid the pink of a half-glimpsed breast, the gleam of an arm or leg under lace: 'Don't forget that I am not only distinguished, noble, sumptuous, but also the most voluptuous of all, and the most satanic,' insinuates black. Above all others I find this prince of darkness too short—like its seven comrades, despite their divided trains that sweep the ground, get caught up in doors, twine round the legs of chests and firmly swathe the feet of armchairs.

Too short, this fake libertine mourning in soubrette's skirt; too short, this gauze-winged dream that doesn't conceal its attachments to earth!

Great *Couturier*, do you recall an evening when you showed us, after truncated Salammbos, abbreviated Mélusines, sirens treated like Alcibiades' dog, and many a ravishing 'little model' with low waist and high hemline which I privately christened 'the fiancée of the legless cripple'—do you recall showing us a bridal robe loaded with pearls, a long, long robe which descended above invisible feet the steps of your 'presentation stage'? It descended, gliding as if by magic. Six yards of train followed, lace and tulle frothing over its still, calm water. . . . Didn't the cry of admiration that burst forth at this sight, great *Couturier*, resound in your ears like a warning, or at least a piece of advice? No? So much the worse.

Underneath

'This way, Madame!' said the elderly saleswoman. She barred my entry to the little trying-on room, closed by a velvet curtain, which I was about to penetrate, and led me smilingly to the opposite end of the establishment.

'There now! We're better off here, aren't we? It's more homely.'

I did not share her opinion. The homeliness in question was that of a sort of vestibule-cum-drawing-room between two glass swing-doors, afflicted by piercing draughts, with a gloomy light falling from above.

'If you've no space for a fitting, Madame R., why don't you just admit "I've no room"?'

'Oh Lord! What must you think of me!'. . .

She raised her wrinkled hands with their painted nails and I heard the bracelets of ebony, hollow gold and good imitation jade clash as they slid down her forearms. Her wise, wrinkled eyes sought the ceiling, then returned to mine without insistence and she smiled showing all her teeth, one of them—of pure metal— gleaming.

'You're teasing, Madame. One should never tell you anything but the truth. And you know, telling a client the truth produces a strange sensation, as if one were doing something one shouldn't. The truth, Madame, is that I have three empty salons in the long gallery, but. . . . Oh Lord! . . .'

The bracelets clashed and Madame R. pirouetted on her well-shod little feet. She is sixty-four, with hair dyed a dark red and the outline of a young girl. She conceals neither her age nor her wrinkles, which she makes up with bright rouge. Under the rouge, the powder, the bracelets, the short black dress with its two panels, there is nevertheless a shrewd old woman who succeeds in resembling neither a procuress nor a mad grandmother. She is, dare I say, a born saleswoman. She might have managed a dress-making establishment had she not lacked a kind of cruel severity and the wish to dominate. Her gift lies in finesse, and only finesse. She loves the long, empty hours, the bustle, the luxurious salons. She likes irony, scandalmongering, a piece of chocolate at four o'clock, the hidden cigarette, the bag of cherries. She 'earns well' and feeds her family well, a solemn family in sombre woollens from which she escapes every morning, concealing her private delight from herself. . . .

'You'll scold me, Madame!' she whispered with a contrite grimace that gathered the lax skin of her neck in convergent folds under her chin. 'Yes, I do have empty salons! Yes, I have brought you to this draughty corner! It's very wicked! But . . . but I couldn't stand it any longer down there!'

'You couldn't stand what?'

She closed her black-rimmed eyes, painfully swallowed her saliva like a choking hen, and whispered in my ear a single word, revolting and mysterious: 'The smell.'

Then she fluttered from one door to the other, cried sharply: 'Mademoiselle Cécile, you're making fun of everyone!'; languidly demanded: 'Mademoiselle Andrée, when you're ready,

Madame Colette's three-piece!' and cast off from a chair, so that
I might sit down, a cloak of gold, moonlight and purple tissue
which she trod underfoot like a queen. She 'played for time' like
a good actress and let me meditate on the word, the word full of
vague horror and fascination. . . .
'The smell of what, Madame R.?'
She did not keep me waiting but retorted in the plain language
of an aristocrat : 'Why, the smell of hairy women, then!'
'How so? Is X. . . dressing a revue then?'
Madame R. simpered, suddenly prudish.
'The house of X. . . only dresses the right people, as you know
perfectly well. The right people—and artistes, of course.'
She dropped her voice into a more serious register, rounding
her eyes like an impassioned preacher : 'About the smell, Madame,
I retract nothing! I've said what I've said! I'd repeat it under the
knife! I'm old enough to remember a time when one could enter
the salons of the House of X. . . at any time without breathing any
odour but the scent of corylopsis and ylang-ylang. Perhaps there
were times when there was an excessive odour of sanctity, but
still. . . . Nowadays, Madame, it smells of a steam-bath here, a
steam-bath!'
She seized a snippet of *lamé* caught between two wardrobe
doors and used it as a fan, closing her tragic eyelids as if to say
'I've said too much. I give up'. But, since I kept silent, she reopened her eyes precipitately and said hastily : 'What can you
expect, Madame? Once a woman used to wear underwear, fine
linen underwear that cleansed her skin; now, when she takes off
her dress, turning it inside-out like skinning a rabbit, what do you
see? A long-distance walker, Madame, in a little pair of trunks.
A baker's assistant in bakehouse get-up. No chemise, no linen
drawers, no petticoat, no combinations, a brassière sometimes,
yes, often a brassière. . . . Before coming for a fitting these ladies
have walked, danced, eaten, perspired . . . I'll say no more. . . .
It's a long time from their morning bath! And their dress, worn
next to the skin, what does it smell of, their dress that cost two
thousand smackers? Of a boxing-match, Madame, a fencing
championship! *Twelfth round*, unpleasant smell. . . . Oh Lord!'
She exhibited the hand-clasping, the affected declamation,

acquired like a tic by women who often meet men who imitate women. But her disgust seemed genuine and her nostrils were pale. I recalled the phobia that used to afflict a corset-maker who took all her meals in a restaurant to escape the effluvium that filled her own establishment. . . .

A model appeared, a sort of tall blond boy, hair shorn close on the nape of the neck, coming down over the forehead to eyebrow level. Beneath the flesh-coloured evening dress the minor jutting of two small breasts confirmed her nudity. Unblushingly she lifted her skirt and extracted from her stocking a narrow wisp of fuchsia-coloured gauze to wipe her nose vigorously. Her comic gesture evoked in me the recollection of a rehearsal of a play where the author intended the villain to tear half the clothes off the *ingénue*. In the imagination of the sexagenarian playwright the victim was to remain palpitating for a moment, undone like a spoiled white rose, clasping to herself the scanty lace, the exciting froth of underwear in a snowy cascade. . . . The run-through revealed, not the froth and snow, but little panties in saffron silk net, four taut suspenders, and a portion of saffron chemise marked with a large monogram like the inside of a hat; the stagehands may have guffawed but the author certainly didn't laugh. . . .

The coarse words of Adolphe Willette sounded in my ears like an enraged bumble-bee: 'They have done away with feminine underwear, the vandals! Why, even the butcher knows that a leg of mutton has to be done up with a paper frill!'

Make-up

I ran into my friend Z. . . one morning just when he was pushing open the door—all thick glass and ironwork—of a well-known perfumier.

'I've caught you in the act,' I said to him. 'You've come to buy

Colette

an expensive phial of those lotions that fashion allows men and are consequently labelled "Gentlemen's socks" or "Unleash the wild beasts!"'

'No,' answered Z. . . . 'Come with me, I've no secrets.'

We proceeded across a vertiginous mosaic that reflected us like a lake, to run aground in a delightful harbour between one blonde saleswoman and another. Amiable rather than pretty, they were worthy representatives of an old French luxury trade, which calls for incense-bearers clothed in black serge, whose pious hands are free of jewellery.

'Give me,' asked Z. . . , 'some lipstick.'

'Which one? The light or the dark? The nasturtium or the creole? There's also our liquid rouge, *The Eternal Wound*, which is very popular.'

Z. . . sat down with a determined air.

'I want all of them. At least, I intend to try them all.'

The less pretty of the two blondes cast down her eyes.

'It isn't possible to try them, sir. You see . . .'

'I do see,' interrupted Z. . . . 'All right, I'll buy all your rouges and then try them.'

Five or six small cylinders of gilt metal and a minute phial were handed over to my friend, on a tall counter covered in suède. Very seriously and with a cynicism I found disconcerting he painted his lips conscientiously.

'You're hideous!' I cried. 'Your clipped moustache over that scarlet mouth . . . have you gone mad?'

He passed his tongue over his lips, bit them, wiped them with his handkerchief, then it was the turn of a nasturtium rouge from which I sensed, at a distance, the bitter smell of banana.

'No good!' complained Z. . . in a low tone; and he wiped away the orange traces of the banana lipstick.

For a moment a dark-red cherry rouge claimed his attention. Musingly, he smacked his lips in gluttonous fashion and murmured: 'Not bad . . . not bad. . . .'

One of the two salesgirls, impassive, gave her opinion: 'May I say that the nasturtium rouge, for your complexion, sir, is the one that . . .'

I didn't wait to hear any more.

'My dear friend,' I said drily to Z. . . , 'I've seen enough. I'm off.'

'Wait just a moment, dear friend, I haven't tried the liquid rouge yet. Miss, what are the ingredients that go into the liquid rouge?'

'It has a base of Oriental roses, sir, with the addition of a touch of essence of cloves. . . .'

'Cloves? Curious. I'm tempted by the cloves. . . . Would you wrap up this lipstick for me too? "Stolen Cherries", if I'm not mistaken. Thank you. My dear Colette, I'm at your disposal, shall we stroll to the end of the avenue?'

Curiosity triumphing over revulsion, I waited for Z. . . and let him walk along with me.

'Fine weather,' he remarked innocently. 'And I'm so pleased with my purchases. My wife will be delighted.'

'They're for her? Why didn't you say so, then?'

'No, my dear. They're for me. This make-up that turns my wife's mouth pimento-red, strawberry, tomato, delights the eyes of those who see her, but . . .'

'But?'

'But it's I who eat them, so to speak. I'm in love with my wife. And she adores me to distraction—but not to the point of offering me an epidermis without powder, a mouth of natural pink. As a young married man I endured the twofold caprice of fashion and my wife. The fresh flower that I kissed, plastered for a whole season with a decomposed violet rouge, exhaled the sickly smell of infusion of violets. One winter I browsed—pouah!—on rancid pink cold cream recommended for chaps. And what can one say about the unpleasant flavour of a certain fiery red, the colour of an irritable urticaria, reserved for fêtes under the chandeliers and for dress-rehearsals? . . . I took the best course. I dodge my un-happiness. Since our conjugal love does not wane, I intend to choose the rods that chastise me and I buy my wife's lipstick myself.'

He sighed, then continued: 'If only, while biting her pretty cheeks, I could remove the bilious-coloured powder that covers them! Under that jaundiced yellow, heightened by an artificial flush, my tooth might rediscover an unsuspected blonde flesh tint —don't you think?—that I may eventually forget . . .'

'But at night, doesn't Marcelle show you her true face, properly washed?'

Z. . . raised an arm and a stick to heaven.

'Washed! That's not the half of it! Scrubbed, polished, scraped with an ivory spatula, rubbed with an ether swab and boiling water, finally carefully coated with a camphor pomade to prevent wrinkles . . .'

'Camphor?' I interrupted. 'Not that wonderful glycerine cream any more, that Marcelle used to claim was so efficient?'

'Alas, no . . .'

Z. . . took my arm in conspiratorial fashion: 'Dear friend, would you be very kind and do something for me? Start Marcelle off again on the glycerine cream, which I recall as sugary, even a little vanilla-flavoured. It's certainly time. Because I'm afraid. I'm afraid of the mudpack, that blackish rubbish that women plaster their neck and face with, without a quiver or vomiting in disgust. The Great Collector at home, between two linen sheets decked with lace, ah, if you only knew . . .'

'*Manure*—a beauty product!'

With this word, which he accompanied with a bitter grimace, we arrived at the Z's establishment. . . .

'Come up,' said the disturbed husband abruptly. 'My wife gets up late, we'll catch her at her *toilette*. I'm afraid of what may have happened in my absence. . . .'

He had good reason to fear. His charming wife, unrecognizable, was allowing the dregs of a cesspit to dry on her face in a scrupulously evenly applied layer. But she had no time to appear embarrassed, occupied as she was with sharply scolding her little dog.

'Go away, you nasty thing! Hide yourself, you horror! I don't know why I don't send you down to the country! I'll forgive you anything, but not that, d'you hear, not that! . . .'

Magisterially she turned towards me a face encrusted with mud, in which her blue eyes smiled, lotus blossoms of fetid swamps, and explained to me, indicating the dog: 'Just think of it, dear! A little creature I'm so fond of. . . . She's been rolling in something dirty!'

Hats

How are we going to recognize, in thirty years' time, the woman who was so pretty in 1924? I'm very much afraid that we shan't recognize her. Those who were so pretty between 1890 and 1900 announce themselves to us in streets and churches and the theatre, everywhere where, as we say in the Midi, 'one wears a hat'. Would you wager that I could point out to you, among ten or twelve old ladies, the one who was so dreamy and ravishing at twenty and who registered long silences because her silences enhanced her romantic beauty more than words? Her face has renounced everything and her black serge dress smells of the sewing-room, she no longer even thinks of filling in her wrinkles, of powdering them, she does not dye her dusty pepper-and-salt hair. She does not sigh: 'Ah! If you had only seen me. . . .' Only her hat has a delicate mission to fulfil, for, unfashionably, unusually, spread over a light brass framework, the crown very small and the brim very large and wavy, she sports a hood of black lace.

Make no mistake, this is the hat of a twenty-year-old blonde, with blue eyes, whose rather pale mouth and transparent cheek show to advantage under a lace canopy. This is a hat for a day of victory or betrothal, the hat she wore, had copied, adopted, the hat of which she used to say, with an irrefutable air: 'This hat is really me.' She has aged without taking counter-measures—if not, what would her children, her son-in-law, her husband have said? —but not entirely. There are days when she still essays, for the sake of an unknown and stimulating audience, the smile at the corner of the mouth and the haughty gaze that we find so laughable, the smile and the gaze that she had at twenty, with the lace hood.

You are impelled to smile—and I am no better than you—when you meet that other old lady, she who artlessly provokes us with the aggressive felt head-dress, turned up on the left, befeathered on the right, of the Grande Mademoiselle. So decked out she resembles an elderly academician, proud as a monkey. We laugh too soon, before discovering, on her aged face, the relics of one of those militant beauties who affected the plumy feather and the so-called 'musketeer's' asymmetric brim. You may be sure that a timid Areopagus, secretly devoted, named her at the peak of her brilliance 'Bradamante'! The magic of such a name impresses the weak-minded, though the vogue for the ensheathing corsage and the arrogant felt hat passed without Bradamante giving them up.

Today an imploring family still sometimes adjures her 'Look, mother . . . I assure you, grandmother . . .' to return to a sense of reality and she promises to do what they ask. She even visits her dressmaker, 'a remarkably intelligent girl, with a central position, who should have all that's needed to be a success'. She tries on one of the little shapes that current fashion dictates. 'My God, it can't suit me as badly as that. . . .' And then she tries it on again, ridicules her faded countenance, smooths her white hair, claps the little hat on the edge of her forehead once more, frowns, is perplexed, decides at last: 'There, it's not that I don't like it, this little cloche, but it needs . . . you understand, Mademoiselle, the brim isn't quite wide enough for me. Haven't you got a hat a little more . . . a little bigger . . . or, if necessary, you could make it for me specially. Wider, and more—look, a turn-up at the side would show my profile better and we might use something on the right, a—I don't know exactly—an ostrich feather, for instance, to complete the ensemble.'

How shall we recognize, in thirty years' time, the Bradamante of today? Frantic, formal, a prey to dreams but more reverent than her grandmother, she hides, like the hooded Rosalinde of 1885, under the universal cloche. The cloche, I say, the cloche, and still the cloche. Behind, its brim touches the collar of the long jacket or short coat. In front, the brim descends like a visor half-way down the nose. Beneath, the right eye, slightly more obscured than the left, bears the stigma of an arbitrary confinement: it acquires the habit of being a little more closed than the left. Obliged to scrutinize everything with a downward gaze, the women 'bear up into the wind' like badly harnessed horses. Cloche, tailored costume, multicoloured scarf, I was forgetting the stockings the colour of pink gravel. . . .

A young man I once knew made a date with his young woman at the entrance to the Métro and darted forward as soon as he saw her appear, neat in her tailored costume, her neck bound twice round with a scarf, the little cloche coming below her eyes, hair invisible, neck shaved, ochre and carmine on her cheek. 'You're here at last!' It was someone else, very much the same. A second young woman in prescribed form emerging from the abyss, the young man bounded forward a second time towards the cloche, the cheek, the scarf, the stockings—he had to try three young women before he hit—if I may so put it—on the right one. Chastened, he greeted his real young woman with a chill reserve and, while she rebuked him loudly, still a little bemused, he identified her: 'A beauty-spot beneath the eye, right, jade-green earrings and fourteen glass bracelets on the wrist, if I remember rightly.' But at that very moment someone trod on his foot; a female voice emerging from a small cloche hat begged his pardon in the tone of a dry reprimand. He heard the clashing of a dozen or so Czech glass bangles; he spied, along cheeks browner and pinker than natural, two long pendants of imitation jade, and received the tail of a motley scarf in his eye. It was then that the young man became possessed by a transport of fear and anger. He bent forward, bit the beautiful cheek of his over-anonymous young woman, and bore her away, newly branded, like the elect heifer of the herd.

Breasts

How do you like them? Like a pear, a lemon, *à la* Montgolfière, half an apple, or a canteloup? Go on, choose, don't be embarrassed. You thought they didn't exist any longer, that they were all over with, absolutely done for, their name ostracized, their amiable or indiscreet turgescence dead and deflated like gold-beater's skin?

If you spoke of them at all, it was to condemn them as vagaries of
the past, a sort of collective hysteria, an epidemic of ages now lost
in night, isn't that so? If you don't mind, Madame, let's bring
things up to date. They exist, and persist, however criticized and
persecuted they may be. There is a dour vitality in those who
hope. 'Next year in Jerusalem' murmured others of the oppressed
over the centuries. Those I have in mind whisper perhaps : 'Next
year, in the corsage. . . .'

Everything is possible, the worst seems probable. Enough of
hedging! Admit the truth once and for all : *breasts exist!* There
are pear-shaped breasts, breasts like a lemon, half an apple (see
above). Anarchy mounts—I wish it merited the title of an up-
rising. What, is the breast being refashioned, then? By the emplace-
ment yours have abandoned, I swear it, Madame. You're in a fine
fix, as they say. Is there to be news of horrors? There is news. Even
better, there are fabrications. Relax, Madame. Let a deep sigh of
happiness stir your squared boxer's teats, or your agitated rhetor-
ician's chest, for now you may choose. Little cups in light rubber,
painted in natural colours, await you. You hesitate between four
or five different types? Bah, you buy them all, for they are all
charming. Oh! the modest breasts of former days, the arrogant
charms for the white tunic embroidered in mother of pearl, and
those two mandarines beneath the Spanish shawl! The technique
of using them is as simple as possible. An almost invisible band
links the two spurious 'assets' at a proper distance; two other
bands, passing under your arms, tie behind your back. Veiled with
lace or *crêpe de Chine*, these cups, if empty, conceal the void and,
if full, gather and immobilize under their domes the secrets of the
overflowing parts. . . .

Are you satisfied, then? No? I see how it is. The result is too
perfect. It's true. A kind of neutrality, a deadly serenity, informs
the sham breast and this itself arouses suspicion. Wait, Madame,
I've not finished being helpful. I offer you . . . take them, these
two tulle pockets christened 'hold-alls' by an over-witty woman.
'It's not ill-meant,' she asseverates, 'it just had to be thought of.
Nothing can outmanoeuvre my hold-alls. You've too much of
them, they overflow on all sides? I gather them for you, I cen-
tralize them, each in their place, come on now, everything must

go back! *Yours* are not wide enough and are too long? I grasp them and knead them for you, I mould them into proper shape—it's only a question of knack—and beneath my tulle, yours can aspire to Venus! Madame has noticed the little hole in the centre to allow the nipple through? That's a mark of genius. That gives life to the whole undertaking!'

I should have wagered, Madame, that I would have over-whelmed you with this stroke. I see you are lukewarm and undecided. Ah! One can't revive a cult at one go, you still reject the twin miracles, so worshipped once. Your nihilism still rests on that unrelenting sentence: 'Nothing too much.' Here we are, at the height of summer. You're leaving for the Normandy seaside, the daily bathe. The women there feel compelled to show themselves brown of limb, flat-bottomed, with no more hip than a bottle of Rhine wine, while the gentlemen are narrow-waisted, laced like Cossacks, and fine-chested. I am inopportune, with my tricks as a precursor of breasts. I need only have first glanced at the new bathing costumes for women, stolen, this year, from the little girls' shelves. Away with yesterday's swimsuit! Or better, hide it, I beg you, under the little checked sleeveless apron that my daughter wore two years ago. Cut at the level of the thigh, the dress of a five-year-old tot in shiny red taffeta with black braid will make the baby happy when mother has given up bathing. Small panels, knots at the back, a six-inch skirt beneath a childish tunic, smocks hitherto reserved for the schoolroom, the elegance of the elementary school, there, that's for Dinard, that's for Deauville! I concede that bathing, breasts, scare you. You are afraid, sheltering them under Claudine's smock, of giving yourself that little 'Chas-Laborde' look that attends every dumpy woman dressed *en gamine*, and you are right. Well then, why not use, between flesh and skin, the supplementary epidermis recently invented, the body-stocking of pure rubber which holds you tighter than a lover from armpit to groin, and even lower. Its hidden strength, uniformly exerted, appears only in use. What matter if it reduces the shape of the female body to the mere contour of a cylinder! Sausage you must be, sausage you shall be. And while a slow strangulation accelerates your heartbeat and congests your cheek you can savour the subtle pleasures of an odoriferous perspiration that gathers the rubber's sulphurous essence, the human body's acidity. . . . I need say no more. Adopt this elastic hair-shirt, Madame. You will find that it serves both vanity and virtue.

Paperweights

This one? Fifteen hundred francs. See, it's signed and dated. . . .

I see. I see that at the centre of the hemispheric paperweight of thick glass there snuggles a caramel flourish whose section presents the figure of a star, a rose, a small squirrel, a holothurian, a duck, or the branched, ramifying hexagon of snow-crystals seen through a lens. The whole, designed in bold colours, evokes the bottom of the sea, a garden *à la française*, a jar of Viennese acid-drops, and costs fifteen hundred francs.

Fifteen hundred francs. I consider the object dispassionately and compare it with the one I have, which is even more beautiful. In the days when my very dear Annie de Pène and I used to haunt the flea-markets, we paid three francs, or a hundred sous, for these playthings now so sanctified and revalued by fashion. We hid them, so as to browse in secret on their puerile monstrosity. Annie had a thing about a paperweight where imprisoned air bubbles shone like globules of mercury above a drowned pansy.

'But,' she would say mournfully, 'I know that the one with the forget-me-not and the swallow belongs to a Madame P. . . who won't sell it, and the very thought of it makes my life miserable!'

She laughed; the laughter lit up a golden fleck in her brown eyes, the most mischievous, the most penetrating brown eyes that ever adorned the face of a blonde. Already infatuation was born. Her more discreet victims concealed it or, taken by surprise, excused themselves as if for a monomania: 'What d'you expect . . . it's frightful, this glass object, but it belonged to my great uncle . . . my mother always had it on her writing-desk. . . .'

Annie de Pène used to prophesy : 'You'll see, they'll get on to them soon enough, these paperweights! Just now, I'm fed up with the chemist in the rue de la Pompe. Only this morning I bought some bicarbonate of soda from him that I didn't need, and some chest liniment that upsets my heart, in the hope that he'd sell me his paperweight with the red rose. Another ten francs thrown away, and for nothing!'

She claimed, rightly, that these glassmakers' masterpieces found shelter with the concierges, and she would suddenly enter a lodge during a walk : 'What floor is Monsieur Defaucomprey? . . . Is Madame Etcheverry on the third floor? . . . The workshops of Messieurs Barnavaux and Coquelourde, please?'

The time it took to put the question and hear the reply was enough for her. Sometimes the darting, brilliant chestnut gaze discovered on the mantelpiece—rounded, bulging, like the luminous cryptogram of the shadow zones—a paperweight. . . . Then Annie, all honey and careful phrases, would start a conversation, praise the baby, stroke the cat, finally approach the paperweight, her imperative desire, in lessening circles. . . . But one day when she asked in a tone of perfect assurance for an improvised 'Monsieur Gaucher' the concierge replied without quitting her armchair : 'There he is now, just on his way down, call him or he'll be through the arch without stopping . . .'

'No, no!' interrupted Annie hastily, 'I only wanted to leave this for him . . . you can give it to him when he gets back. Don't forget, mind!'

She dragged me away, cowardly abandoning a yard and a quarter of excellent suspender elastic that she had just bought.

Well, now they're the rage, these pustulous, incestuous products of the English sweetmeat and the magnifying lens. They've also something of the medusa who perhaps inspired them. Nevertheless, the ladies who currently collect paperweights are well known, Mme Lanvin, Mme Bouniols; Germaine Beaumont and Pierre Battendier shared the rare pieces collected by their mother, Annie de Pène. The Hôtel des Ventes, though it has seen so many others, was in an uproar at the auctions when an unknown collector broke up his collection last year. How long will the new fad last? Longer than one thinks, as it always does when fashion alights on a nobly and entirely useless object. The paperweight now belongs to fine art, just because of its uselessness. It presses no paper, it does not hang from the wall, it cannot be made into a lamp like a vulgar Persian pot, it is not embroidered in cross-stitch like an old print, nor does it cover a lampshade like a precious silk, and no one has ever been heard to suggest that it could be adapted to make a handbag. It evades every degrading usage, the exploiting temper of the modern woman who sacrifices everything to furnish a house and sighs before a slender upright Virgin of the fifteenth century, 'What a marvellous pedestal for a table!' It's not the paperweight that will be turned into a divan or into a 'stylish' telephone apparatus. It can't be cut up into sheets to make a boudoir canopy, like a humble screen from Coromandel. It mocks at the ingenious construction of powder-boxes and shrugs a shoulder, so to speak, at the onyx fashioned into a cigarette-case.

In answer to the uninventive collector who asks herself 'Should it be a god, a table, or a bowl?' it has chosen to be a god. It reigns, no more convex than the forehead of an obstinate spouse, good for nothing, polished, receiving the incense of the faithful. Its crystal soul reveals its every thought, and it thinks little. It is both various and simple, witness of the fervour and the ignorance of those who shaped it. A flower, a little silver sheep, a cactus, a dreamy confusion of sea-creatures, a spreading cross, the emblem of the Legion of Honour . . . that's enough. Our imbecility does the rest. But we must also take into account, to the credit of today's plaything, its shape, so like a sphere, and its thick substance, translucent and distorting. The crystal sphere, an abyss, a snare for images, resort of the weary spirit, source of chimeras, maintains its mysterious attraction for man. When I asked Annie de Pène 'Why do we like these glass balls?' she replied : 'Don't bother me. I know nothing about it. A glass ball, it makes one's mouth water. It's probably a sin.'

Novelties

You take a marabout,* you shave him. And to fill the cup of his
ignominy you degrade him, before exposing him for all to see. . . .
If these lines chance to be seen by a Moslem it will give him a
dreadful shock. To humiliate a saint of Islam thus!

Happily, it's only a matter of fashionable wear. As for degrading
the marabout, well and good. Pink or red, violet or blue, he'll be
none the uglier for it . . . but shaving him . . . why not shear a
chicken or depilate an angora? The rabbit and the marabout, both
shorn, are paradoxically allied with that other monstrosity which
dishonoured our hats for so long—the glycerined ostrich-feather.
(I trust that Joseph Delteil will allow me to dedicate to him, as a
delicate offering, these two singularly linked words; I can't forget
that he is the author of *The Incestuous Sponge*.)

It is a strange industry that appropriates a downy animal
covering—light, warm, smooth to the touch—to destroy it by
chemistry or electricity and then to announce 'Behold this unrecognizable skin from which we have removed the living grass
and left the stubble! Behold these bound bundles of feathers,
with the last of the winged down still adhering! Behold this
miserable, nearly bald broom, whose remaining strands have been
stuck together by an ingenious treacle! You may wear these
remains as proudly as plume or caparison and, what's even more
remarkable, no one will laugh!' A fact. It would make me cry
rather.

Quick, let's get drunk to forget it. The drunkenness of deliverance, the great wind of change. The little cloche sounds its own
knell. Just when one had given up any hope of ever dethroning it,
the little concave hat suddenly expires. Its dominion had lasted
for more than two lustra. Now, we're told it's done for. By whom?
Pah . . . by unimaginative usurpers who mistake eccentricity for
courage : the hexagonal skull-cap, the top hat, the pastry-mould,

* *Marabout* can mean either a Moslem holy man or a marabou stork whose
feathers were used for decoration.

73

the inverted bucket, the old-fashioned chamber-pot. Let's put on our heads the truncated bucket which 'gives an Oriental look', the 'amusing' mould, the hexagon said—who'd have thought it—to rejuvenate, the 'stylish' top hat and the 'becoming' chamber-pot— I could give you a thousand examples. Let us savour these ephemeral indulgences whose days are numbered for, in the shadow, there waits and watches, assured of a triumphant return—the little cloche.

Charming extinguisher, friendly shelter for tired eyes, you're on the shelf now. Born of a rudimentary logic, it is the tubular hat just now that crowns the crabbed geometrical masterpiece known as the tube-dress which, like Jeanneton's doll, has neither front nor back. O sadism, O mortification! To inhabit, even if only for a few hours a day, a stove-pipe, the interior of a drain, of a stick of macaroni. The modern woman takes a peculiar delight in this. And whenever fashion reduces the breadth and increases the length of the malleable female body, certain accessories of the toilet become deformed in the opposite direction. Just as the long stalk of the Brussels sprout adorns itself at the right moment with tiers of edible tumours, so the tube-woman hangs from her neck and ears excrescences of hollow silver, notable for their size if not for their weight. Silver was ever a poor, sad metal. Earrings of tarnished silver, tarnished necklaces of silver spheres, take up a lot of room, have little lustre, darken the skin, and anyone but a Negress would disdain them in favour of glassware. These not so brilliant spheres do not even capture the distorted reflection that dances in the centre of the silvered garden globe, their scintillating rival. But they are surprising in their sphericism on a wisp of a woman, flanked in addition by an umbrella. An umbrella? Is that really an umbrella? I quiz the object that Madame Blanche Vogt forgot at my place. She dropped in and I imagined that she had come straight from some Cancale estate by the sea; for she was wearing a dress of light silk, bright red, printed with violet and yellow flowers, shoes of scarlet kid, and flesh-coloured stockings. These maritime appurtenances reached their climax in a little umbrella of bronzed taffeta, a few inches high and broader than it was long, whose handle was decorated with a terrible and probably prehistoric knob; but it was a modern caprice that had carved in the thickness of its hard wood garlands of little flowers painted in natural colours.

I haven't yet returned this strange umbrella, this chunky dwarf, to its owner. I've arranged it beside a carved wooden siren, also dwarfish, next to a bottle-base in greenish glass picked up on the beach, polished, mellowed, translucent and turbid as a jelly-fish, next to two rare shells with pink lips. . . . Strange, my friends exclaim at sight of the siren, the glass bauble and the shells, but they have no cry of surprise for the gem of my collection, the flower-decked truncheon skirted with cockchafer taffeta—in fact, the umbrella.

I meant to tell the ottoman, an old flame that returns, newly done up, from afar, what I thought of it in two words; two words touching on its ill-humour in enveloping us, its misplaced gravity, its temper that takes offence at a drop of rain. But here I am side-tracked by a musical reverie. The king of weavers doesn't stop at inventing materials, he also invents their names. Hardy neologisms, sounds of arabesque richness, calm as Tibetan wool, you caress the ear with a harmony that derives from savage chant and waggish invention. It's not for you I speak, kasha, cat-named kasha :

'On your ravishing breast that your modesty concealed*
Crosses and recrosses in beauty a scarf of kasha !'

But, when I read the roll of crepellaine, bigarella, poplaclan, of djirsirisa and gousellaine—I forget how many !—I am seized by a phonetic rapture and begin to think in pure poplacote dialect. Allow me, in taking leave of you, dear reader, to glove myself with filavella, to put my rubespadrillavellaines on my feet, to wear my djissatutbanecla hat; now's the time, at low tide to go fishing among the anfractuosities of rockaskaia, congrepellina and the zibeline sea-bream.

* *Cacha.*

Late Season

Winter approaches. A bold statement that dates from a few weeks ago and in particular from the day when I saw the first chestnut-seller install herself beneath the massive arcade of the porte Saint-Vincent. Before her, English elegance, conquering the heights of Saint-Malo, had heralded frost. Fashionable London of Saint-Malo does not shrink before the audacious innovations that astound the eye and capture the soul of the artist. No doubt of it, it must have been admiration that held me captive at sight of a young Islander, serene despite the shower, beneath a cape of black marocain with monkey collar. Some artifice of fashion simulated, at shoulder-level and on the lower part of the cape, the greenish plaques that grease imprints on any black material. Under the cape could be glimpsed a ravishing shirt-dress in braided cotton, in old rose turning to yellow. And the fringe of black fur that hemmed the bottom of the garment was not so long that one could not see, as coquettish as unexpected, two bare feet shod in espadrilles very cunningly decolourized by one of those techniques of which shoemakers of genius guard the secret. And what to say of the hat, of mauve national material and Scottish ribbon? How to praise the handbag-reticule in brushed painted leather, the necklace of green bobbles encircling a lorgnette?

Mindful of this dazzling memory, I sought in vain for an analogous ensemble in the great collections, where there was nevertheless a surprise in store for me.

'Is it you?' I asked Lucien Lelong, 'who is launching the dress in braided pink cotton, covered by a marocain cape . . . ?'

Before I had finished my sentence the young and ebullient *couturier* had evaded me, crying: 'Mme de X's *culotte*, now! What, it's not ready? It only needed gathering at the bottom and fixing two pieces of suède on the. . . .' The rest was lost in the clatter of doors. The door of a delicate lacquer salon opened and there emerged a thin acid voice: 'No, Madame Jeanne, no revolver-pocket. And the base of the jacket to reach the level of the trousers, not an inch more!'

The word 'ski' issuing from invisible lips enlightened me just as I trembled to see myself, to keep up with everyone else, condemned to the smoking-jacket and to the horrible so-called fancy trousers which contract with the jacket an indissoluble union devoid of love or reason.

Winter sports, I've more to say to you. From December to February you nibble at the female skirt, subject to wave and sun from July to September. You have a place in the year determined by the snow-bearing east wind, the west wind that melts the glaciers. But you have for accomplices the hunting season, sea-bathing, African exploration, riding, which—like you—strip Woman of her ancient shackle, the dress. Nowadays every season tolerates and favours the trousered woman, and the *couturier*, endowed with a hound's nose, changes into breeches-maker, knitter, military tailor, rather than lose half his profits. He profits from the woman's boyish infatuation and, cutting his losses, more or less does away with the now useless transitional costume, mid-way between the morning's sportive leggings and the soft draperies of evening. The 'good, safe dress' has had its day. But the Saumur breeches for ladies prosper, and the *lamé* also.

Gold *lamé*, silver *lamé*, copper, steel—they are alike in their rustle, always a little like chocolate wrappings, in their grating chill and in their smell. The enduring vogue for *lamé* indicates the grossness of the female senses, particularly the sense of smell. For the scent of a *lamé* dress, dampened in the course of a warm evening, oxidized while dancing, surpasses in acridity the strong aroma of a removal-man in full activity. It smells of ill-kept silverware, of old copper coins, the brass-cloth; its silken texture does nothing to attenuate the odours that impregnate it; on the contrary.

The other day a slender friend—all my friends are slender—was amusing herself at her *couturier's* trying on some evening dresses she coveted. 'I'm a small 42!' she announced at every opportunity. Like a stickleback with its nest, she agilely traversed those narrow drainpipes that are labelled, according to their material, as a morning walking-dress or a ball-dress; she went in head first, made her exit with her feet, danced a peacock step before the mirrors, mimed fashionably the amiable scoliosis that was already in vogue in Albert Dürer's time, and steamed, I swear, like a little horse at dressage. A dress of gold and steel *lamé* on a green foundation attracted her, not so much, however, as another of silver *lamé* on black; but then there appeared a copper *lamé* on brown which, as my friend vividly expressed it, 'knocked the rest into a cocked hat' and yet was dethroned by a silver and gold *lamé* on pale pink. Privately, I criticized the irritating uniformity of their design : a metal tube, quite straight, based on a foundation of material. One particular dress, slit from top to bottom, revealed an under-layer of green crêpe and the saleswoman, reassuring my perplexed friend, informed her that 'many of these ladies wore the split sometimes in front and sometimes behind'. She added, mysteriously, that the coming winter would see an 'even more practical' evening gown, thanks to two laterally placed openings above the hem : 'You turn your dress upside-down, you put your arms through the openings and the result is that the embroidery or the material is now on top and looks quite different. What do you think of that, ladies?'

My slender friend did not reply immediately, reduced as she was to the condition of a hermit crab inserted into an unyielding casing, arms raised and blindly beating the air above her invisible head. I felt that I ought to fill in the moments when, as they say in the theatre, people dry: 'I think,' I suggested humorously, 'that it might be simpler perhaps to teach your clients to walk on their hands. . . .'

An angry look reminded me, too late, that nothing is to be gained by being facetious at the expense of taxi-drivers and dressmakers: 'In France, only those who sell Christmas cards and mah-jong sets need bother about English habits. As for walking on hands, we may leave that to the Duchess of Sutherland, who, so it seems, can outclass anyone.'

Furs

She has a car, but she has not got a pearl necklace.

I have, you have, we have a pearl necklace, but they have, will have, might have had a fur-coat.

The car of my cousin is smaller than the pearl necklace of my aunt.

If your grandmother had had a pearl necklace, your mother could have bought a fur coat and sold her car. . . .

In a year or two it will be obligatory; meanwhile the use of the little manual of conversation and syntax from which I quote is optional. In all, it contains three hundred phrases constructed by felicitous combinations of the words 'car', 'pearl necklace' and 'fur coat', with nouns of the second order such as *château, Deauville, aeroplane, blackmail, carat, suicide, concealment of capital,* etc., and thereby capable of universal application. I am told that a *de luxe* edition contains a list of famous necklaces, furs and cars. This list, kept carefully up to date, makes it possible to state that a pearl necklace and a motor-car are interchangeable in precisely opposite directions, but that a fur, if it is not definitely associated with its owner, disappears without trace like a spring soaked up by desert sands.

Certain young women—a woman who possesses everything is inevitably young—own necklace, car and fur together. Instead of remaining in stagnant serenity they relinquish the cares of necklace and car to devote themselves to a prudently graduated collection of fur coats. Hierarchically, the coat progresses from mink to sable, by way of chinchilla.

I knew an artiste—an artiste of the woman-of-the-world type, that is, the minimum of charm with the minimum of talent—who, between a peerless mink and a pedigree sable, lacked the gradation of chinchilla. She retained a constant bitterness because of this and the smile of a woman who has lost an incisor tooth. Another artiste, young and charming, finds herself at present within reach, if I may so put it, of a sable coat, the waiting, the passionate quest for which, produce in her the physical trepidation, the dancing from one foot to the other, that can be seen in children tormented by a long withheld desire. She has got to ill-treating her last year's chinchilla and to mishandling and treating—I swear it!—as a 'little tart's fur' her own two-year-old mink which she accuses of having turned red. . . .

'Master' furrier, since that's how you christen yourself, you can count on thousands of slaves. You know that furs and roles have changed, and you are no longer to be heard saying to a customer, as you bow her over the threshold, 'Your servant, Madame'. Debt-ridden, the customer bows a shoulder under the hand of your smart purveyor, male or female, and knows the cost of the 'Goodbye, little one!' that you throw her from the top of the stairs. She hasn't stolen it, Our Lord furrier. Remind her, whenever necessary, that she is the humiliated descendant of those women who waited, shivering in the dark of a cave, for a male to throw some still-bleeding pelt round her nakedness. You won't need to remind her of the surrender with which the prehistoric little woman had to pay for the animal's skin.

'For that's one of the things a woman doesn't forget. . . .'

But you care little, furrier, for this voluptuous kind of trifle. You invent, and how! Never were there fewer furry animals, or more skins. Rabbit, treated in a hundred ways, has not said its last word. It was merely an impalpable snow falling from your hands on the skin of the rat that promoted it to the inaccessible chinchilla; now you have to marry the wild beast and its victim and you offer us, as serious as a Batignolles trapper, 'gazelle, panther-style'. Hybrids that embellish the sordid dialogue of saleswoman and client, while the smallest purchase of a little skin confounds natural history. It was an honest dealer in skins at Toulouse who boasted to me of the beauty of a large width of burnduck: 'Look, Madame, see how the colour is the same from one end of the skin to the other. It's very fine burnduck.'

'Is it natural?'

'Oh, Madame, you can't mean it! Real burnduck isn't strong; this is made from little shaved mink. If you prefer this panther for the fine facings and bottom of a coat, you'll be pleased with it; we aren't like those people who make their panther out of good-for-nothing gazelle, I can guarantee it!'

'Really?'

'As per invoice, Madame! All our panther is made from real kid.'

Amateurs

Sanctifying and extending a privilege hitherto reserved for MM. Sacha Guitry, Fauchois and Verneuil, the Casino of Monte Carlo this year launches the author-actor. Down with the professional! After all, what does the public expect from a lead player bearing a famous name? Talent, emotion, admirable self-control and the clarity of diction acquired through much labour? It's not much. It's monotonous. 'Let us then,' says the Casino Theatre, 'engage the authors themselves and let them loose in their own works. We don't yet know what the public will make of it, but real actors will doubtless experience a moment of gaiety at this novel spectacle and, frankly, it really is their turn. This kind of theatrical gala will at once combine a childlike improvisation and a delightful inexperience.' In which belief the Casino Theatre engaged Tristan Bernard, Jean Sarment, Jacques Deval, hinted at Maurice Rostand, co-opted Léopold Marchand and Colette. Then it sat down, this Casino Theatre, on its ample white backside, rubbed its hands in anticipation, and watched the antics of its squad of author-interpreters while waiting for the moment to laugh. . . .

It's still waiting. Beside the blue sea it dreams of this use of dramatist-interpreter, to which its authority as Monaco's Casino Theatre shall have accorded official acknowledgment and existence, of this amateurism, if I may so describe it, which only asks to become professional. Where now is the promised farce? Where now the light-hearted improvisation, the studio absurdity? Why, here are authors who rehearse as if they hadn't other fish to fry, who know how to walk on to the stage without catching their feet in the carpet, who make up like English ballerinas, take their time and give the audience the glad eye! We have here outsiders who don't fuss about working continuously through the day and half the night, who don't blink before the footlights and who travel with their bottle of gargle! But it's a betrayal! It's not funny any more at all!

My dear Casino Theatre, don't lose heart. It's much funnier even than you think—first for us, the outsiders, who engage ourselves to present our own texts to the public, here one day and there another, and who amuse ourselves to distraction. Maybe Jean Sarment does not share my opinion, but that's because Jean Sarment, a born actor, an author born and bred, no longer has a hobby-horse to ride to death. Ask our natural Tristan if, more than anything, he doesn't like to play in comedy? Ask Jacques Deval if he didn't experience the keenest and most reprehensible pleasure during the time when I had him rehearse the part of Chéri? If you should catch my collaborator Léopold Marchand before his mirror, his face coated with make-up, then, driven by exaggerated professional motivation, he will alter his boxer's face and change in turn into an aged general, a bistro waiter, a Red Indian, a leper and an Indian fakir! There shine in him the dazzling qualities of the amateur interpreter of the first rank— and I don't say this just because Léopold Marchand measures over six feet—the same qualities that dignify Jacques Deval. Jacques Deval counted the lines of the part I offered him and grimaced: 'In my own piece,' he said nonchalantly, 'I'd have ten times as much to spout. . . .' So he turned down the part of Desmond in *Chéri*. Léopold Marchand did not dare to imitate him but cast a grim eye at the excellent Basseuil, a professional, who inherited a more important part in the same piece. And he attempted to console himself by purchasing, for a ten-minute appearance on the stage, a fifty-louis suit as well as a pair of boxing-gloves for seventy francs, special shoes, an English sweater that cost several pounds sterling, and a mauve check cap that made me smile. . . . But one cannot criticize the born amateur with impunity: 'Do I criticize you,' he said acidly, 'for your three

Lelong dresses? Three dresses for three appearances, one for each act!' Masculine surliness will resort to the lowest arguments. What's the point of arguing?

All the same, it's still the case that the company of author-actors 'sets the fashion' as they say. It will last . . . as long as a fashion? There are some very enduring fashions, such as the shirt-dress. . . .

Before me the sea is a fierce blue, the palm-trees a vivid green against a backdrop of advertising bill-boards. But the violets smell of violets and the Italian grape, Madeira-coloured, is within reach of every purse. I might easily forget my dignity as author-interpreter if the furtive yet gigantic shadow of my collaborator did not momentarily block the square as he leaves a perfumer's shop where, I dare say, he has acquired some stick of make-up that was missing from his amateur's collection. Punctually, and with papal severity, we shall both be ready in advance in our artistes' box this evening, like the brave amateurs we are. The producer has no worries so far as we are concerned. Forgotten are the anxieties evoked last week by Tristan Bernard, when he disappeared to go gambling between two appearances in his role. . . .

Dear Tristan, whatever you do, you'll never be an amateur!

Empty Pockets

Well, that's that. We've done the rounds but we admit that we're flat out. Exhausted, drained, here we are seated on a modern cushion given us too late to be sent, a rose pinned to its bulging *lamé* belly, to a friend. From now on, terrified, we watch the approach of Easter, hatching its eggs. . . .

The children have been stuffed. Nauseated with sweets, cinema and circus, they are back at their hygienic school, where they will be restored to health. Among themselves they speak less of their own presents than of the ones their parents have received. 'My papa has a new six-cylinder . . .' 'And what d'you think, when Mama opened her jewel-case . . .' They are the children of today, greedy, impatient. They accept the cinema while waiting to travel, the mechanical toy while anticipating a motor-car. My daughter, aged eleven and a half, announces the make of every car as it speeds by, and she is always right. She calculates under her breath and asks: 'How many years' ordinary New Year's presents would it take to make a five horse-power?' The poor child doesn't realize that ordinary New Year's presents don't exist any more. December has brought chestnuts at twenty francs a pound, roses at eight francs apiece, truffles at a hundred francs the kilo. The little Pont-aux-Choux soup-tureen was marked up at a thousand francs in the window on New Year's Eve; it will be less in January, but we shan't have any money left to buy it.

January, month of empty pockets! The snow of the mountain-tops calls us, but everything has to be paid for and snow is as expensive as white marabout. What woman would dare tread it without having refitted herself with Saumur breeches, double and triple stockings, nailed boots, sweaters, fur coat, scarves, eider-down-gloves? The tourist is ruined by his equipment before even reaching the mountain-slope; what use will they be, those deep, buttoned, leather-lined pockets? Let us endure this evil month, anxious as a theatrical producer's forehead. With a diver's courage more than one woman this month plunges into some neglected chest, into wardrobes given over to darkness and camphor. The purse may be empty but one must nevertheless keep up with the spring fashions, though the holidays have put a large part of the wardrobe out of action. The pearled tunic, fatigued by dancing, is on its way out; indoor fireworks and pudding-sauce have aged the velvet sheath-dress by a year; and this obstinate rain can't have been helpful to the hygiene of the afternoon dress in crêpe marocain.

'We must see about it,' say the women. They see about it. Between January and March, Madame, you will meet your newly adorned friends and you will cry out in admiration, but with a desperation in your praises that demands an explanation: 'This?' your friend will say. 'But this is my three-piece from X. . . . Look, it's fifteen months old, my dear, and I'm not ashamed of it!' This is uttered in a frank, honest, high voice that adds, more gently and offhandedly : 'Have you noticed that the new collections have gone back to exactly the same details in the neck and shirt material? It's very strange.'

Empty pockets, high hearts—this is the month for grand feminine resignation. My friend Valentine exhibits, in January, the embarrassment of a peahen at moulting-time. Each New Year, like an equinoctial tide, brings her its unvarying manifestations of economy. The week of Twelfth Night, she nibbled her piece of flan at my place and the *vin de paille* loosened her tongue—a result that might have been brought about just as well by a glass of water.

'It's all over,' she tells me. 'I give up.'

It crossed my mind that she might be taking the veil : still, I made inquiry.

'What? Why, the *couturiers*, of course! Thank heavens! And I've no regrets, understand? I've just discovered an absolute treasure . . . a little dressmaker, my dear, who for two hundred and fifty francs can make me exactly the same dresses that I pay —used to pay, it's all over now!—eighteen hundred to three thousand francs for at X. . . .'

'No! Is that possible?'

'Absolutely, I tell you. It's better finished, even, than at X. . . because X. . . has too many customers and he botches things. So you see, for the price of one dress from X. . . I've just ordered eleven dresses. It's not worth going without! Real pleasure, real smartness, lie in variety, believe me!'

I congratulated my friend Valentine. She seemed so happy that I did not remind her of her avowal of Twelfth Night, 1924, an avowal during which I learned that, tired of modest and ineffectual dresses, she was leaving her jobbing dressmaker to become a client of the famous X. . . .

'You understand, it's all over. I shan't be taken in by those little dressmakers any more. Thank heavens! There are ten dresses, my dear, ten dresses I'm giving up quite new. Money thrown away, bad temper, four thousand francs in the gutter, that's what comes of trying that little dressmaker! Now, at X. . .'s I get for my four thousand francs two marvellous dresses which won't lose their shape and won't go out of fashion, that I can always wear happily. To be really smart doesn't mean having a lot of dresses; on the contrary, it's wearing the indisputable style of a great house.'

Silks

From obscure depths, where sometimes glides the slow reflection that illumines abundant lazy springs, there rises an enormous umbel, a kind of star. Its dome, flush with the surface of the water, bears the colours of the fiery begonia, the full-red rose, its drowned edges descend to the red of hot metal, of pomegranate stained purple by shadow. Behind the empurpled floating creature sways a trailing branch, fronded, of algal-green. . . .

However, we are only talking of velvet, and a printed flower. The creator of the design declares : 'That's a poppy . . .' and so he believes. But I know full well that his flower—bulbous, umbilicated, delicately segmented, fringed, and trailing a filamentous train—is a jelly-fish. If I tell the designer that it's a jelly-fish he will protest with the haughty manner of a misunderstood artist. The primordial sea is a long way off. The monster or the flower it engenders in our minds emerges, as does the fruit of the water-chestnut, at the end of a stalk so long that we give no thought to its submerged root. But the beauty of the material displayed reveals the secret of inspiration : at the heart of richly moiré velvet, touched by the watery sheen that plays on a light-absorbing surface, the poppy has become a jelly-fish.

I touch, I contemplate these modern silks, the most costly of feminine adornments. Sure of his supremacy, proud of his magical workings, he that weaves them says gently : 'I am supreme.' What point in modesty here? All is magnificence, inflated even more this year by certain monstrous features. Consider this giant gloxinia, that gapes like a little maelstrom at the corner of a great square of silk! The edges of its mouth are tinted the colours of the rainbow, as happens with cataclysmic phenomena. It is as beautiful as a rainbow, as the eye of an octopus.

On an implacable background of gold there turn and climb long, black, half-open pods whose stalks are daughters of the noxious viburnum and the snake. Applied to the flat hip of the nymph of 1925, they will incline her towards evil spells, no less than these lanceolate flames, a fire that is not quenched, purple, green, sun-yellow, that thrust their several tongues towards a bare throat.

What gold, silver and red copper, mixed with the silk! Over the material designed for artificial light there reign the splendour and brutality always imposed by epochs when fashion suffers from poverty of form. The little rectangular tunic goes back to, recovers, the luxury of Byzantine gowns. When the designer sleeps the weaver wakes and works miracles. Using more or less torsion he curbs or cossets the brilliance of the metal thread, evokes a background, interposes between design and spectator a mist of illusion. One piece of illusion detains me for a long time as I seek mechanically with my finger to judge the exact distance of this floating spider's web in pure silver, here concave, convex there, that separates me from a curtain of half-seen roses—yellow, red, pink, against a distant black sky. . . . It's clear that a certain kind of phantasmagoria is popular here, an optical deception that is akin to wit. Avenues of enormous, multicoloured lozenges affront the eye, then recede with the vertiginous diminution of nocturnal reflections. A play of lines plots deceptive perspectives on an artless crêpe, while on another crêpe the eye takes in, from bird's eye or aeroplane height, tree-top after tree-top, crinkled foliage emphasized by a little stroke of vivid lightning-blue.

There is no pleasure without fatigue and that of the eye, if it is prolonged, is particularly dispiriting. Too much gold, gold embroidery on a gold background, too much light and line, too much damascened lampas, eventually engender the lassitude caused by overrich museums. Yet our satiety is deferred by an artistic device not at once apparent, that consists of using an invisible grey, if I may so put it, applied to the reverse of a leaf, an ardent petal, insinuated between two red gleams, between two segments of green. A grey that caulks and stops the fissures where colours fly together, a concentric grey like the zone of feeble reflection that bounds a breach in smooth water.

Let us take our ease in those gardens which, flowering this winter, await the sun and the women of the summer to come. The rose abounds there, a rose faithful to the pictorial tradition our mothers cherished around 1880. Such material is decorated with veritable floral 'portraits', portraits of rich, rather heavy, well-fleshed roses of scrupulous accuracy. Farewell to the 'stylized' eye-shaped rose, farewell to the rose shaped like a snail! The roses I brush against bathe in a light mist, in an air atremble with heat, and I think of those miraculous machines whose steel finger, applying a mother-of-pearl hue here, a splash of light or the green mirror of a moist leaf there, never errs. . . .

Other roses are strewn on other silks, in rustic and ruinous taste; there is the rose borrowed from Persia, the rose of carpets, flat, crushed, laid out to be grateful to the bare foot. The gentle orange seeks the company of the bright rose and the mauves of the sweet-pea are enhanced by a shadowed white ground, mysteriously besmirched. But the dishevelled poppy needs no contrivance. Its torch flames out against the white, against the raw green of the young corn, and burns with such fierceness that women may well be afraid of it, come summer.

But they won't be frightened so easily. Come summer, they will go away, a grass-green skirt round their loins, a red poppy at their breast, fork-tongued lilies at their heart's height. The master of these gardens of fabrics tells me how readily his guests become infatuated, feverishly plunging their bare arms into the murmuring waves of silk. But they are not overawed and, the first ecstasy over, unastonished, they seek a star to garner for their corsage, a meteor to plant in their shorn hair. . . . Whosoever weaves the moon, the sun and the blue shafts of the rain, knows that neither prodigality nor splendour exhausts the depths of feminine avidity. So he restorts to certain perversities.

This year he has been cloistered with a choice bundle of priceless skeins spun by silkworms, murmurs an incantation, baptizes the web with a talismanic elixir, and brings to light amid cries of astonishment . . . the most perfect imitation of a little hound's tooth woollen, at twelve ninety-five the metre!

Logic

Bravo, bravo! They've made up their minds, most of them. The dark days of February, crabbed icy March, April of the two faces —one violet with cold, the other warmly pink—have seen them clothed in yellow oilskins, greenish gaberdines, topped with a little hat glistening with water, minus umbrella and hands in pockets. Bravo! They've braved the vertical rain, the slanting wind, the horizontal snow that adhered to the eyelashes. There they are, the practical women, the pioneers of 1925, good managers today, tomorrow's voters, those who . . .

. . . Those, O Dithyrambic, who have paraded their old and new virtues all winter, at zero temperature and below, on two soles no thicker than a finger-nail, fastened by three little patent-leather straps across a flesh-pink silk stocking. And don't try to tell me about the mottled or ribbed stocking they tried to popularize this year! It was admirable, the ribbed stocking, on the avenue du Bois in the mornings, I mean between twelve and one. It attracted attention, produced as it was in five or six versions. But all winter, in the puddles, spattered with mud, blemished, pitiful, grotesque, indecorous, you must admit one has seen only the pink silk stocking and those wretched little slippers. Oilskins, gaberdines, lynx and beaver collars, topcoats of panther-cum-mole and jaguar-cum-kid, yes, yes, women have pampered their bodies, sheathed in all the necessary fur and quilting, but their care, their coquettish and hygienic ingenuity, has not reached below the knees. Why? Enthusiast, give me a reason. The vagaries of Fashion have a goal and often make sacrifice to aesthetics. But this! And the bare-fleshed stocking beneath the tailored costume! And this poverty of the leg, its cold hue emerging from a rainproof! And the defenceless foot, sullied by a shower, preposterous under a fur hem as big as a child's body! And the attitude, either shivering or cynical, of a woman seated in a drawing-room, seated on the banquette of a bus! And the unfinished appearance, so oddly scamped, got up in a hurry, imparted to a town outfit by two legs clothed as for an evening's frolics!

Having decided to shorten skirts still further, to lead women towards the 'seven-year-old look' (and five francs extra by age, as the catalogues say), Fashion hesitates, not daring to risk, at least in town, the Asiatic trousers that are the unique resort of modesty and hygiene. I should add 'of common sense', since it would enforce some concealment in the great lump of a woman, rare surviving instance of the extinct chubby genus, in the sylph mounted on stilts, neither of whom hesitates to exhibit, beneath the pearly mesh of a '44, fine', twenty inches of legs fit to offend the good Lord—and even his creature.

No, Enthusiast, no, out-and-out Feminist, don't try to make me share your lyricism and don't expect me to foresee any good from a female legislator who is incapable of a warm-foot policy, from a female deputy who, with fingers numb from cold and stamping her feet, winds up a session in somewhat cavalier style to run to the hearth and the radiator.

All very well if, hardened, women become used to trampling the brown slush, the transient whiteness of the snow, with an invulnerable foot! But hardly so. There have been nothing but complaints all winter and our barefooted wanderers danced with the cold from one foot to the other like a cat on hot bricks. Haven't you heard them, in a restaurant : 'Quick, *maître d'hôtel*, a hot-water bottle, a brick! I can't feel my feet any longer. Oh, my dear, this cold! I've been unable to keep my poor feet warm all day and I know I'm going to have a red nose this evening! ... My dear, just believe me, the skin of my thighs is all chapped because of these very short dresses. . . .'

All the same, Enthusiast, do not look down your long nose. Think of the good weather ahead, the warmth, of the thin winter sandal at last yielding place to the thick golf shoe, to the rubber-soled shoe, of the female foot, in July, simmering to boiling-point on odorous rubber and chrome leather. Amuse yourself, already resolved to applaud them, in enumerating the small inventions we owe to elegance. Celebrate here and now the return of the dress-necks that reach up to the ears, the sleeve that lengthens with the summer and shortens in winter. Sing the great knot tied under

the chin, the three turns of muslin, the Royer-Collard lapels, the
enormous boa in cock-feathers reserved for the dog-days, and sing
also, while you're at it, the suppression of our hat-brims. Come the
fine weather, for us the nose that peels and the eye that waters in
the powerful light!

Logic, feminine logic, astounding decisions, sudden, possibly
long-meditated changes, secrets of little boyish heads, arrogant
above sheaths of gold and pearls. . . . At the *couturier's* a Byzantine splendour promenades on shorn collegians. Lelong drapes
ravishing little emperors of the decadence, sexless types accom-
plished in grace, so young and so ambiguous that I could not
refrain from suggesting to the young *couturier*, on a day of up-
heaval in his court of models: 'Why don't you employ—oh, quite
innocently—some adolescent boys? The lively shoulder, the well-
poised neck, the long leg, the absent breast and hip, there are
plenty who'd give good value . . .'

'I understand perfectly,' interrupted the young master *couturier*.
'But the boys who get used to dresses very soon acquire a gait, an
exaggerated feminine grace in comparison with which my young
female models, I assure you, would come to resemble transvestites.'

Everyday Adventures

Yesterday's Age, Tomorrow's Youth

For me, there are no theatrical recollections to evoke Duse, who died this week. Twice, in Rome during the war, the cinema offered her for my delectation. On the first occasion she was playing in the film the part of an aged peasant woman. Beneath the knotted shawl, beneath the calico and the dark apron, she displayed hair of a luminous whiteness, an erect, firm body, and eloquent hands capable of saying everything that a somewhat constrained, even intimidated, countenance refused the screen. During her great scene these hands, lifted towards a high window, called to a much-loved child. La Duse turned her back to the audience, which saw only the calico blouse, the kerchief tied over her hair, and the hands at the ends of outstretched arms, such hands—loving, beating wings, extended and elevated by their shadow to the very edge of the window—that, at that moment, sobs and sighs escaped the sensitive Italian crowd with which I mingled.

On the second occasion, a few days later, I had sought in another dark, cool cinema some shelter from the Roman spring, exploding everywhere in wistaria, irises, lilac, and so fiery that even the *ponentino* brought no relief. A friend said to me very quietly : 'Behind us, that woman in black, that's Eleanora Duse.' I recognized the luminous hair, swept up in a slanting flame above the brow, restrained by a black hat, and the large, deep eye-sockets, where the eyes swam in a shade that enhanced their brilliance. Only the small nose remained the nose of a young woman, a demanding ironic nose, a nose prompt to anger and disdain.

This famous face, turning to right and left, followed the episodes of a wretchedly dramatic film and there could be read in its every feature a great and tender simplicity, without trace of suspicion. But the interval, bringing back the light, also brought a good many admirers around La Duse. She received their homage standing and shook a number of hands. She did not smile, held her face rather defensively, and the little nose, offended, quivered with disdain.

'See,' whispered my enthused Italian companion, 'see what a great lady she is!'

I have never witnessed such hauteur, doubtless involuntary, in Sarah Bernhardt, who blossomed in the love of the crowd, the unknown, the passer-by, and who gave a smile in return for the thrown flower, a kiss or a salutation launched in the air.

When I chanced to be a passing guest at her table, four or five months before her death, Sarah's youth and octogenarian coquetry almost left me speechless, and I was all eyes and ears for her vigilant chatter, her pale, exalted gaze, her hands—agile ossicles playing beneath a skin as delicate as the new skin of healed burns. She poured boiling water on measured doses of powdered coffee, filled the cups herself, while asking my opinion—for the malicious pleasure of voicing her own—of those who, stumbling in her footsteps, assumed the roles she had created. What desire to please, what near-posthumous effort still to shine! What determination to forget, to make others forget, the present physical decay and to reconstruct for us, by a single movement of the eyelids, drawn up to the summit of the forehead, by an imperious rap on the table with her dry, resonant fingers, by a fugitive, evanescent smile, the Sarah of former days, the eternal Sarah!

They were not fond of each other, these two dead women. They are at rest, having neither known nor wished for rest during their lives. Perhaps, in some unknown place, they pine and complain, La Duse that she can no longer, on the stage, weep the tears of a woman in love and betrayed, Sarah that she has ceased to simulate so marvellously the feminine suffering against which the theatre rendered her immune.

Did they suffer in growing old? Not for long. La Duse respected the wrinkles on her face, though there was as much negligence as dignity to be divined in her scruples. Sarah attained old age without feeling it, but she touched up her features with colour and make-up with an Oriental and intelligent taste for adornment. La Duse, because she had loved and never got over it, kept the same open wound in her bosom; Sarah, cradled and sustained by the fanatic adoration of the crowd, never weakened on her single leg. . . . After them, who no longer counted the years, survivors plan to count the days and hours, to mortify themselves and keep

on guard. For our age has witnessed the flowering of a rather
disturbed and rather self-ashamed style on stage and screen and
in literature : first there is the adolescent starlet, the film heroes
haven't always reached the age of matriculation, and out of twenty
new novels half relate, minutely and gloatingly, the first giddiness
of youth. It takes a hundred and fifty pages to prepare their fall,
the rest is rushed through in forty pages—the rest being love. The
Daphnis and Chloë of today, seeing themselves in the stream,
sigh : 'When we were young. . . .' I know a little girl of eleven who
takes stock of herself in the mirror and grimaces : 'I tell you,
Mama, that dressmaker makes me look old!' Another, at twelve,
acts bewildered to rejuvenate herself : 'What a child I am!' No
gain for candour here; on the contrary. Was it with great smiles,
limpid by artifice, that they won and betrayed the confidence of
trusting parents, all those little 'lost girls' who went off furnished
only with a school satchel or a carton of milk? Sometimes one is
brought back and then silence closes over her, after the grand
inquest in the newspapers and the maternal lamentations. 'It is
thought that some shady individual tempted little Suzanne away
. . . smothered her cries. . . .' But no. This simple, crude and tragic
picture is not—as one learned too late—the truth. Little Suzanne,
little Eugénie, in fact the little girl, too little, is a child of our time,
matured in the light of images, the dazzle of arc-lights, the bat-
teries of looks, the sound of words, as out of season as a first fruit.
With the adventurous brow of the ignorant, with a chill and
foolish bumptiousness, the diplomacy of prisoners, it is she who
walked deliberately into a trap as a stream yawns open into an
azure gulf, it is she who negotiated with the man lying in wait.
Every child is unfathomable. But what to think of the vanished
little girl who, brought back, restored to her family, goes out again,
melts at night like a cat between door-jamb and half-open door?
We, who are only simple adults, we dare not think of the little
girl who, without a quiver, puts her hand into the hand held out
from the shadow, the hand that perhaps will close on the childish
neck to leave a collar of hollowed imprints, the colour of violets. . . .
One mustn't shiver overmuch, condemn too eagerly. Lyricism
and tragedy express themselves as best they may in everyday life;
a predestined child will employ new methods to distress her family,

that is, to try to be grown-up. The generation that engendered two famous tragediennes still streamed with romantic tears. Which of our mothers would enjoy the fevered, ambitious adolescence, obsessed with stanzas, of a Duse or a Sarah? Yet our own reticent and stolid children nurse the same disease, the same promise, for all escape is lyricism and conforms to what Hélène Picard has called 'Poetry, the one great sin. . . .'

Assassins

Stimulated by a facile press, the curiosity of the crowd extends to the four lunatics painted by Géricault. They are five portraits, precise and devoid of mystery. It is rather odd that there is less secrecy and horror in these madmen's faces than, for instance, in the study of avulsed, mixed-up limbs enhanced by a small strip of linen and a little pale blood, or in the enchanting head, with eyelids invaded by shadow, of the *Dead Young Man with Closed Eyes*. But I note, looking more closely at *The Mad Assassin*, a detached expression, eyebrows raised in vaguely injured astonishment, a kind of haughty indifference, that I am not seeing for the first time. If I ignore the madman's inflamed complexion and twisted mouth, the rest of the face reminds me of Landru, whom I studied throughout a long hearing. This well-mannered man suffered a most tumultuous session that day. The subtle attorney-general and Moro-Giafferi, carried away in a wild delirium, abounded with threats, venomous allusions and shouting, and the flutter of their sleeves ventilated the chamber. The public, sympathetically excited, showed an equal abandon and the sound of their voices re-echoed. Above the uproar, Landru, with a uniform monochrome pallor, preserved a silence that expressed an opinion. His rare responses were uttered in an agreeable tone of voice. On two occasions only, during a period of four hours, he turned to-

wards the over-excited public and his gaze wandered without
insistence, dark under astonished eyebrows, showing towards all of
us a barely perceptible censure. All around him there was talk of
flaying, bones and burning; a surviving fiancée came to the bar
but met with small success there, suddenly intimidated, once more
submissive to the calm, dark, unfathomable eye that neither sought
nor avoided her, brilliant as a bird's eye and, like a bird's, devoid
of language, tenderness and melancholy. An eye created to see, to
spy, to diminish, to conceal emotion, to weigh up every passer-by
and every spectacle. An eye as serene as that of the first men, an
eye that contemplated the shed blood, death and pain without
blinking a lid—as very small children do, as our ancestors did
before they had invented pusillanimity, when they still enjoyed
the blood freed from its fleshly prison, the water springing out of
the ground, milk spurting from the udder and the juice of crushed
grapes. This beautiful, inexorable eye did, however, as I watched
it, settle on the blonde plaits and the neck of a woman who bent
over a pad, sketching, but he showed neither weakness nor desire
and turned away almost at once, so indicating the ascetic limits of
earthly lusts. . . .

A peaceful English countryside witnessed the reappearance of
a Landru, under the name of Mahon. The same disappearances
of young girls, but the remains—more recent, incinerated or
buried by a more novice hand—are more eloquent.* The English
murderer is young, of cultivated intelligence, his face and speech
impress the audience : 'How pleasant he is! And such a gentle
appearance!' For tradition, and public naïveté, expect a murderer
to be branded with a bestial and violent face. A bestial and violent
man will go as far as to kill because he is under the influence of
drink, exasperated, or driven by rage and alcohol. He is paltry.
He does not know the pleasure of killing, the charity of bestowing
death like a caress, of linking it with the play of the noble wild
beasts : every cat, every tiger, embraces its prey and licks it even
while it destroys it.

---

* Patrick Herbert Mahon was hanged for the murder of his mistress Emily
Kaye, then in her late thirties, in September 1924. Though a philanderer,
Mahon was not responsible—so far as is known—for the 'disappearance of
young girls' or for any other murders.

Landru did not gain the benefit of irresponsibility; no doubt we shall see that Patrick Mahon, too, is of sound mind, intelligent, good-humoured. The fact is that neither of them is an accident of degeneration; they are survivors, relics. Possessors of an animality lost elsewhere, they radiate a gentleness full of shadow, bathed in the grace still possessed by those peoples chance has preserved from European contacts. Do we not know that Patrick Mahon had a singular attraction for 'hinds and stags and other wild animals'? The detail is worthy of note. I believe that no deeply civilized being can charm animals. An animal readily displays its distrust, that is to say its independence, of those entirely given over to humanity. Mahon charms animals; that appears to be a romantic feature to be added to the history of his crimes, whereas in fact it is one further abyss, and because of this I despair of his ever being able to make himself understood by an English jury, or even by a French jury.

The wild bird recognizes and follows him, flying above his head. At sight of him the dog's hair bristles upright along its back, it reflects and submits; the cat rubs itself against his leg as against a tuft of valerian; his mare, should he essay another mount, snorts with flared nostrils and lashes out with jealousy. . . . Fired by a rabble of obeisant creatures, desined to cause feminine rivalry, the ingenuous Patrick Mahon doubtless trod a happy road. A gentle monster, content with the facile act of killing, but whom our time constrains to maladroit and boring butchery. . . .

Marcel Schwob, who knew everything and guessed the rest, refused one day in the Tuileries to admire an old man, covered, like a dry tree, with tame birds. 'I don't like these bird-charmers,' said Marcel Schwob to his wife, Marguerite Moreno.*

She protested and he became incensed, as he never missed an opportunity to be. He uttered paradoxes in short bursts: 'No, I don't like them. They make me frightened. They are sadists. Bloodthirsty sadists. Torturers; and usually they murder children of both sexes, flay them methodically, and put them into round

* Marcel Schwob (1867–1905), of Jewish origin, was a critic prominent in the Symbolist movement. Marguerite Moreno (1871–1948), the actress, was a close friend of Colette; one of her most famous creations was the title role in Giraudoux's *The Madwoman of Chaillot*.

hat-boxes, which inevitably leads to the uncovering of their crimes, since during the transport of their victims, cut up into pieces, the string that ties the parcel slips and the whole lot is spilled into the street. . . .'

Animals

The fox-terrier of la Courtine has just miraculously escaped a double peril: the explosion of ten tons of dynamite and the unbridled curiosity of man. Stolen, it is restored to its master; thus its little romance is over, it ceases to be a matter for discussion. The other dogs, those that la Fourrière hands over to the laboratories, go on. Researchers, with science as their authority, will be able to cut them up, alive, into small pieces, drop them from a height to see if they are shattered by the fall, or deprive them of sleep for sixteen days and nights continuously for the purposes of an iniquitous monograph. . . .

Animal trust, undeserved faith, when at last will you turn away from us? Shall we never tire of deceiving, betraying, tormenting animals before they cease to trust us?

Our manner of exploiting domestic animals offends common decency. There is no forgiveness, according to peasant wisdom, for the proprietor who plays havoc with his own property. Yet one dare not say how many rustics, when their cow struggles to give birth and pants as it lies on its litter, take a cudgel, close the stable doors, and beat the cow so savagely and so fiercely that it finds the strength to get up, to try to flee, so that its despairing leap delivers it abruptly of its fruit, often inflicting mortal injury.

There will always be kids that arrive at the market hung up by their trussed tender feet, heads down, blinded with apoplexy. There will always be horses who, condemned to death, arrive at the place of their deliverance over miles of road, on three feet, on

Colette

bleeding unshod feet, their wretched flanks straddled by unfeeling riders. The rabbit will always surrender its life with a frightful scream, at the moment when the pointed knife puts out its eye and penetrates its brain. The sensibility of our civilized tourists is outraged, in Africa, to see the sharp goad of the donkey-driver sink into the donkey's open wound, carefully kept open; but just read, in an illustrated magazine this month, about the method of catching, housing, feeding and finally disposing of ortolans! At first they quiver in barred traps in their thousands when hardly bigger than large hornets, then a dark loft awaits them where those captives who do not die consume a measured amount of food. There, their health declines in a singular fashion that turns them into balls of fat and their feathers sometimes fall spontaneously from their stretched skin, as delicate as the membranes of bats. This is the time—as the magazine conscientiously explains—to kill them by 'crushing their beaks'. A photograph shows us a good ortolan killer, a model worker, who can crush the beaks of two birds at a time. The work, paid at piece rates, breeds virtuosos; this one smiles the smile of a fine fellow.

At the rate of two or three dustcarts a day the mounds of stones removed from the fortified walls of Paris diminish before my windows. They have been getting smaller for two years now and I calculate that the operation may last another three at least. Each morning the cart—the typical cart, the unique specimen, the cart in fact—arrives empty. Two men fill it. The work of four human arms, the operation does not proceed without slowness and rest periods; I'd like to see you juggling with those ten-kilo blocks! But the workers have perseverance, if not alacrity, and the cart fills. Then one of the two navvies shouts 'Gee-up!' at the shaft-horse, who's generally preceded by a lead-horse. The shaft-horse leans all its weight on its collar, the lead-horse gathers itself on its hind-legs, and . . . the cart doesn't move. For the earth of the fortifications, a yellow clay softened by the slightest moisture, has yielded during the loading to the deep imprint of the four wheels and engulfs the cart a little more every minute. 'Gee-up!' Each effort leads to another. The leather-thonged whips—I thought they were officially forbidden—go to work. The yellow clay is like a leech under the cart, sucking at the hooves, and the scene, protected from being overlooked by a high fence, assumes its traditional character of noisy torture. Helpless, glossy with sweat, with bleeding stripes, these fine and desperate draught-horses endure everything the human creature, ignorant of animals, ignorant of the craft he claims to follow, can invent. On Thursday, if I recollect aright, the departure of the filled cart took two hours and the exhaustion of two prize horses. Two cubic metres of stone went off at walking pace towards an unknown destination; their driver, at any rate, tired by his exertions with voice and whip, did not fail to stop at the first place for a drink.

It is an ugly sight to see an armed man treating a defenceless animal severely. The inaction of the passer-by, detained by the curiosity of an overloaded cart, constitutes one of the immoralities of the street. Man has the right to rest before a working animal only if the normal exertion of his servant produces normal results. In my lilac-covered district I no longer care for the markets that, twice a week, cause a bustle in our little provincial squares, their walls overflowing with laburnum and paulownia. For the green vegetables, ruddy carrots and pinkish potatoes, crimson-footed rhubarb, the dressed meats, all the edible riches, all the expensive victuals, arrive, I know, at the slow pace of teams sick of life and bound for the slaughter-house. Whence comes this cruel indifference of the boss, the prosperous tradesman, the market-gardener profiting from his garden or the buyer at les Halles, for his four-footed employees? They are only rough donkeys, never groomed, ill-fed horses. Canvas screens conceal—but I lift them—the collapse of these screws while they munch at a pittance where an oat-kernel is like a currant in a pudding and rest with one leg across the other. Sometimes a dog drowses under the arch of their belly. Horse and dog expect nothing of their master but his return. But they would tell you that that's quite enough. They see him return, full of shouts, mysterious, animated by inexplicable caprice. They hear the sound he utters, ready to submit but not to flee, they see in his eye the mood of the moment. Only a man who has been chastised is capable of shunning man and hating him.

It is man who has affixed the word 'wild' to the name animal. About this, ask the opinion of those who have lived in solitude,

who have invaded a hitherto inviolate animal territory. Question
the trapper spared and followed by the bear, the hunter surprised
by the clemency of the wild beast and its condescending play.
Without doubt they will teach you that we are the eternal curiosity,
the unlucky passion of every animal, their treacherous climate,
swollen with storms. Once they experience our daily inclemency
they retain a nostalgia for it for ever. Subject to man's incompre-
hensible anger, if one should groan without trace of rancour 'Ah,
what bad weather!', another will sigh with the despairing gratitude of an ill-treated lover, 'Still, it's better than nothing at all. ...'

What did it want, the ocelot of the tropical forest, the wild
creature splashed with black like a flower, when it purred all night
beneath the hammock of the white hunter? It fled at dawn, for
it possessed the timid feline heart oppressed by broad daylight
and shy of revealing itself. Like every wild animal it had trembled
at its first glimpse of man the unknown. It had guessed at impossible happiness and had manifested this in a medley of loud,
raucous cries, insults and groans; it had scratched, licked, bitten
and rubbed its head against the knees of The-one-who-never-
understands. So it went away at dawn, having offered its trusting
sleep, the soft murmur of its drowsy happiness, and the witness,
imprinted in the grass, of its beautiful form, flanks long like the
flanks of women.

Flowers

I dedicate to them, these imprisoned flowers, a little of the pity
that goes out to caged animals. Almost alive as they are, these
die the more quickly for having travelled, having found a miserly,
shifting, shallow soil. As the plant perishes one can guess at the
life it had there and how tenaciously it held on to it. Its flagging,
the pathetic inclination of its floral head, constitute a genuine
syncope, accompanied by pallor, since the plant now reveals the

whiter underside of petals and foliage. If it receives watery aid in time, it is restored in the most dramatic fashion. How many moments have I lost—if I can call them lost—with flowers as avid for moisture as the anemone, the tulip, the hyacinth, the wild orchid! Swooning with heat and thirst, their stalks, plunged into water, imbibe so much, so greedily, that the energetic movement of the flower, its return to the vertical, become visible, jerky at first and by fits and starts when the head is too rich and too heavy.

It is a pleasure sweet to a writer to witness the rebirth of a tulip in a crystal goblet. The ink dries on the pen while before me a creation, interrupted by a transient death, raises itself towards perfection and will attain it, shine for a day, perish the next. . . . I can do better than watch the tulip regain its senses; I can hear the iris blossom. Its last protective silken layer rasps and splits down the length of an azure finger which uncoils at the proper time and, sitting by oneself in a small quiet room, one may start suddenly if one has forgotten that, on a nearby table, an iris has suddenly decided to blossom. Consider how there are, at the Cours-la-Reine, thousands of irises, renewed by continued flowering. The early morning sun delivers those whose time is come and I am seized with desire for that morning when, in the dawn that filters through the curtains, I may be able to cock an ear for the perceptible sighing of so many irises delivered simultaneously. . . .

They flower without pause, suffering too, so it seems, panting with their canine tongues hanging out—see the median vein, the ramifying canals, the fleshy and transparent border. It's their own perfume that suffocates them, so cloying is it; lingering, inclined to trail, closely seconded by that of the petunia. The bed of irises is a torpid pool that our passage cleaves with difficulty. Nervous women blanch there, pushing away with their hand the insupportably languorous perfume exhaled by all those heraldic tongues, some of which bear hairs like those of leopards. As for the roses, the female visitors extend not only their nostrils but also their mouths, as if at a fountain. After which these thirsty doves loudly proclaim the unprecedented odour of a new rose, the more beautiful for having gradually conformed to the will of a horticulturist who wanted it to resemble a peony, a hollyhock, the flat clematis or the double cherry.

One has the scent of well-cared-for skin, another of a mild cigar, or apricot or pineapple. But which of these equals a rose with the scent of a rose? Lips linger on the latter, nostrils flutter; the woman who inhales it closes her eyes: 'Leave me, I feel as if I had at last come home.' A home that she would endow with the names of Sensibility and Reverie and Literary Affectation, if she could but name it. But she knows only that the scent of the rose is enough to impregnate a woman with a vague and sibylline poetry, as if it were ten centuries ago.

For years now we've had no cause to mistrust the begonia. It has appeared as an emblem in the end-of-year reviews, where the lobster—hairy variety—has been of comparatively little account beside it. To suit popular caprice the begonia has developed strangely. Already, enlarged and cultivated, it resembled an exceptional begonia, then a monstrous begonia. This year we stand stunned before its megalomanic flower, which aspires to replace the hollyhock, the nasturtium, the peony, even the rose. A blaze of incomparable, presumptuous colours adorns it, it claims the most beautiful vibrant reds, a yellow that sheds light all round, a unique fleshy saffron. But smell it; it has less fragrance than a clod of earth and, if you touch it cautiously, it has been unable to lose its vegetable stiffness, its flesh as brittle as that of a young radish.

I have no time for these disguised vegetable characters. Those that puff themselves up so exaggeratedly leave me cold. Some growers miniaturize the brabancon and the fox-terrier, others bring a blush to the hydrangea. Let us be fair to the latter: they admit, even at their exhibitions, that they are not concerned with art. Here is the blue hydrangea alongside the pink, the purple-blue, then the white, arranged in kitchen-garden geometry; it's enough for each swollen head, with its globe of a flower erect on the stocky stem, to fill its compartment. Someone will be vexed—the chrysanthemum.

Something of romanticism embalms a rockery devoted to the spears, the bells of foxgloves. They remember their original sand, their fine burning natal soil, hot to the walker's foot in July. Their race has known the sun that calcines the rocks of Fontainebleau and they remain unbending beneath the stifling tent at noon. But dying and prostrate at their feet are the small scented folk, dull, delicate, ancient, provincial. They have names that stir the heart: herb-bonnet, sage, cinquefoil, lupin, the hairy cornflower. Yet who stops for these? A single gaping gloxinia could swallow them at a gulp. Beware the gloxinia! Velvety fat *arriviste*, it glares at the begonia. . . . Oh, to be the first to possess a gloxinia as big as a bedroom pitcher, what a dream!

At noon the little lotus-pool steams and there rises from the depths of the calyces the stagnant, somniferous odour that annihilates energy and appetite. Every flower cries for mercy, and the garden-lovers go to lunch. In the torrid, steamy enclave where the orchids are massed, 'the most beautiful flower' poses for its portrait. This prize beauty, a cattleya, proffers its certificates and swoons against a background of black velvet. Its foot is swathed in a silken binding, as it might be a prize charger. Around it there are only blue throats darting an inflamed stylus, wings barely retained on a threadlike stalk, ophrys and orchis camouflaged as striped fish, fruits, wine-coloured bees, humming-birds : vegetable contrivances, traps to catch butterfly, bird, insect, even man? What complicated design modelled the most cunning orchid of all, the most impenetrable, the one that succeeds in imitating—I give you a hundred guesses—the flat and honest corolla, the everyday mauve and commonplace blue of the simple pansy that flourishes in the nuns' small garden? . . .

Doubles

I should like to know what nostalgia is being experienced by the former cashier of the Opéra-Comique, now incarcerated.

Does he regret his honest life or the enchanted hours that saw him, suddenly long-haired, by the side of a young woman? Does he, so used to balancing accounts, say : 'It's worth having got rid of all that'? No doubt he mourns the chill conjugal dwelling and the esteem of the *quartier*. For the perverse regret their valley blessed with pure dew all the more, since the just do not aspire to such forbidden delights. M. Picard is perverse, there's no doubt of it. He was brought up in that school of demoralization constituted by an impeccable life, made up of amiable duties, beside a spouse beyond reproach. Before sinning officially he was acquainted with excess and intoxication, thanks to the inexorable repetition of the same daily virtues. Even wheels like a change of speed and, alas, nothing altered Picard's pace. We may wager that he took scant heed of the household set-up, that safety-valve for cramped bureaucracy. Sad rotation of the days, the slow vortex of wretched drunkenness, the sickening lack of colour in life, these are what corrupted Picard rather than the proximity of the theatre and the nearby costumier's. . . .

A young sage who died gloriously during the war, called Maitrot, taught boxing and physical culture. He judged all things soundly, from the height of shoulders fit to destroy a temple. He showed me great friendship, which I reciprocated, and it was he who dissuaded me from applying myself to sessions of slow, re-peated, rhythmic movements which I had essayed to overcome a keenly felt sorrow.

'None of that,' said Maitrot. 'Movements by numbers, they do those in school, in groups, in the open air and then it's when you've no worries. You're in trouble : no gymnastics with movements by numbers.'

'Why, Maitrot?'

'Because of the poisons. You see people who do what they call physical culture in movements by numbers. I count and count : one, two, three. . . . The stomach flattens, I admit, the poise improves, but at the same time the morale of these persons suffers, and their physiognomy too. "I don't know what's the matter with me," they say. They're suffering from self-induced neurasthenia. It's the poison that's in the numbers. Because, if you count you must do exactly the same movements over and over again, you poison yourself.'

'But how do you explain that, Maitrot?'

'I can't explain it. I'm sure, that's all. You want to beware of figures that you count out loud or softly, and of regular movements. The body isn't constructed for the same movements always, nor is the soul.'

Strange language from the mouth of an athlete, who thereby revealed a vocation as psychologist.

I have read, I don't know where, of an exemplary woman employee who suddenly threw down her work in the factory, insulted her bosses, and was seized with an acute nervous crisis because she had just calculated that she had finished her eight thousandth buttonhole. . . . Was it at the foot of a column of figures or else when greeting his concierge for the four thousandth time that Picard experienced his premonitory heart-sinking and revolt? He does not say so, he would not know how to say it. He talks instead of sentimental encounters, of falling head over heels in love, of frenzy. He would lack the words to explain how, suddenly, and to save his life, he had to jump into the skin and soul of another man. . . . But what other man? He had no choice. A bandit, his time up, allows himself the luxury of a sudden confession, drowned in blissful tears. Picard-cashier could not don a thief's disguise or Picard-husband become inconstant. He learnt what it costs to keep a secret and was eventually sufficiently shocked to admit everything. He managed, perhaps with a last touch of guile, to sacrifice the make-up box at the feet of his legitimate wife and, without the knowledge of his judges, to do penance to his directors, already disposed to clemency—he wants the public confessional, which he prefers to the simmering *pot-au-feu*, to the faithful lamp and companion.

Poor companion, sadly resembling the woman maligned by Marseille folklore in several bantering anecdotes:

'Hallo there, Marius.'

'Hallo there, Pascalin.'

'Is Madame Marius well?'

'Well, Pascalin.'

'Does she manage the house? Does she look after the cooking? Does she do her dressmaking?'

'Yes, Pascalin.'

'She looks after the children? In fact, she still has all the virtues?'

'Yes, Pascalin.'

'Hmm. . . . That's bad!'

It was not only with make-up, with false hair, with rouge to touch up a sagging mouth, that Picard manufactured his clandestine appearance, divulged by the newspapers. Colour and greasepaint would not have sufficed. But after applying the last touch of make-up he gave spontaneous life to the newly painted mask. The eye played tricks that he later forgot, the mouth, braced in its smile, resembled the underside of the chin, dragged the neck and shoulders into an attitude of defensive coquetry, his gait reacted to the carriage of his head, the bracing of the shoulders; then Picard left his hotel room, destined for another existence. Intoxicating departure, perhaps the best moment of the metamorphosis! For after this departure there came disquiet, fatigue, the summons to become a lover. . . . Only the moment of return could stand comparison with the dash of departure : the right, the pleasure to become old again, ugly again, to reclaim the bowl and the *tisane*, the security of having finished with deception until the morrow, all these relegated to second place the pleasures of imposture. To the gentle tinkling of the spoon against the cup of infusion, Picard enjoyed what was probably the cruellest moment of his destiny.

The assassination of a woman in a furnished apartment twenty years ago revealed the honourable name and the age of the victim, an octogenarian seductress, and her double life. More romantically than Picard, she died rather than called for the help that would have unmasked her. Some time later I was astounded to learn that I had met this heroine two or three times at the little family 'five o'clocks' at a friend's, where Madame . . . let's say Madame Protée, in triangular mourning shawl, *chapeau fermé* tied with a string over her white locks, rejoiced us with her gay grandmotherly vitality. She walked well and laughter dwelt in her wrinkles. A gourmande, she slowly savoured the creamy chocolate, eyes closed. Her duplicit maturity, based on firm decision, went on in strict parallelism interrupted only by her indiscreet death. A headstrong Ninon of Montmartre, she benefited also from the unassailable standing of a fairy grandmother and never got into any difficulties. She lived unsuspected on one or other side of the watertight division created, in their meticulous fashion, by her old hands. I have to take a good look at her, at the back of my memory, to remind myself how, eyes closed, a cup of chocolate between her gloved fingers, she sometimes seemed to abandon herself mysteriously to the two greatest sins of an elderly lady—*gourmandise* and reminiscence.

Cinema

No cars were parked at the entrance to the Musée Galliéra last Thursday; which led us to believe that the room reserved for 'Art in the French Cinema' would be empty. Just the reverse, it overflowed beyond the doors with a silent audience of mingled children and adolescents. This fine and modest audience, which had arrived uncomplainingly under a hail of rain by slow and inconvenient modes of transport, close-packed now on the benches of a stifling room, received its just reward. Together we watched what is denied us by those screens where the only rivals to American epics are *Didi découche* or *Patochard cherche sa belle-mère*. Two magic words had drawn me thither for I know that, cinematographically, fantasy, marvels, incontestable miracles, are to be sought only in what is called the educational film.

One part of the presentation took us on tour in France, over the summits of low hills, along rivers sluggish in their flat, cramped valleys; as well as this, the tired voice of a teacher explained that the shape of these hills, this watercourse, these trees, depended on an invisible subsoil—cretaceous, siliceous clay. A field in the Perche showed proud draught-horses,* the satin of their coats gleaming and dappled over the play of muscle. In a granite quarry, stone-hewers lifted the blocks, carved out millstones with the chisel. . . . Schoolchildren! Surely you will never forget the happy light, like that enveloping a soap-bubble, that shone on the cruppers of the horses with the aquiline foreheads, or the strange,

* *Percherons.*

many-toothed shape of a black tool biting into white stone; surely your memory will retain the movement of the quarryman's two dark gigantic hands which, before your very eyes, hacked the friable block, striped with pure white, to show you that kaolin is hidden away like truffles; that, like the truffle, it is invested with thick clay! Children, from the height of a transporter-bridge you saw the wheat flowing like lava at the port of Marseille, in a wave so solid that we seemed to hear its aqueous murmur. . . . Children, resist those who still protest, in the name of the imagination, against teaching with the motion picture! They are not fools or simpletons who assert: 'To feed the childish imagination with precise images is to deaden and restrict it. Teaching by cinematography turns the child into a receptacle for images and condemns every sense, save the visual, to inertia.'

At first sight this argument does not seem negligible. For our civilized senses lose no chance of impoverishment. I am assured that, deprived of music, cinema-halls would become the agents of communal slumber; I am also assured that, confronted with a film, the child hardly thinks at all. It may well be that it thinks very little, faced with some confused activity where human movement has pride of place. The beating of the heart, the to-and-fro of the eyes, supplant thought while the screen is showing the hero pursued by kidnappers or murderers and revolver shots explode in wads of cotton-wool. The interruption of the subtitles suffocates like a stoppage of breath and I'm inclined to believe that the child's mind finds no place to settle therein or to turn fruitfully inward. The exciting film, rapid pursuits, all those sports whose speed surpasses the normal rhythm of our heart and lungs, eliminate those thoughts that are not mere recording or painful pleasure.

But give the child, the adult too, cinema spectacles devoid of romantic action; neither the child nor the adult will be niggardly in expressing his surprise, the quality and vividness of his pleasure and interest. I recall, during the showing of the film called *Way Down East*, that the audiences, each evening, gave voice like one man to a long murmur of appreciation at an incomparable countryside, silvered by the rising sun, of quivering willows and a great river, soaked by the morning dew. Despite the courage and talent of Lilian Gish, it was here that the emotion of the moment found its sigh, its release and regrets.

Similarly, last Thursday at the Musée Galliéra, there were two moments when every young hand clapped, when mouths exhaled their content, their 'Ah' of respectful ecstasy. The first time, in slow-motion, a sea-gull was lifted from the ground, immobilized in the air, cradled in the wind. The undulation and banking of its wing-quills, the mechanism of its tail rudder, the whole secret of flight, the whole simple mystery of aviation, were revealed in an instant, dazzling the eyes. A little later the speeding-up process recorded the germination of a bean, the birth of its searching rootlets, the greedy yawning of its cotyledons from which, darting its snake head, the first shoot burst forth. . . . At this revelation of the plant's purposive, intelligent movement I saw children get up and imitate the prodigious ascent of a plant climbing in a spiral, circumventing an obstacle, groping at its stake. 'It's looking, it's looking!' cried an impassioned small boy. He dreamed of it that night, and I too. These fantasies are not forgotten and excite a hunger to learn more. We desire for our children and ourselves, we desire, after the poor workings of one's imagination, the extravagance of reality, Nature's unrestrained fantasy; we desire the fantastic fable of the germination of the pea, the marvellous story of the metamorphosis of a dragonfly and the explosion, the forceful expansion of the lily-bud, half-open at first with its long mandibles on a sombre swarm of stamens, an avid potent process of flowering, at sight of which a little girl said quietly, rather scared: 'Oh, a crocodile!'

Spells

The brother of a soldier, killed in the war, has the use of the dead man's bicycle. He has a fatal fall, leaving the bicycle to a newspaper-seller who is knocked down and run over by a lorry. The fourth owner of the bicycle, chased by the police for burglary, runs away; he is arrested, but the policeman who rides the 'fatal bicycle' to the police-station is knocked down and run over by a car. . . .

This is a jolly story that comes to us from England, country of the haunted castle and the malevolent opal. Over there the vampire is still in good standing. But if there were a possibility of buying the bicycle in question, would you buy it? Not I. And I would not wear the malevolent opal on my finger, if I knew the history of the bicycle and the ring. I can't help thinking that the last victim, the policeman, had the time before straddling his mount to become acquainted with its fatal power. He was responsible for his own downfall; I believe that, instead of giving way to the car, instead of crying '*Hep!*' in English (I don't know how one says '*Hep!*' in English), he had a moment of indecision, despite himself, and the car was on him. . . . Note that on each occasion the bicycle remains more or less intact; I stress this point so as to evoke in my readers the realm of the fantastic and the damnable pleasure savoured by the superstitious. The gleam of planetary fire that ravages the opal, that I am not afraid of. I mistrust only the opal of evil repute, the ring that your grandmother wore on her finger when she lost her life on a boat-trip and that she herself had had from a mysteriously murdered grandmother. But the bracelet of woven hair inspires no more confidence in me than the opal, once I know that these threads of tarnished gold were cut under the Restoration from the tresses of a dying fiancée, a fiancée who, a fiancée whom. . . .

Haunted houses, now those I know something about. The rat behind the panelling runs in a hundred surprising ways, and when he plays, his shrill little rat's laugh makes the hair of the unsuspecting stand on end. The death-watch beetle, terrifying name, is to its familiars only an insect set on banging its head against the wall, a head shaped like a hammer, hard as the wood it taps at regular intervals : toc-toc-toc-toc-toc-toc-toc, often in a series of seven. Ah! You prick up your ear! Seven? Why seven? I couldn't say. The tropical gecko also cries seven times and when it goes beyond this number someone dies in the house. . . . You shiver, eh? Under pretence of reassuring you I fill you with new terrors.

Let us speak of other charming hosts who, come summer, assume the responsibility of maintaining the reputation of their castles, English or otherwise, the great grasshopper with a horse's head and the stag-beetle whose horn scrapes against the window-pane in the dark or on the wood of the table like a scratching finger-nail. Let us mention the gently sobbing owl, capable, when flying against your face in the darkness without so much as a sigh, of imitating the fold of a shroud or the icy breath of the tomb! Four or five small twilight or nocturnal animals, an artfully modulated draught, and that's goodbye to the case of the haunted house, at least the haunted houses one talks about and which receive noisy publicity. There are others. . . . There are dwellings saturated in defunct humanity, the murmuring overflow of unknown souls. Sometimes beneficent, sometimes lethal, these dens crammed with an invisible population make their influence felt on the insensitive living—you, I, our neighbour, our friends—who translate it into inadequate words : 'I don't know what's the matter with me, I feel uneasy in my new room . . .'; or else : 'I feel much better in my new house. I'm not so irritable any more.'

One of these places, favoured by one who shall be nameless, is well known to me. A dark courtyard obscures the view and the friend who moved in there parcelled out in a single day all the furniture, the divan-bed, desk and ash-trays. It took us only forty-eight hours to discover that a guardian spirit had settled in before the furniture : a spiritual warmth, unobtrusive company, encouragement that came from no one knew where, an even respiration of the walls accustomed to human contact, nothing was lacking in this basement dwelling, scorned though it was by the sun. Then who was haunting it? A single former inhabitant, even one of the powerful dead, would not account for it. I may happen to sleep there for half an hour, a sleep well watched over, or to eat there with a motiveless cheerfulness, while the detestable mezzanine light, obliquely filtering in, stagnates in grey splashes at the bottom of the white plates. . . . Quite different is the almost rural comfort of my little house in Auteuil, blessed by thrushes and nightingales. No doubt, both here and there, a closed door there, a bed of climbing roses here, is found the one whom I designate in all seriousness by his name—the vampire.

Ah! Now we have it! Honour to whom honour is due, the greatest and the most frightening. You can tell him thus. Pale, a little green even, hands . . . and with a mouth like a wound, right? Your guess is too crude, all the same. It's very likely that your most ostentatious vampire is no more than a harmless candidate for tuberculosis, enhanced by Peladan's great eyes and a hair-do that I used to say was a chemist's before chemists became sporting types. Your true vampire, unhappily for his victims, dispenses with outward characteristics. He usually has a fresh complexion, a smiling approach, a wandering eye. If it is a woman she is charming, idle, gay, with an infantile manner of devoting her time, her presence, to admiring and liking you. The male vampire presents the same absence of special features and the same amiable manner. Man or woman, the vampire is generally liked. His most frequent phrase is 'What shall we do?' For he awaits some motivation, he seeks it if necessary. Like every incarnation of shabby fiendishness, he is 'nice'. Very nice, and you say so, you repeat it *ad nauseam*. You seek the vampire, who is seeking you. Whenever he departs he leaves you depressed, yawning by fits and starts, saddened as if by a debauch. He takes away everything you need, everything that assures his subsistence, and it may be that as he leaves he will get further plunder on his way, using the residue of your own energy. Will you die? No. Besides, an access of energy may save you, realizing that the vampire, uncertain how long to stay, will not desert your dried-up veins of his own accord. But you will measure your effort by the calibre of your enemy, his leechlike prowess, the frightful trap of his vacuity which you fill, blindly, with the best part of yourself.

Pedagogy

June: month of cherries and strawberries and the first bats! All the nests are empty, the rose condescends to all our suburban gardens, prisoned between four walls. Bagatelle is ablaze with roses, a profusion of roses loads four wooden arches behind my house. Unbending roses, upright on their inordinate stems, at the large florists and short-stemmed roses on the hawker's tray, cheaper than leeks, which are also trussed in bundles. Hot roses, crucified against villa walls, exhausted by the sun. Plump, flushed roses, pride of the level-crossing keeper: 'They haven't any at the château like these'; the poor man's wild roses smelling of spring-onion because of the hand that picked them, the rich man's roses, one of the latest inventions, no bigger than a bee, simple, red, slender, whose yellow bristly heart, all hairy with stamens, releases such a wild fragrance as to be almost embarrassing. This is the month when the rose, blooming everywhere else, deserts our children's cheeks.

They reach, thank God, the third month of their longest term and can do no more. The majority do not suspect this. My sturdy daughter, who in any case has the advantage of a suburban school, betrays unknowingly and obviously the signs of what I call, each year, the inanition of these children. For them the school year is the boundary of their entire existence. October, mild for those children under the serene influence of a well-run boarding-school, brings the fluttering of wings, the trepidation, the excitement that flushes the baby at his first unaided steps. . . . Christmas fosters in them romanticism and lust for love; from that time on they grow up very quickly under thaw and shower; with good luck Easter lures them on with a St Martin's summer. May, June frankly display their fatigue, a sort of sensible or agitated disenchantment. This child of mine debates with her seasonal malady, triumphs over it, outpaces it; but it follows her, it catches up with her, and she lets herself be caught, though she does not officially admit its presence. She says: 'It's funny, I don't enjoy myself as much as in winter and yet here we are starting a newspaper, Jacqueline and I.' She says: 'You know, I haven't got the same best friend any more. Why?—Oh, I don't know! And yet I thought she was the best.'

She arrives tempestuously, crying: 'We've got two days' holiday! And do you know why? Because of Doumergue! That's a good effort of his. Oh yes, now we want to make a revolution so that they have a new President again, and we shall get another two days' holiday!' But the access of joy is short-lived and the signs of rejoicing subside in diminishing outbursts. The cinema, the bicycle ride, I throw these at her like mouthfuls of water to a fever case. I know that all this, to be truthful, is lustreless, done with, hardly gayer than the daily grind. I know that one should change the year, emigrate to a new world, emigrate to a new world and die at this time.

Here and there people complain about exhaustion, demand release. Hot weather régime, cold weather régime, no doubt that's what studious youth demands, embedded in a teaching cycle that's too old, that successive ministers approach with uncertain hands. The retarding cold, the sleepy heat, the spring, languorous or unsettling, we adults quite rightly put up with their effects and blame them for our exhilaration or our listlessness. . . . Fatigued by its own growth, our child, however, must contribute the same amount of work throughout the year, the same in dog-days or frost. The hard, the blind rule that sets a little girl of thirteen, a boy of the same age, before an exercise-book at 30° C., at the hour when the birds fall silent and the blue blind stops rattling against the window-pane! What mature man, what oldster forgets the particular temperature of his summer *baccalauréat* or diploma? Yet, sheltered by an age not yet affected by dreams of university, we witness the prodigies of resistance attained by our offspring; we are compelled to admire them when we run through the students' manuals and exercise-books: 'This is really too much! A grown-up couldn't cope with it!' Let us admit that only a child can cope with it. What memory, what resilience! It's time we no longer abused a cerebral malleability that is not unlimited and is endangered by prolonged and sterile effort.

Almost all the modern educational establishments deal with

the situation by using short and varied lessons. The sterile effort, so terribly demanding of the young spirit, results from causes not envisaged in educational circulars. Initially, the child is vulnerable only through his senses. Later his intelligence benefits from an enlarged sensibility. But at the beginning of his time at school some blemish or physical tic apparent in his teacher, some peculiarity of accent or pronunciation, may sometimes lose the teacher the interest and attention of his entire class. Ragging of the teacher by pupils, violent insubordination, spring from a secret horror—visual, olfactory, auditory—that the child will not acknowledge even to himself. Always unfortunate and less well rewarded than a rejected suitor, that is the mysteriously stricken pedagogue who imposes and engenders sterile effort. The pupil hears him without understanding. Trustingly the pupil raises to his master a petrified visage that supplicates and suffers before subsiding into an unhappy indifference. Hours, months, pass thus, the teacher vainly expending his magnetism, the pupil his attention. Their opposed forces are dissipated to little advantage. How many actors there are who can tell you that at certain times in their career they despatched to the other side of the proscenium words whose phonetic value and meaning were suddenly lost in the void?

This phenomenon of ingratitude is commoner, more constant, at school than in the theatre. As abettors of juvenile exhaustion and waste of time, oughtn't we to deal with it? I think so. Perhaps, if pedagogy sprang from vocation rather than ambition and if higher education produced graduates experienced in the art of addressing a crowd of children. . . . What then, a *Conservatoire* for teachers? Certainly. To talk to a child, to fascinate him, is much more difficult than to win an electoral victory. But it is also more rewarding.

Tits

The poplar seed no longer clouds the air, so light as to indicate the direction of the wind even when we do not feel the wind itself. It is the sweet of the year and sappy, ephemeral blossomings accompany it—hyacinth, narcissus, tulip. It is composed of discordant greenery, various as a lawn of silver-green or jonquil-green, of pimento-green to bluish-green : the Parisian Bois has just reached its fugitive maturity.

By now spring would be over for us had not the tits, because of the cold, been late with their hatching and the sparrows too. It's not ten days since the befeathered little tits jostled each other in their nests. And if my narrow garden retains till June the charm of an uncultivated tomb, abandoned of men, it will be because all work with spade and rake has been deferred, silenced, round a nest of tits.

What harshness is needed, I asked myself, to lose the trust of animals? Refinements of torture are vain and never exile an animal long from us. A kindly gesture bestowed by us on an animal arouses prodigies of understanding and gratitude. When I fixed two nests hollowed out of two birch billets to two uprights in the garden I secretly thought of them as a superstitious votive offering. . . . The vow knows only one path, it rises; mine reached two wall-nightingales. They came, greyish-red, darker than the shrew but, like it, a forager, and began their delicate pillage all about the house under my inspecting eye. One day the round window of the nest was blocked by a thread of floss-silk, stolen from a blouse. . . . This pink thread, as it floated there, spoke as clearly as the lace curtain in the window of an apartment : I behaved circumspectly, especially as the other nest belonged at the same time to a blue tit.

The latter, princess of wild birds, can do nothing without *éclat*. Where she reigns one sees only her, her back blue as the metallic wing-case of the dung-beetle, the willow-green underside of her wing, her brazen begging, her quickness to flee. She is laughing and combative and greedier than anyone. Would you say she is fierce? But it is man who speaks thus and how can a man have any idea of what a tit's fierceness may be? It hunts and scavenges from waking to sleeping and it goes to sleep late. Between the hatching of its eggs and the flight of the fledglings its daily round defies observation. Two blue flashes, blurred by the swiftness of their flight, lit up for me my small burgeoning enclosure. Male and female, just as they disappeared into the round window of the hollow trunk, perched for an instant on the end of a bamboo stake and swayed there like a flower; their brood fed, the sound of a fan, a streak of blue and yellow fire shot out of the nest again and the waiting raised the pitch of the piping little invisible ones, which resembles the twitter of an exasperated kiss.

As for the more audacious and active, the small female, I've seen her dive beneath the low jungle of crowded young begonias. She entered at one end of the flower-bed and hunted about there like a rat, running agilely on her marvellous little claws; she shot out at the other end, arrogant, head erect, a caterpillar dangling from her beak or else moustached with two insect-wings, belli-cose. . . . Did she find the time to eat? No doubt, since she found time to sing again. Her little copper-coloured sistrum interrogated me, she feigned anger if I approached the nest. But it was only a tit's play, followed by acrobatics of amity and association—head down, hanging by her feet, swaying with a thousand flirtings of her tail and chucklings. Fierce? Perhaps. The tit is as gay as a wild beast. It is meticulous in the manner of those model housekeepers who fly into a rage if there is a stain on the parquet : the threshold of her nest does not bear a trace of white droppings. Fierce? How pretty she is when she kills! The worm snatched, she finishes it off with repeated blows and cuts it up with an executioner's fairness. Fierce, yes, no more and no less than innumerable lovers. . . .

For I've not been able to regard my tits' maternal instinct as a fault. The gardener sent for, they summed him up in five minutes, well aware that he smelled of earth and leaves and that he brought to light, shifting compost in a wheelbarrow, new plump vermin. The cat they had long ago forgotten, knowing their nest to be out of reach. They merely chose, to get the little ones to take their first flight, breakfast-time when the sun is low and the garden deserted and flew off to the wooden belfry.

But I was rewarded more than once, until last week, at the edge of the racecourse. Nothing indicates to the eye a nest of tits abandoned by its brood, but the surrounding racket is news enough. . . . What cries! A constant high-pitched pedal-note of inharmonious squalling, fed by unmatchable vitality, emerges from the tree that bears the nest. Thin as a small cigar, grey still, a glimpse of yellow beneath the wing that beats as quickly as a butterfly's, the little birds quiver with emulation, turn by turn, on the edge of the natal chalice, felted with wool, floss-silk, selected moss and horsehair. The mother warbles on a twig, repeating a lesson that can readily be translated: 'No flying now! Or you'll catch your wing on the first branch and you'll be on the ground, in the grass, where I can't help you. One little jump only, with me. . . . Then another jump on the twig above, and another, another, always higher, to the top of the tree. . . .'

She bosses about four or five ignoramuses, scolds them, encourages them, shoves them with her wing, infects them with her own enthusiasm, leads them on, exhausted, to the top whence one can discern the green racecourse at Auteuil furrowed with birds.

There, momentarily, they are all silent. Is it vertigo that keeps them quiet? They contemplate the open air, the virgin territory that is theirs from now on. Is this not the moment of the greatest anxiety for the tit, blue amid her grey nestlings? Brief anguish. One of the little ones takes off from the tree, aims at an isolated chestnut-tree on the lawn, follows a course like a racing yacht, and berths triumphantly. Never, in three nests, have I come across any hesitation, any appeal for help, from the timorous young sparrow. The tits are expert in the air and gymnasts on the branches. Birch-trunk or hanging cradle, the natal nest never sees them again. They depart before their blue wing-quills have yet developed, pilferers, throaty, intoxicated with combat and coquetry, and capable of devouring, through its round eye-socket, the brain-substance of their own kind.

Heat

The torment of heat is reserved for the city dweller and the inhabitant of the desert, for more than elsewhere the mineral kingdom lends the sun's fury an implacable character.

For a few days in the desert I have experienced the mounting heat, received and reflected by a soil from which the scorching sun raised a spiral pillar of sand. But at least, at Bou-Saâda, the Saharan night shed its few hours of clemency, the cold that assumes a violet colour in the mind as it descends with night from the mountain-tops. Paris, during the dog-days, knows no truce, no relief for its affliction. We are a poor lot, who go about in winter wearing silk stockings and pierced leather shoes, and in summer in sleeved jackets, collared, tied and waistcoated. A poor lot? Why pity them? They have the elegance and the correct clothing that they deserve and have themselves chosen. The heat in Paris is like a nightmare. Thousands and thousands of human beings at their windows have nothing to look at but stone prisons, quadrangular blocks, rectangles of hot zinc, cubes of iron or cement. When the thermometer shows 'despair in the shade' there is something inexorable in all this cubic limit of gaze. I once knew an office where men suffocated from June on and where, when they looked up, they saw through some railings, a long dark corridor of a court-yard dominated by a tall white chimney, struck by the sun on its widest aspect during the latter half of the day. Deadly succession of right-angles! If, during these torrid months, plant-life is as necessary to us as nourishment, it is because it contains and engenders an inexhaustible supply of curves. 'Mercy!' begs dried-up man, 'a glass of fresh water—cylinder or circumference to ease the soul. . . .' I don't forget to rest my eyes and my brain on spheres of crystal and glass, the year round.

In our city, alas, each guild gets cooked in its own way: the one in trousers of thick stiff corduroy, the other in jackets with sleeves worn by the wood of desks. The caged book-keeper is half-dead in his detachable collar, and the saleswoman totters at her post in the obligatory black dress with no comfort but the stoical gaze of the frock-coated overseer, pale and choked, upright like the legendary dead man, secretly pouring with sweat. In our country the torrid noontide demands the same activity, the same toiling mass is exposed, to perish under ever crueller rays, and each human box harbours within its thin walls dazed sufferers, children to whom night brings no repose, who utter their small, repeated cry till dawn.

Cast a glance at the working-class houses, the tops of the thickly populated buildings: no shutters, blinds that dim the light but admit the heat. Those roasted on the fifth floor think with envious ill-will that the ground-floor tenant leads a privileged existence in a cellar. Soon we may see the last of those ancient Parisian buildings, entrenched camps of microbes but thick bastions where the temperature fluctuates hardly more than that of the stone chambers in the tower of Elven, in Brittany. In summer their deep carriage entrances are the shady paradise of the seated concierge and of a few elderly women with shade-spotted hands. A draught from the tomb emanates from these entrance-ways in July and brushes the forehead of the passer-by, who slackens his step, sighs, and foresees for himself too, beyond the tomb, the eternal happiness of the man seated at a cool threshold.

On the evening of the terrible Saturday of 12th July even Auteuil was no better off than the boulevards, and its inhabitants complained angrily that the sun poured down on them the same heat as on the natives of the 9th *arrondissement*.

Your born Auteuillois tends to the sybaritic, since he possesses the Bois and its lakes. Basically a villager, he still speaks of 'going to Paris', defends himself as best he can against sporting activities, and pities the 'centre', not without malice. But he becomes indignant when, as on the other day, the sultry weather does not, in respect for the 'seventeenth', halt at the level of the way that an aged kinswoman, ten years ago, used to call the 'Grande-Rue' of Passy.

Accustomed, after dinner, to inhale the scent of limes, of privet, of mown grass brought to its door by the faint west wind that has caressed the Bois, Auteuil—deceived, injured—lived very meekly indeed on that Saturday night. Around half past ten I went, at the pace of the condemned, to see what was going on in Passy. The whole of Passy was lying prostrate on the burnt grass around la Muette, and the motionless body of some woman, lying face downward, her head between her crossed arms, seemed a victim of death rather than sleep. The lovers I saw all lay apart. No gaiety rose from the families who had eaten there, amid the greasy wrappings and the melon-rinds. Sometimes, in the half-shade, there sprang up some slender, light young girl, whose youth still impelled her to run and jump, but like the Olympic champions she suddenly sank down again, her white dress subsiding like the last flame of an unfed fire.

Round a shady green bush five or six silent beings resembled those who warm themselves at a winter brazier, intent on profiting from a singular cold radiation, a concentric zone of coolness of which the bush was the mysterious centre. A woman held out her bare arm, a child its two hands, and for a moment I shared their patch of oasis.

An arriving 16 tram took me back towards Auteuil. The imminence of midnight, and of Sunday, was reviving some village life despite the still air and dust-white sky. A little dance to lantern-light, not far from the avenue Mozart, resembled all the Saint-Jeans, all the fourteenths of July, of my natal province, and I was glad that the tram stopped just there. What honest youth! They danced among themselves, free from intrusion, the draper's daughter in the arms of the cooper's son, the jobbing dressmaker with her female apprentice, two little girls of ten did the polka, and the blonde servant-girl from the tobacconist's whirled round grasped by the smart waiter from the café.

Seltzer water, grenadine, beer, syrup of lemon. . . . The smell of the pine-branches nailed to the musicians' platform reminded me of beflagged fairgrounds, prizegivings and polished dance-floors. . . . Nothing was missing from this conjured past, not even the trusting parents sitting in a row on yellow iron seats.

From the height of the platform of the empty tram I breathed in this peaceful past and present. The young folk were dancing on the tramlines and I was not sorry that our halt was prolonged. At last I spoke to the conductor, leaning contemplatively, like me, on his elbows :

'Is there a breakdown along the line?'

'No. We'll be getting going again.'

'When?'

'In just a minute. We're waiting.'

'Waiting for what?'

'For them to finish their fox-trot. We didn't want to disturb them.'

Conflicts

'You're looking forward to getting there?'

'Oh yes, Mama!'

She dreams, and does not enlarge on her tepid acquiescence.

'Are you thinking about the sea, the beach, the terrace?'

'Oh yes, Mama!'

'What's the first thing you want to see?'

The hazel eye sparkles, a dimple hollows the right cheek, a childish glow reveals that this is the face of a little girl of eleven.

'I'm going straight away to see if the shell is still in the little blue box, and the sea-horse I painted green!'

She bounds up on both feet and goes away and the friend who is visiting me follows her with a condescending look : 'She's rather babyish for her age, isn't she?'

To which I reply with an offended mother's 'Yes, thank heavens!' Purely reflex on my part, as I'm not offended. It's a long while since I troubled to explain the child to grown-ups. I've been too occupied in understanding her myself. Left alone with my child I'd have refrained from asking so many inane questions, the equivalent of : 'Hold out your paw, nicely now !' I consider that my daughter did well enough, from respect and politeness, to speak in suitable terms while keeping to the truth.

Yes, sure enough, she'll go first to find her blue box, with its sleeping shell. Unique, heavily symbolic, the ritual objects dwell in a secret cupboard. When my daughter arrives at the weathered shore of the Ile-et-Vilaine she won't run to the romantic headland to claim from the sea the sea of yesteryear. She is too removed from our simplicity, which has no more need of symbols. Each season brings her nearer to it; high school, with its civilizing influence, makes her ever more ordinary. Nowadays she utters opinions which are the opinions of a clique, a sect, a group; she may even share them, that's her right. We have just extracted a few neutral words from her, but she is well aware that her silence is her own. It is there that she gambols in security, there that she ripens in awareness of risk and responsibility. We respect, she and I, the boundary I guard so jealously of the two mental domains, hers and mine.

Children! . . . Where you are concerned we can only wander undecidedly, advance gropingly. How does it happen that, in bringing you into the world, we lose that shrewdness of recollection that would enable us to understand you? We lose it for ever, a total obliteration; we lose it like the knack of flight that comes to us in dreams, as the new-born loses its knack of swimming a few hours after birth. Chance, rather than perspicacity, allows us to rejoin, to understand children; then they are our ephemeral conquest. A gentle patience works with them, but not more than a strong hand. We are disgusted by the brutality of some parents, yet without reflecting that this verbal brutality and its accompanying harshness of feeling are neither more nor less unproductive than a more seductive strategy. The words brim with antagonism. . . . Alas, one must struggle with what one loves, in love as in motherhood. Yet love adapts itself in *grosso modo* fashion and for a long while possession may suffice as final settlement.

'Trust . . . an open heart, the delightful blossoming of the child in the maternal breast . . . the crystal-clear spirit of the child. . . .' Literature is quite dewy with such expressions. I sometimes wonder whether this kind of doting writer ever had children. At other times I begin to doubt their sincerity as much as their intelligence. A troubled faith usually binds the child to its parents. A faith that suffers and has need of heroes and saints as it contemplates human failings. We can never be great enough for our sons, even if the best they recognize in us evokes a filial fanaticism within them. But fanaticism is a matter of pride. Between doubt and fanaticism there is barely room for tenderness; slow to well up in childish hearts, born of grief, sometimes of deserved punishment, almost never of joy, it is a consolation that ripens late. Arbitrary, as independent of our merits and virtues as love itself, it manifests itself as timidly as love and heralds the first crack in the inexorable serenity that haloes childhood. It is the weight of tenderness that draws hitherto intact young creatures towards the weakness of confidences, which are to trust what the fitful light and shade of a shutter flapping in the wind are to broad daylight. The dawn of victory for us, a happiness we must keep hidden—however, the struggle starts again, the stern thrilling struggle. I dramatize? No doubt. The truces, the happy surprises, make me tremble more than need be, certainly more than is apparent. What deep love can dispense with an atmosphere of drama? The extravagant desire to give all, poisons motherhood, as if to punish it for its passionate origins. But from the earlier flame what remains to the mother is that the child is more demanding than the lover, and will not share; that it chooses among the gifts one thinks to offer it; that it remains inflexible where a lover would forgive, for a child hugs its grievance, fixes it in memory, disinters it twenty years later, fresh, gorged with a mysterious, vampiric life. . . . So the mother refines and purifies within herself what love has left untutored, rudimentary. An incorrigible lust for giving will always attach itself to her like a blemish. But little by little she gives up demanding tear for tear, transport for transport. More patient, she will accommodate the good that she would once have ravaged in amorous fury. The repeated check shapes her, at last she acknowledges the mystery of the loved creature, she who but recently tested her beloved prey with sight and scent, she who could see a square of paper in a pocket gleaming through the material, she who used 'Why?' and 'What are you thinking about?' and 'Do you love me?' like a double-edged weapon. She is proud to sport an appearance of reason every time in her life that she thinks of renouncing the possessive spirit. . . . As if she were capable of anything other than possession! No matter. An ageing adversary, faced with a child in whom, the better to wound her, there flourishes all that got the better of her, she savours the profits and perplexities of her practised tactics. For her there is no longer any equal footing. For in that period when her living creation relaxes and surrenders, during the peaceful seasons when youth refreshes itself, when the child returns to childhood, the mother secretly appropriates what she likes best and delights in it. 'You exist. Every moment you demonstrate my capacity. The fact is that you can do nothing against me, except to make me suffer. So long as you exist, I am the stronger. You are the owner of that cheek, that updrawn lip, that eye shaded in its deep socket, and that fresh-complexioned expression: so many weapons that will be fatal to others, but thank God I've already succumbed to them, for years now, and it is almost to defy you that I find, in what was once my downfall, my present fortune and subsistence. . . .'

Summer

Another year for octopuses. They reduce the number of shrimps and little rock-fish of the coast. I try to learn from them something of their nature; but my patience is exhausted by their astonishing sagacity. Should I forage for a little while with a shrimping-net in the submerged 'wharf' of a lobster or conger-eel, a strange caress gropes at my ankle in the green water, a delicate, cautious entwining that suddenly clasps round my leg a fetter at once soft and burning, like certain flat water plants, whose stickiness does not allay its smarting: it is the arm of a little octopus, that is only induced to untwine itself because its prey is too large for it.

If, at low tide, I hold the baited shrimping-net at the edge of a salt pool, the agate shrimps come to palpate the raw meat with the tips of their bristles. They dance their shrimps' dance, one leap forward, two leaps back. In the middle of their transparent body a bright jade-green phial marks their full stomach. Intelligent, they pose themselves with bravado on my bare foot dabbling in the pool and stab it with their inoffensive beak. A sea-perch, all head and fanned-out fins, whisks its short tail, demands to be caught, if only for a moment; but who's interested in this inedible hog-fish? Even the cats won't have it. Dreamily, floating askew, heavy and agile, the 'clenched fist' then reveals itself and grasps the bait with an assured pincer. But it surveys us from below upwards, its articulated crab's eyes study our movements, it listens to us thinking and at its own pace regains the shadow to change into a pebble, a weed, an eddy of sand. It made no attempt to slice, with one scissor-stroke, the shrimps prancing on their own, or the little sea-perch, and I've never managed to surprise the struggle between the species which do, however, feed on one another. . . .

Betrayed by the crab, I often remain empty-handed beside my empty net and the mocking quadrille of shrimps. The weather is mild, the wind brushes the grubbing of potatoes, the upturned earth, the hay and the damp seaweed. . . . It's always just when my thoughts desert my half-hearted fishing that a firm grasp seizes the edge of the net and tests it with a brief shake. A long blackish finger, two, three long blackish fingers, of an indescribable heart-stopping suppleness, are knotted round the iron crown of the net; another reptilian finger, directed over the pocket, prods the meat bait, tugs at it, calls yet another finger to its aid. Should the meat yield to this tearing, the slender, studded, powerful fingers carry it off in one go. Should it resist, they are guided by a kind of fury. One attacks the meshes, tears, and carries off with the scrap of raw beef the bottom of the net. But neither during its approach nor in the course of the struggle have I seen the centre of the octopus, the thinking nucleus of the eight arms, the creature's cold and placid eye. It despatches the active parts of itself to a distance, recalls them, magically projects them. Small as it is, it sometimes excites in us a giddiness that is entirely cerebral, for its suckers are not tenacious and they are inoffensively pneumatic. It succeeds by fascinating the sea creatures, overcoming enemies of superior strength. I watch in vain for an encounter with an accustomed antagonist, I wait for its tentacles to seize its marine prey before my eyes. When we make an appearance it seems that all struggle

ceases between wild animals, aquatic or terrestrial, that they shiver
with a shared anxiety at sight of their common enemy, man.

On the other hand, our presence stirs up the quarrels of domestic animal with domestic animal. For a fortnight there have been
living here three bitches, two Siamese cats, one of which is feeding three kittens, a languorous and interminable black tom, two
dogs and two aboriginal cats. Of the thirteen, the three Parisian
felines ignored the existence of the canine species, the sea and the
countryside. The accord was miraculous, in the narrow human
sense we give the word. A prolonged, definitive, olfactory investi-
gation suffices for the cats. The bitches, warned in a few words,
exhibited the dissimulation and politeness we expected of them;
and anyway, the nursing cat taught them, in a few seconds of
terrifying apparition, that a nursing cat is the equivalent of a
horde of demons. A pair of finches, occupied—counter to all tradition and probability in the month of August—with a nest where
two unfeathered fledglings cheep, nested above the front door and
showed themselves not wanting in cordiality, fluttering above our
heads, gathering provender in flight, picking it up from between
the dogs' paws, and chirping under the noses of the cats, offended
and scornful at such presumption. As for us, the two-legged ones,
we are still delighted by the charming and preposterous sight
of a terrace where cats and dogs slumber in the hours of heat,
hovered over by trusting finches. Such peace is dear to us and we
cannot refrain from stroking this one, congratulating the other on
its perfect urbanity, cradling the long tom in our lap whence it
slips away, stretching, spread out, like an almost fluid putty. . . .
Then the scene suddenly changes. The congratulated cat opens a
dragon's mouth and punishes some innocent; the bitch one is
stroking bristles, the hair of its back like a sole's backbone, and
chases the smallest dog from its shade; a Siamese, drowsy till now,
crawls in strategic demonstration against a low-perched finch; the
other Siamese explodes into oaths, treating the tom as a child-
stealer. . . . Everything is spoiled, the sentimental sky of our
earthly paradise is darkened, because we have just cast there the
demoralizing shadow, the unlucky hand of the master, of him who
leads animals astray, discloses his love and jealousy, and would
see himself without rival in their once pure hearts.

Beauties

Madame P., too much of a beauty, disfigures herself. Another beauty, Romanian this time, kills herself because of the first wrinkle. Man, be satisfied, be glorious, both sacrifice themselves for you. Of the two victims the most naïve is certainly the one who bathed her perfect features in sulphuric acid. A lot of good it has done her, as they say. All she can hope for now is not to hear, falling from ungrateful cherished lips, the word once heard by a beautiful would-be suicide who had just placed a bullet in her shoulder and was not dying: 'Imbecile. . . .'

Whenever a woman tries to remedy the inconveniences of an amorous passion she either makes a mistake or else swaps an evil for a disaster. She is beloved by fate alone and loses all in sinning against it. Let us suppose that Madame P. had continued to dazzle and desolate her rivals with her unique splendour, to wound a jealous and madly infatuated husband to the heart. Would the set-up have ended in drama? I am sure it would, but in what I dare describe as a normal drama: the husband's suicide, a duel between the said husband and a suspected lover. All that is within the tradition, I might even say the banality, of fierce and ordinary love. 'I'll kill you,' threatened a jealous woman. 'That's your affair,' her husband very sensibly replied. Nothing guaranteed Madame P. the development of predestined tragedy.

But, forgoing the four or five gestures consistent with the logic of her life, she chose the monstrous challenge that confounds the simple issues and fixes the unhappy woman in a deadlock, disfigured and left to contemplate the prospects for her love.

It's nothing to be born ugly. Sensibly, the ugly woman comes to terms with her ugliness and exploits it as a grace of nature. To become ugly means the beginning of a calamity, self-willed most of the time. In destroying her beauty Madame P. shows that she counts on the nobility of soul of a hitherto tormented spouse. 'Now he'll be happy,' she says. Alas! If once he loved her material form, he may have forgotten long since that she was the most beautiful woman in the world. Obsessed, on the other hand, he thought only of this beauty. He cursed it, abused it, blamed it as the source of all his troubles. Poor man, what is he left with now? The right to display, peacefully now, the being of whose treasure he once wished to be the sole possessor? Allow me a moment to consider this widower, this rich man driven mad by overflowing possessions. According to the newspapers, he is 'inconsolable'. He implores the medical profession to restore his reason for living, his reason for hating, for suspicion. If he has any charity, will he not cry inwardly 'If only she were dead!' For already he can see further than the rash woman, he is capable of picturing the course of future events, the sudden sleep of all the passions, and the appearance, in a setting still redolent of impassioned wrongs and sensual conflict, of courtesy, disinterestedness, kind attentions, all those virtues that would have waited patiently to be ushered in by mature age. . . .

That's enough pity to offer the one who has not suffered the irreparable effects of vitriol. Well, to whom shall I extend it then? To the self-burnt? Excuse me, but I cannot. I cannot concede that a proprietor has the right to lay waste his own property. Madame P. puts me in mind of the stupid whim of defiance that finished off Felicity, a Normandy farmer. Felicity governed and worked to exhaustion her nephew, a man of all work, who used to grumble unendingly 'Oh, Aunt, if only I could see you in the well!' One day Felicity cried impatiently 'Like this?' and jumped into the well. The nephew married the pretty little servant-girl. . . . But this anecdote is not intended as a fable.

The other beauty who, this week, celebrated her fiftieth birthday with a very successful suicide, deserves that I should think of her with regret, if simply to blame her for knowing only how to be beautiful. The fear of ageing, a commonplace neurosis, does not usually wait for age and spares neither sex. Mlle de V., aged twenty-six, once confided to me that it ruined her appetite and sleep in advance. This was doing things on the grand scale, prematurely to prospect the feminine hell peopled, once age has come, by so many 'beautiful Mesdames So-and-so'. In contrast with such frenzy, the deceased Romanian might have taken the path of so many pharmaceutical establishments, violet-ray laboratories, laboratories for blue light, dyeing, massage and surgery, that she would never have found the time to quit this world. But this proud woman doubtless lived a withdrawn life, imprisoned with two equally pitiless spies—her mirror and her lover. In which of these two did she witness her declining image for the first time?

I was talking about her to a friend, a spruce quinquagenarian, who judged her with light peremptoriness. 'Pooh! These are a foreigner's ideas. We French women, we shall never lack for occupation once love is over. We have the family, scandalmongering, the love-affairs of others, and greed.'

I nodded assent, reflecting on a recent glimpse of two women who had been beautiful, celebrated and rivals. The one, hardly aged at all, blowzy and gluttonous in front of a plate of Spanish *puchero*; the other, all claws and velvet like a cat's paw, her cheek still smooth, her light blue eyes blazing with eternal malice. . . .

Offspring

In Germany a butcher kills them, salts them and eats them. As for us, we buy and sell them, put them down and take them up again, deck them out and exchange them. From time to time some child is discovered hidden away in a cupboard in the midst of darkness and filth; every month brings its news-item of a child branded with a poker, bruised with blows, starving; public opinion, represented by neighbours on the same floor, brings it to the attention of justice after an interval that is usually a long one, for public opinion, scrupulous, likes to garner the evidence in minute detail. . . . To repeat the expression of a small girl I know, 'It's becoming quite impossible to be a child!'

We now have a more or less complete list of the Galou pseudo-offspring. These, as it happens, seem hardly to have suffered. If one or two were lost, it was from inadvertence and not from brutality. But what can one think of the mother who handed them over, in all propriety, to a monomaniac of maternity? We are horrified by the pale and shameful little renunciatory contract drafted by one of the defaulting mothers; but it's because we don't read often enough those newspaper pages where the traffic in children publishes its advertisements between the bargain piano and the 'twice worn' fur coat. It is there that an authentic marquis, whose days are numbered, refuses to die out altogether and wants his name to survive him by ennobling some cherished commoner's head. There that a family without issue cannot contemplate sterile old age.

Rights, clandestine cares, are exchanged for a little money; it is not a matter of enormous sums, for the secretive adoption is one of the rare commodities whose cost has not quintupled since the war. . . . How easy it all is, how romantic, inadmissible and every-day! Every kind of traffic seems authorized when it's a matter of suppressing or banishing an inconvenient child. In my own local cemetery a pretty truncated column marks the place of a new-born who lived for a week. It was the child of a lady—a young lady, rather—who came to stay in Puisaye for three months, heavy and ravishingly beautiful, and went away lighter, having delivered her fruit to a local doctor. The doctor died too, but much later on, after having added to his medical rank the ephemeral title of Minister of Finance. But who ever knew the name of the beautiful sinner?

I date from a time, I come from an area, where the traffic in Parisian 'foster-children' provided an income for nurses, wet or dry. My elder brother, a country doctor, used to take me on his rounds and I could guess, from his sombre expression, when the time came for his tour of inspection of the Parisian infants. For one child who flourished in his rural squalor, ten cost us laughter and appetite just to look at them. We would arrive without warn-ing to find the little patient alone in the farm building, swaddled in its cradle, dummy in mouth and eyes black with flies. Or else it cried endlessly, given over to the care of a four-year-old. One of these, at eight months, was nourished on lard, cabbage soup and cider, like a grown-up. 'But what he likes best,' his nurse proudly assured us, 'are gooseberries. Ah, *he* doesn't want to go back to Paris!'

And he did not go back, and for good reason. . . .

Brittany, Puisaye, it was the same hecatomb. Did I not this week come across, at an antiquary's at Saint-Servan, a sturdy piece of Louis XIII furniture, a squat cabinet, a sort of deep side-board with two thick, hermetically closing doors. 'It was inside this,' said the merchant as he opened it, 'that they used to put small children—see, the two planks that made the cradle are still there—and then they were shut in and like that the parents could go to work in the fields without their little ones being eaten by the pigs.'

Have the last twenty-five or thirty years altered the fate of these foster-children? Surely. First, there are not so many children now. And then, nowadays, they don't wait for a child to come into the world before getting rid of it. A simplification that resorts to criminal surgery and that has abolished the familiar picture that used to dishonour—for instance—a certain railway station in the open fields where the nurses, back from Paris, well provided with squalling infants, money and alcohol, used to take a snack. . . . Prostrate or feverish new-born infants, the sour odour of milk churned up by the train, new swaddling-clothes, a dirty pink ribbon, a coarse black hand rocking the basket that sheltered four or five little ones higgledy-piggledy. . . .

As a small girl I was scared by these kidnappers, who were for the most part no more than simple or greedy peasant women. But my sensitive elder brother lost, in their context, courage and in-clination for his profession. My mother, loving protector of all nascent life, did her best to save these still secret children. On two occasions she took girl-mothers into her service, saying no more to them than 'Lift up your corset now, my girl'. Poor morality? That was the narrow provincial judgment on this morality, too elevated for it.

Nowadays it is the child-welfare officer or the eugenist who provides for the most urgent cases. Given the dearth of French children, France may well take nurselings from no matter where, and in the manner of the strange Madame Galou. It is not difficult to collect bastards and orphans. It is less easy to protect against their own parents the lamentable number of little Poil-de-Carotte who sigh : 'Everyone can't be an orphan. . . .' Between the spoilt middle-class baby—unhappy autocrat who divides two doting families the better to reign over them—and the little skinny martyr, fodder for news-items, there is room for more than one kind of unhappy child, beginning with those households where divorce assumes the periodicity, and almost the frequency, of a cure. Vandérem will tell you that these children, whether well brought up or spoiled, can pass for the happiest creatures in the world. Nevertheless, for lack of love and instinctive attachment, these same children feel unstable and anxious and would regret, had they ever known it, the patriarchal peace of the Orient, the harem that witnesses the growth of the mingled laughing sons of Fatima and daughters of Aïscha. They cast a happier shadow than do the obstetric clinics, those pink-washed walls and the columns of the enclosed patio, at the centre of which a dreaming urchin, leaving his play, leans randomly against a female knee or checks his impulse at some breast which, though not having borne his growing weight, is nonetheless maternal. . . .

Mausoleums

The friends of Marie Bashkirtseff* are up in arms and reveal that decay threatens the tomb of one who was a restless young woman, glory-struck and a peripatetic invalid. I see no harm in vigilant friends scraping off the moss and restoring the stone, though I prefer those tombs that are loaded with unrestrained vegetation and spared the rake. I respect the devoted care of the hands that clean the crown of pearls, change the water in the little vase and

* Marie Bashkirtseff (1860–84), the Russian-born author of a remarkable *journal intime,* in which she records her struggle against the consumption that finally killed her.

rub down the engraved marble; but, in my view, these are attentions better suited to a little villa for the living than a chapel for
the dead.

I haven't recently visited the pleasant cemetery at Passy, where
rest the famous dead. The last time I was there was when I
repaired to the tomb of Renée Vivien* and then I was accompanied by one of the most lively of the living—I refer to Annie de
Pène. She showed me over the garden, pleasant in all seasons but
enhanced by the clear autumn weather.

She traversed the narrow paths with familiarity, picking off a
dried-up rose, rearranging a bouquet with those marvellous hands
of hers that touched everything with assurance, made fruit and
vegetables more appetizing, could break a branch and throw a log
on the fire. Annie pursed her lips at Renée's tomb, found fault
with some faded violets, and laid beside the dead flowers some
fresh violets she had brought. She never stopped talking but did
me the honours of the enclosure and named the inmates as if it
were a drawing-room. 'That's Marie Bashkirtseff over there, this
is that charming little Henriot who died of burns. . . . I tell you,
Colette, this is the best sort of cemetery for a woman. The others
are big, crowded, it's a scrimmage! But here, my word, it's the
devil to get in, you have to know someone. . . .' Her gaiety was no
insult to the peace of the dead and we spoke of Renée Vivien as
if she might have been waiting for us, five minutes from there, at
her home in the avenue du Bois. Annie shook her stubborn
Norman forehead in irritation. 'Finished at thirty, what stupidity!
How can one live eating so little, feeding on raw fish and grapes,
hiding from the daylight behind stained-glass windows in the glow
of three brown wax candles: Renée Vivien would have done
better to eat my stuffed chicken or my creamed haddock. But
perhaps a poet can't eat stuffed chicken without risking ceasing to
be a poet. I know nothing about it; I'm afraid of poets. And yet
she was a charming creature, this tall fair girl who's asleep under
the violets and who never discussed her poetic gift. I must say, I
prefer invalids who don't tell you about their diseases!'

* Renée. Vivien (1877–1909), pseudonym of Pauline Tarn, born in London
of an English father and an American mother. She lived mostly in Paris and
wrote sensuous verse influenced by Baudelaire.

It's true, Renée Vivien never spoke of her 'disease'. She did not recite verses, demanded neither praise nor criticism. A foreigner, she thought and wrote our language with purity, but she might have found it hard to comprehend those words that still vibrate in Marie Bashkirtseff's underground chamber : 'To succeed . . . to arrive. . . .' Yet even Renée Vivien left a body of work.

I think that her soul was like her face, which was fair, coiffed with fine flaxen, golden hair, and childlike from the forehead to the small English mouth. Laughing brown eyes, a kind of mobile artlessness, kept her countenance ever young. I used to say to her 'Renée, you've only the body of a writer', teasing her about her long, long, insubstantial, stooping body. It was what she wanted, this long thin body, ever more frail, ever thinner, and she foolishly went without eating.

I don't think that anyone has had much to say about her dark, sumptuous and changing apartment. At the back of the courtyard of the same building Robert d'Humières sometimes inhabited a bachelor establishment, ornamented with exotic souvenirs and a white cat. Apart from a few Buddhas and the antique instruments of the music-room, all the furniture moved and changed mysteriously at Renée Vivien's. A collection of Persian gold coins gave way to jade, were replaced by a collection of butterflies and rare insects. She wandered about among tottering marvels and displayed them with an exile's pleasure : 'I can't find my new Buddha! Marie, Marie, where have you put the Buddha I got yesterday?' How charming she was, one sometimes saw her as the farouche priestess of some strange sentimental cult! Towards her guests she behaved with the eagerness of a well-brought-up young girl, watching them dine while nibbling at grilled almonds and fruit. She also had a young girl's sudden blush and a liking for tall stories and over-strong liqueurs. She cried like a child, then laughed one night when, overcome by shadow and unable to eat beneath a canopy of sombre hangings starred with occasional candles, I brought along and set down by my plate an offensive, inadmissible and indispensable paraffin lamp worth five francs seventy-five.

I may not seem to evoke a poetess, gravely devoted to her art. It was just that she worked unobtrusively, with little noise. At

Nice I often surprised her sitting on the edge of a cane divan, writing verses on her knees. She would get up with a guilty air and excuse herself : 'I've just finished. . . .' Even in death she remains far removed from her Slav neighbour, anxious for fame, who would have given ten years of her delicate and burning youth for a sprig of official laurel. Beautiful and young, early of the elect, it may be that they lean over the bar of Heaven to see what we preserve of theirs. So let us give to each what they loved on earth; let us restore the tomb of Marie Bashkirtseff and, for Renée Vivien, let us encourage the grass, the viburnum that climbs and hides her name, the wild violet. . . .

Newspapers

For anyone who spends more than six weeks on a miraculously inviolate shore, with no sound but the battering of the angry sea, the faint, silky ripping of the calm tides, the mewing of the gulls and the plaintive note of the red-foot, reading the newspapers becomes astonishing. 'An hour's delirium' is what we call the period after the arrival of the postman here.

We are not scared off immediately—Paris keeps up with us for a long while when we leave it in July. A grey mist of crimes, thefts, infanticides and embezzlements, spreads over the summer news-papers, passes before our surfeited, unresting gaze. The long columns resemble provincial streets, empty and silent, where a sudden echo repeats the brief explosion of a revolver-shot, perhaps a single cry. It's July, the time of rejuvenation of our senses, sur-prised and exiled to the point when, in the early days, holding a newspaper stretched and flapping in the breeze, we say : 'Another woman cut into eight pieces, what a bore. . . . Aren't they done with their parricides and stories of kidnapped children?' But we call out at the top of our voice, arms raised : 'Come and see, come quickly! The shadow of the cloud is violet on the sea! And there's a rose on the rose-bush! Run, run, or you won't see this animal, I don't know its name, I've never seen anything like it, it's got feet like a grasshopper and a golden head, quickly!'

Gradually equilibrium is restored and ecstasy becomes habit. Replete, equable, dedicated to physical enthusiasm and mental serenity, every day our life becomes better and further removed from what it was in our urban epoch. The fine weather, the lunar months, the harvests, the colour and caprice of the storms, the prognostications of the birds, the quivering desire for sociability expressed by the wild game, normal life in fact, bathes us and we live, initiate and at peace, at the heart of its miracles. Beautiful refuge, where we discover in the distance what we have abandoned! A single day, a single glance, do not suffice. The rock fissure, filled with sea-water, does not reveal its treasures all at once. Only gradually does our persistence fathom the depth of a glacial green, carpeted with sea-wrack, discern the crab's moving jaws and the living beard of the shrimps among the delicate weed, the agonizing drama of a small conger-eel cut in two by a crab. . . .

Little by little, having laid the newspaper aside, we return to it; and little by little the phantasmagoria and horror of daily life in a hundred civilized places reaches us. At five hundred kilometres from Paris the unaccustomed smell of newly printed paper stands for fever, ambition, ferocity, often macabre comedy. As we read, a drowsy naïveté evokes in us a loud exclamation, a communal indignation. There's reason for it.

'Did you see about this stolen necklace? Yes, a necklace worth five millions, isn't that enough to tempt the Devil? And did you see where a prisoner and a warder conspired to rob the prison safe? Oh . . . it's outrageous, damn it!'

Friends arriving from Paris and stopping by listen to us indulgently. It's true that we question them as if they've left a Gehenna where people kill one another, where the 'flics' hurl themselves at the heels of men who flee, scattering pearls and wads of banknotes in their tracks. The newspaper, all surface news, no longer has a bite for these crusted city-dwellers whom we shall come to resemble after the equinoctial tides. But my word, what a harvest in one week! In seven days God allows himself less vagaries than his own creatures. '*A train runs into a sandal factory. Three jewellers, terrified at the sight of a cotton-wool bomb, hand over three hundred thousand francs to a miscreant in a hold-up. A business employee slashes a woman passer-by. An engaged couple go for a walk in the bois de Vincennes; they are assaulted by three false policemen who ill-treat the young man and abuse the young girl. A lawyer and his mistress fight a revolver duel. A seventy-five-year-old father is thrown out by his children and left on a chair by the kerbside. Fifty-seven millions, left in a car for an hour, disappear . . .*', etc., etc.

How the fate of these robbed, slashed, ill-treated individuals excites our curiosity and compassion! How well we understand the word, reduced to the singular, that the peasants use. Contemptuous of any political implication, there are many of them who still speak of '*the* newspaper', with no other specification of the invasive, perturbing gazette. Let us admit that a facile technique, a concise lyricism, almost everywhere inform the news-item, jewel of the front page, the guts of what, typically, is called the 'body' of the paper. Humour smiles there, among the hecatombs. Eros juggles there with tibiae.

Perhaps what is lacking at the sessions of the League of Nations, so that the fate of the world might compete in interest far afield with the most recent tortures of Biribi, the disappearance of a sempstress and the assassination of a sexagenarian by a pretty young woman, perhaps what is lacking is the ingenious, enthusiastic, tragic, pseudo-naïve bard who edits here, there, everywhere, the news of the day. I picture him, this Proteus, given a free hand at the Geneva Conference and giving all his attention to a jaundiced diplomatic smile, producing for the public, like so many impassioned articles, the chain and seal of Monsieur X. . . , the monogrammed portfolio of Monsieur Z. . . . A light touch with the colour of a capital execution, a hint of the Assize Court, what success. . . .

But the protocols of Geneva are edited by upright career journalists, by secretly ardent politicians who conscientiously 'play the game'. It is not these we shall ask to relate, with due extravagant seriousness, the adventure of the American multi-millionaire who sees his two daughters elope with two of his servants. Is it just our natural rusticity? Is it the talent of our specialist colleagues, and the sickly satanism they know how to impart to fifteen inoffensive lines? I don't know; but we are thrilled and stunned to learn that an 'exclusive' clan of Massachusetts millionaires has gone into mourning because of the double misalliance, and that the father of these two rebellious near thirty-year-olds declines henceforward 'to be seen in public'.

Wings

It is beyond dispute that I can fly in dreams. You too. I add 'in dreams' because my efforts, like yours, have not succeeded—by a sound, a strangled sigh—in crossing the frontier that separates the two worlds, only one of which we designate, arbitrarily, as 'real'. I can cross a valley; pivot, to turn, on one or other of my flying arms; and swoop down, head first, feet raised to gain speed, then straighten my trunk to regain the horizontal for climbing or landing. And how I sport with the wind, in this entire universe! Entire, because it possesses its pale day-star, its nights less dark than earthly nights, its plants, its population of the loved dead, of the keenly staring unknown, its animal life especially. The most recent animal I encountered there dates from last week, for the full moon, which sends cats delirious, authorizes my brief visits to this boundless continent. A black feline, as big as a Great Dane, was waiting to fight with me and we fought gravely, not in frenzy but as if for sport, while meantime I noticed the shape of its eyes, more horizontal than those of cats, and the particular pink of its mouth, opened whenever it wished to frighten or bite me. A very real animal, in fact, whose contact and appearance inspired my dreaming double with no more than normal curiosity, the normal desire to vanquish a strange animal, and the confused ill-formulated conceit of bringing off a victory *up there*: '*They* will be pleased with it; I'll display it to *them* as if it had always been mine. . . .' But it was the same with the beautiful black feline as with that little tortoise with the bird's head, so friendly, that climbs in the trees and cheeps . . . you know. No, you don't know. The bird-tortoise remained on the far side of the gate with the great black feline, the intelligent sociable serpent, the dog that silently regards me and puts his hand in mine, the man who holds out an open notebook which I never have the time to read. . . .

Thanks, no doubt, to my perfect digestion, animals and people in my exclusive nocturnal empire are courteous and peaceable, even in combat. The flights that carry me over a familiar valley of dark fir-trees do not break my bones and I land, instead of falling, in the middle of the bed after one of those jolts as severe as any earthquake. Did the same flight haunt the dreams of a Maneyrol, a Barbot, a Simonet, of all those who seek the dream-remembered motorless soaring, the everlasting wing? An aviator obsessed with gliders assured me that, while it takes our wingless species long study to control an aeroplane, an ancient science intervenes when it comes to the glider in which man progresses as if seated in the midst of an enchanted cloud, drunk with a newly recognized but ancient gift, in the newly conquered air. I can well believe it. All is marvellous that astounds senses as deadened and mutilated as ours. Flight exists for us only in dream, the complete being is he who sleeps and is newly born, for the new-born swims at birth like the sightless kitten and puppy. But its human condition holds it back and denies it one more element; two months later the 'little man' can no longer swim.

I ruminate on our downfall, lying stretched out on a shorn meadow where the seeds of the last dandelions rise, ballasted by their minuscule oblong fruit, tufted with spun silver. They progress slowly, visible for a long time against the misty blue of the sky; they stop and rest in the air without descending. It is also the season for the thistle-seed to emigrate. This flies in a different fashion, an iridescent hedgehog rolling on the tip of its bristles, descending the length of an invisible slope, climbing an aerial hillock. Two cormorants cleave the sky, not too high for me to fail to distinguish the angled articulation of the outer third of their wings, which constitute their private mystery of living mechanism.

They have arrived with the high tide and only pass over us to where the long estuary of the Rance beckons. Our faithful sparrow-hawks do not need these folded wings to execute, in a flash, the path of their patrol from Saint-Malo to Cancale, from Cancale to the nest which I respect; propellants hidden in their widespread, unmoving wings bear them up against the strong wind. . . . Flight, abandonment to the lost element, thirst that even the aeroplane cannot satisfy, torment of the creature, stretched crucified on the earth, who lifts his gaze on high. . . .

My tame finch does not concern himself with the sky. He lives like the hens and runs about in mouse disguise to terrify the cats. He runs, picks up the crumbs thrown to him, climbs the stairs using his feet, and sadistically acts the cripple. Cripple? Ah, if he only wished. . . . He does wish sometimes and climbs with a jeering cry into his modest finch's heaven, his sky, so low, informed with earthly smokes and smells. Little fawn wings, feeble beating apparatus of a sedentary bird. . . .

September gathers the swallows and sees the summer butterflies perish. Deflowered of their vulcans, peacock and tortoise-shell butterflies, the ground-lilac and the yellow broom have lost their most beautiful and quivering petals. But out of the mauve and yellow bouquet that remains something winged still launches itself : the venturesome spider leaves its web, casts itself off at the end of a silken cable, and rises borne by the wind. . . .

Back to School

They're going back. Their savages' feet, brown and hardened, re-experience the weight of the great shoes we have thoughtfully studded and strengthened with nails. A pair of good 'everyday shoes' for adolescents is as weighty as a shackle and our ballasted children frolicked with a shorter stride during those last recreations that served as dress-rehearsals before reassembly.

I was not moved by pity for my high-school girl, who executes the same gay dance on the threshold of her jail, whether coming or going. Certainly the schools of Paris and its surrounds welcome back, as boarders, many a strapping young woman like her, who will not go without either park or bathing. Neat, hair cut like a well-tended lawn, in pink aprons, it is a pretty posy of children that I run across at any time beneath the trees of Saint-Germain. They are well-conducted and their somewhat boyish vivacity is not altogether devoid of affectation. 'Once is not a habit,' said my own prisoner to me one day, 'I treated myself to a hair-wave.' From acquaintance with her best friends it seems to me that they soon learn to make prompt decisions, to run risks, and to take responsibility for their follies. My daughter's pocket-book notes various desiderata:

> *Buy writing-paper*
> *Soap, toilet-water*
> *A waterproof hat I've no need for: but people look*
> *askance if one goes for a walk without a hat.*
> *Ask Mama if I can become a Jewess.*

I assented to writing-paper, soap and lotion, even the oilskin hat, without a murmur. But on the question of apostasy I allowed myself a brief inquiry:

'Why do you want to become a Jewess?'

'Oh, it's not that I'm keen on it, but you know, at school they're nearly all Jews, so it seems rather like a uniform. . . .'

Roses on the wall, sunny pavilions, musical scales and trills of laughter . . . I'm well aware that this unclouded picture of boarding-school life is not the same everywhere. Gloomy colleges still exist. There is, especially, the extraordinary and inexcusable lagging of the provinces behind Paris in the matter of boarding-schools for boys.

One worries sentimentally over them and I know that every year well-meaning propaganda accuses the boarding system of all manner of disgrace and crime. This year, however, firmer and more numerous voices are raised in its defence in Paris and its periphery. It's from the provinces that the angry denunciations come, directed against the length of the classes, the total neglect of hygiene, and the incurable gloom that shrouds the decrepit buildings where our scattered sons languish. Optimists when they have daughters, our mothers sing the praises and advantages of the boarding system; pessimists where sons are concerned, other mothers malign it and bewail their fate from the heart of the ancestral home, bereft of its greatest pride, its young masculine ornament.

Eternal weakness of one sex for the other! I happen to know five very French families with but a single blossom—I mean that the five couples have each produced a single girl. It's said that the small English girl is unsurpassed in beauty. But it's my view that a pretty little French girl, well loved and of good carriage, has few rivals. My five little princesses know how to use their charm. Family life revolves around them, though with difficulty at times since their parents work. Five sensible mothers insist that their daughters' moral and physical hygiene demands a boarding-school near Paris to ensure the children's comfort and their parents' peace of mind. But five fathers, jealous as lovers, selfish as husbands, resist. What, give up the brief radiant encounter with 'la petite', the dinner-table chit-chat, the evening kiss, the sound of cantering feet? Never! Each of these impassioned fathers defends his treasure with such convinced ardour that I think of La Palférine's remark: 'Cut Claudine's hair? I'd rather see her dead!'

Is boarding-school a prison? 'It was in our time' many a man affirms who is over twenty-five, and almost all who are past forty. I don't doubt their sincerity and I am reminded of two older brothers, formerly entrusted to the College at Auxerre. Dirty, emaciated, devoured by fleas in summer, swollen with chilblains in winter, they endured their torment in dumb hatred. But this refers to a remote period, the period when I saw my sister, too, return from her boarding-school in the provincial capital changed, dispirited and miserable. It was the captivity of these three older ones that decided my liberty. 'Oh no, not for her!' murmured my mother as she looked at me. . . .

The concept of the boarding system is probably a monstrous one. But its application seems inevitable in future. For it is important, in too many cases, to remove the child from what an ignorant sentimentality still calls 'the warm and peaceful atmosphere of the home', in fact the narrow incubator which approximates the elbows and foreheads of two or three generations, the one the issue of the other, the one often the enemy of the other.

Nowadays the private life of parents is less mysterious for the child than the book one shuts away in a library; and how many couples constrain themselves, in front of the child, to the respectable lie, the pretended harmony? Is it certain that boarding-school corrupts a child? One may well wager that it will corrupt him less, and that our offspring will rather derive from fathers and mothers whose bonds are trivial a precocious apprenticeship, the bitterest, in all that destroys security, a sense of permanence, and faith. Whatever we may think, our children do not change; but we seem determined to diminish ourselves before them. Adult stupidity and inertia crack up the father as a pal and the mother as a friend, innovations prone to determine the son as judge and the daughter as rival.

'Away with the corrupting promiscuity of the boarding-schools!' I say the same as you, honest reformers. But I am not sure that whispered conversations in a study corner, books or newspapers passed from desk to desk, spoil and stain the precious fruit more than do your homely lessons of conjugal quarrelling, conversations in hinted words, the negligent looseness of our morals, in fact the spectacle of your fine adult existence as taken in by two large unfathomable eyes, by two small ears that shudder at what they understand, that retain the sound of an insulting word, a servile prayer, or a slamming door.

The Evening Star

Preface

The Evening Star (L'Étoile Vesper) is an autumnal work; but of late autumn, for Colette was in her seventies and a sequestered invalid in the Palais-Royal when she wrote it. She was incapacitated by an arthritis of the hip following an injury, which progressively immobilized her until she had to spend the greater part of the day and night in her divan-bed, straddled by the 'raft', the bed-table incorporating a desk on which she kept her papers and did her writing.

Situated in the heart of Paris, with its colonnades and formal gardens, shops and apartments, the Palais-Royal is a unique survival. Colette had lived there before, in a dismal subterranean 'tunnel', and longed to move to a higher level; this she did eventually, after a long series of vicissitudes and removals. She was now happily settled with her third husband, Maurice Goudeket, to whom she uniformly refers as her 'best friend'. Hers was a red room — with red wallpaper, a double door covered in red satin, and red coverings for armchair and bed. Everywhere were scattered books and baubles — glass paperweights, boxes of butterflies, shells and ornaments, crystal balls. Her bedside light had a blue paper shade, the *fanal bleu* that was the title of another book of this period. In the summer the bed was pushed into the window embrasure so that she might be 'in the garden'. Tended by her husband and a devoted servant, and absorbed in her new-found tapestry work, she greeted a constant stream of visitors: friends, doctors, black marketeers, reporters, members of the Académie Goncourt, of which she was the first woman member and president.

It would be a mistake to suppose that *The Evening Star* was written solely in the Palais-Royal. Colette was not completely incapacitated until her final years. She could still go for drives, could visit the South of France, most conveniently by aeroplane;

and she finished the book in the summer of 1945 at a house called Mauvannes at Les Salins d'Hyères, in the Var. But most of it was written in Paris, and in circumstances which might be thought both conducive and non-conducive to creative work. Though immobilized and in constant pain — 'An accident and its consequences have settled my fate' — she came to terms with her situation, refusing to take drugs of any kind : 'Aspirin changes the colour of my thoughts. It makes me gloomy. I would rather suffer cheerfully.' And it is her cheerfulness that prevents us from labelling her a stoic. She accepted her dependence on others; she was resigned to being crippled and old; but she decided to be a *gay* old person, to continue to savour the joys of the natural world, to create her own local paradise — bounded by her red walls, her blue lamp, the window with the Paris sky and its evening star. She retained her acute intelligence, her wit and acerbity, and she was never sorry for herself: 'I have always taken immense trouble not to show emotion.'

The book itself is very mellow, with the mellowness of Auden's 'Evening — grave, immense and clear'. It ends with these words : 'From here I can see the end of the road.' Subtitled *Souvenirs*, it is a fascinating collection of reflections, essays and reminiscences. It darts to and fro in time, a diary with the dates disarranged. At one moment Colette tells us of her experiences as a journalist at the turn of the century, at the next she is watching American aeroplanes over Paris towards the end of the Second World War or sharing, from her window, the frenzy of the Liberation. There are portraits of those — mostly women — she had known and loved. The style is honed down. The reader is insidiously drawn into her little enclosure to share her physical limitations, her unfettered imagination. We share her days as a music-hall artiste, her lecture tours, her reflections on graphology or sexual perversion, her visits to clairvoyants, memories of her mother, Sido. She transcended her past work to meet and overcome old age, pain and death. She was still eager to learn and wonder at stars, visitors, her own life. She remained a craftsman with an obsessional urge always to find exactly the right word.

She had not had an easy war. She suffered through others —

the indignity of having to receive German visitors, the screams of Jewish women and children being taken away, separately. Her husband was removed to an internment camp at Compiègne and she was without news of him for many weeks; when he did return he lived the life of a hunted man. And yet she could remain observant enough to note how women resented the comradeship their men had found in the camps. She was intensely patriotic; but hers was the patriotism of the small man or woman who could do no more than turn their back on the invader, make a fool of him, maintain an implacable reserve.

Death is rarely mentioned in *The Evening Star*, except obliquely, a reference to an impending engagement. Yet, for all its flashes of gaiety and youth, the work is pervaded by intimations of decline and mortality. Man is the only animal who knows that he is going to die, wrote Camus. Yet one cannot but believe that animals possess a noble melancholy that presages their return to nature; and it is just this sense — in one always so close to the animal creation — that is manifest in *The Evening Star*: 'Nothing perishes, it is I who am drawing away.'

. *L'Étoile Vesper* was first published in Switzerland in 1946. It was offered for sale in very unfavourable circumstances in Paris, without advertisement, on Bastille Day. It is not surprising that no more than 10,000 copies were sold, and that this very moving book has never become as widely known as it deserves.

DAVID LE VAY

One

'*Are you all right?*'

'*Fine.*'

'*What's that you're writing?*'

'*Oh, nothing! I scratch on the paper and then tear it up. When I can't make anything of it, I destroy it!*'

Tonight the sky is lowering, a breath of air through the open window heralds the thaw. It is time to close the sun-faded curtains.

My solicitous companion will go on thinking that I am bored. The healthy always believe that forced inactivity gives rise to boredom. It is a great error, into which I should no doubt fall myself, if, instead of having a defective leg, I lacked an arm. An infirmity becomes an affliction during the first year, when every season, every day almost, informs us of a new restriction, demands a new renunciation, the acknowledgment, from ourselves to ourselves, of having shaken today the chain which is to be more firmly riveted tomorrow. The seasons' cycle over, to acknowledge the fetters of the previous year and their mark is already to accept them like a garment rendered tolerable by age. If we are to be shaped by misfortune, it's as well to accept it. We do well to adapt misfortune to our requirements and even to our convenience. This is a mode of exploitation to which the young and robust are ill-suited, and I can well understand the difficulty of making them appreciate, for instance, that near-immobility is a gift. But give me, for a long illness, the child or the old man, who are alike in endurance once they perceive in good faith that what is commonly termed a martyrdom is more easily borne than a thorn under the fingernail or a bad whitlow. . . .

There's been a ring at the door.

'Madame, it's an ugly customer with two wild rabbits stuffed under his shirt. He says they're worth two hundred francs apiece, but he'll let you have one at a hundred and fifty.'

'Why?'

'Because it's Madame.'

But how can this ugly customer know that I am I when I find it so difficult to realize it myself?

'Does Madame wish to see him?'

No. Neither him nor the little wild rabbit with glazed and bluish eye, marked by the cord round its neck. The dogs of Paris may well stop, petrified, at the scent of this man's passage, true savage of the nearby forests, furtive bearer of dangling heads and matted feathers. . . . I won't see the little wild rabbit.

'I'm going out.'

'In this weather! I don't envy you.'

'Are you all right? You're not expecting anyone?'

'No one.'

It is a half-truth. Yet I can hardly admit to my best friend that I'm waiting for the spring. What should I wait for, if not the spring? I am its creditor, this year. It owes me the autumnal renewal which we haven't had, that febrile spasm which re-lights the candles of the chestnut-trees, brings out the lilac in October, and forces unexpected leaves from the bare branches, in fact the crisis we call St Martin's Summer. For no one thinks, twice in the same year, to call what is spring-like, spring.

The feeling of anticipation applies only to the real spring. Before then, and afterwards, we go by the harvest, count on the vintage season, hope for the thaw. One doesn't await the summer, it imposes itself; one dreads the winter. For spring alone we become like the bird beneath the eaves, like the deer when, on a certain night, it breathes in the winter forest the unexpected mist that warmly heralds the approach of the new season. Annually a profound credulity possesses the world, prematurely releasing the song of the birds, the bee's flight. A few hours—and we subside into the common misery of enduring the winter and awaiting the spring. . . .

'It's freezing here! Pauline!'

'Naturally, Madame. It's to be expected, it's not nearly spring yet.'

. . . which never arrives when we expect it. It arrives — we used to say as children—in a carriage, that is, it rides in and irrupts on a chariot of thunder, lashed by great zig-zags of lightning. Another year, before dawn, it lays icy shards everywhere, on the hens' trough, on the filled bucket, even in the footprints of the cattle by the edge of the pond. As soon as the sun touches them they explode in splinters of thin tinkling ice, and the frost, just when we want to imprint our name on it with a fingertip, vanishes like breath on a mirror.

Or else, as on the day of my last marriage, the springtide wipes out in a morning all the good work of an April already well advanced, fills the sky with grey flock which comes down as snow like a burst eiderdown. And yet it wasn't cold, that morning; what velvety snow! It clung to the yellow catkins of the hazel-trees and fell so thickly that I begged my old friend, and new husband, to stop the car so that I might hear the snow whisper on the bed of dead leaves. It is a very gentle, almost articulate, murmur. I've tried to describe it more than once. To compare it to the quiet praying of a crowd at worship is to fail once more, especially if I omit to mention that it is accompanied and accentuated by another rustling, like the diligent turning of silky pages. Beautiful April snow. . . . The wild honeysuckle of Vaux-de-Cernay held it piled on its new little ears, and the water rushing from the springs was like the blue of a snake.

The menu of the wedding breakfast did not belie this wintry passage in the spring. It comprised melting knuckles of pork, cooked in casserole, dressed in their own pink lard and crackling, moistened with their gravy flavoured by a little celery, a little nutmeg, a little horse-radish, and all those wholesome vegetables which devote their aroma to their mistress meat. We had pancakes too. . . . Can one get married without champagne? Yes, if the champagne is made to retreat by one of those chance encounters that used to brighten our French inns, in the shape of an anonymous vintage, dark and golden as a Spanish shrine, which held its own with the pork and the cheese. . . .

'*I'm back again. What weather! Are you all right?*'
'*Fine.*'
'*I hope you're not working.*'
'*God forbid! Just the opposite, I'm playing.*'
. . . On another occasion the springtide is reminiscent of a submerged rose. It gleams under the water, all gay showers and mosses grown in a few hours. From a green fingernail, at the tip of a branch, a drop drips endlessly, another drop and yet another, feeding the singing subterranean cascades. The seed is moist, the grass is juicy, the bark peels, the sticky clay entraps the foot. But a dull glimmer clings to each ripple of the overflowing water, the iris unsheathes itself in a moment, and the rain is warm. At twilight the river smokes like a rubbish-fire. . . .

A first green film clings to the sides of the trunks that face the north-east. An insidious odour ascends to the ground floor from the cellar. 'What is it that smells so?' What smells so is a full barrel, denatured by this damp mouldy spring, whose wine turns to vinegar. Too late, the cask is delivered of an enormous matrix, a kind of horrible octopus, violet and gelatinous. . . .

A great clamour from the housewives: 'The cider is ruined!' They emerge from the storeroom mourning the cider, brandishing a jug full of a liquid dark and murky as old beer, which has lost all its virtue.

Everything smells sour and acid, like a used-up gherkin, like apple *marc*, like silaged beetroot. . . . It's your smell, you mouldy spring! And yet, if the sun and wind only change their mind, you can still become the fertile muddy road, the sour alley, that leads us to the most beautiful time of the year; there's just time to freeze up this mildew, to serve one last little dish — a passing shower — on the platter-like flower of the laurustinus, and the torrid spring will hurl itself at the blossoms.

It's the most difficult period to evoke. I grasp it by a bud, a wormlike shoot, a viburnum, and pull it cautiously towards me. . . . Silence and heat reign over the bare fields. A varied feeble population crawls, flutters, subsides again. Legs feebly grope and stagger, bellies crawl; everywhere an insect perishes at the brink of life, a milky larva exudes its white blood, the chrysalis bursts like a pod. In the subterranean darkness a massacre is in progress. For every creature so despatched a door was about to open and has not opened. . . . Does the rage to die exceed the rage to be born?

It is the scorching springtime, which stunts the grass and the spears of the wheat. An east wind, no dew, the rosebush drops its unopened buds, the cherry-tree its wrinkled cherries, the young garlic and sensitive shallot swoon away — pity the winged pea-flower which begs for rain to transform it into a pod. . . .

I also superimpose on this strident spring the idea of love, if only to recall the callous selfishness of the loving design, its private barrack-room language — for what modest young girl, besotted by love, doesn't secretly scourge her rival by calling her as ugly as sin and a sick cow? . . . It's strange that this kind of spring remains one of my mysterious recreations as an old woman. . . .

'What are you looking at?'
'The American aeroplanes going over. Fish flying in the deep-ening night. . . . They enter the rain clouds like a stickleback its fluffy nest. . . .'
For it is always prudent to dissimulate. To admit that one is occupied only with memory is enough to wound the innocent. And how to make my questioner understand that, though I'm over seventy, I miss so much, with such obstinate strength and intolerance, a sky, a countryside, and unbounded and inalienable possession? Let us withdraw then, my dead springtimes and I, behind the inflated foreground of my pretended turbulence, to gain the shelter of my true patience.
'Your leg isn't still bothering you?'
'Not a bit. I'm thinking!'
I'm thinking. That's saying a lot, but it's said with enough comic emphasis to reassure the anxious one. Can one really give the name of thoughts to a promenade, an aimless unplanned contemplation, a sort of virtuosity of memory that I'm not the

only one to condemn as vain? I set off, I dash forward along a once familiar path, as fast as I used to pace, I spy the great twisted oak, the poor farm where cider and bread-and-butter used to be generously doled out to me. Here is where the yellow road branches, the creamy white elders, surrounded by bees in such numbers that their threshing-machine hum can be heard at twenty paces. . . . I hear the sobbing of the guinea fowl, the sow grumbling. . . . That's the way I work. . . . Then, suddenly, a mental block, emptiness, annihilation, exactly resembling, or so I feel, what must be the approach to death, the road lost, barred, obliterated. . . . No matter, I shall have enjoyed myself in transit.

I don't always enjoy myself. I may be engaged an entire night in pursuing a fragment of conversation, a name, a word, which are not even helpful to my work. A game, a challenge. Do other wretches, other writers, give chase in the same way? The pursued object leads me unfeelingly on, it is as elusive as game already stalked a dozen times. To catch up with it I find myself singing to it its veiled homonyms, to its vaguely glimpsed rhythm. If it falls asleep, I sleep. My rest makes it careless and I capture it in the morning, innocently drowsing. Wakening before it does, I seize it. . . . I should very much like, for instance, to recapture the name of the traveller who assured me that in Martinique — perhaps it's not Martinique — at about the time of St John's Day — though it may well be some other saint — the ground becomes covered in a single day — more likely in one delirious night — becomes covered with pink flowers. You see that I am not only unsure about the place, the date, the time of day, I don't even know the name of the flowers. What am I saying, flowers? *One* flower, a single flower, a layer, a sheet of flowers, every inch of soil opening as a flower's mouth. . . .

'*I asked for that book you were wanting. You won't get it till tomorrow. Were you expecting it today?*'

Not at all, best of friends. But I'll let you think so. At this time I make only the most unavoidable appointments. Depending on whether my bed, which follows me like the shell of a snail, is placed at one or other window, faces south or east, I may or may not chance to spy certain stars familiar to a nephew of mine

acquainted with the celestial vault. When the stars he has
pointed out to me are not apparent from my vantage point I
invent them and stick them up where they are not. For one who
can barely stir, it's easy to confuse the stern order of the firmament by craning one's neck.

'We don't have any Great Bear here,' remarked one of my
neighbours.

She added, in the same pinched tone:

'We're very badly off for fish-shops in the *1st arrondissement.*'

Tiny pointed lights of distant stars, distracted and dispersed
by smothering clouds, spacious throbbing of the planet's sidereal
rotation. . . . I miss the great planet, Venus of the watery glare.
My nephew explains to me why she is so often unavailable to our
gaze. But I like to remember only those things about her that
please the ignorant. For instance, that she was wont to cheat, in
ancient times, those, with eyes raised to her, who did not recognize in the Venus of evening the glittering Lucifer of morning. . . .
And that we say: 'Venus is rising,' when she is near setting. . . .
With her third name, Vesper, I associate, I link that of my own
decline. Once she used to shine on my childhood, seeming to
rise from the woods of Moutiers, in the midst of a calm sunset.
My father would lift a finger, say, 'Vesper!', and recite some
verses. Then he would fix the feeble little telescope on its tripod,
and aim it at the stars. . . .

Soon it will be the season for me to sleep outside, that is to set
the head of my bed in the embrasure of the open window. From
the garden, if it were not closed at night, you could see my
bird's nest of hair through the balustrade. It's one of the attractions of this apartment to be able to sleep outdoors. Great drops
of rain hurry from the south, the wind flutters and scatters one's
papers, a nightbird cries. Everything enters and expands in the
open room, everything that the nights lavish on the lighted sky —
the waxing moon, the dawn, lightning and stars — save the
great planet which invisibly traverses the Paris sky, effaced by
the sun and setting almost at the same time as it does. To thrice-
named Vesper, acolyte of the sun, I dedicate my own vespers,
and read of her celestial adventures.

Every eight years Venus displays herself so dazzlingly that she may be seen shining in broad daylight and casts a shadow at night like the moon. The year 1849 is a memorable one. . . . *Dictionnaire Universel*, you go too far, I wish I were able to toy with time as you do. In 1849 you were a young encyclopaedia of twenty-seven years, and you watched as glorious Venus, visible from December to May, stayed while she waned from disc to crescent. Tell me then, hoary Dictionary, tell me how it was that, on the fourth of August 1857, Venus of the evening, Lucifer of the morning, 'attained its maximum size and brilliance, then shot rapidly (*sic*) to the summit of its orbit, then fell back into the rays of the great star and disappeared with it'.

So difficult is it to avoid lyricism when speaking of Venus. Abandoning all moderation, the Great Dictionary goes on to invite its readers on no account to miss the transits and the apogee, at intervals of one hundred and thirteen years and a half. . . . I should very much like to try, but I'm afraid that I shan't succeed.

Could I but return, tonight, to Martinique, could I but view some isle fixed in the thunder of God, on which, from one day to the next, a pink flower, a mushrooming of pink flowers, a catastrophe of pink flowers. . . . Ah! What wouldn't I give. . . .

No. What's the point of this wish, this journey, this extravagant flying carpet? One can't arbitrarily colour the whole or even part of the earth pink. It's true that the miracle lasts only twenty-four hours. But an entire day of rosy life is already too long. The flower that, one day, improbably occupies the entire available surface, which bursts forth without leaves, without buds, in short, without plans, future or morrow — what is it to be compared to if not a blight?

The wild buttercup, the so-called *bouton d'or*, lords it over our ill-tended fields, flows in rivers, stagnates in sheets. . . . The narcissi in April on the Swiss slopes — Oh, how their perfume disturbs sleep, what frenzy they excite! — are no more than an inverted starry sky, on a green firmament. . . . There remains the autumn crocus, the poisonous meadow saffron, which infests the fields with its distinctive mauve. . . . But no vegetable pullulation in our temperate hemisphere is vigorous enough to transform a landscape.

I've also been told of some exuberant blue flower in Australia. . . . Let Australia turn blue. It's bad enough to picture a pink universe. Pink meadow and pink mountain, while the shore is reflected pinkly in the lake. . . . The pink onslaught spares nothing in this . . . call it Martinique or what you will. Enough of this blandness. I could enjoy a pickled herring.

'You look very serious. Did anything bother you while I was out?'

'Not in the least. You can be sure I wouldn't deny myself the pleasure of telling you!'

There you have the manners and banter of the married state. The recluse has a keen desire to scandalize the physically active spouse, free to go out, to walk, to return bringing the news of the town, a flower he's just bought, the illustrated papers with their gasoline odour. . . . With so many heady smells from the outside world the recluse's heart, however conditioned to its lot, swells, covets, suppresses a sigh and preens itself:

'It's a pity you went out. Do you know who just left here? Guess. . . . I've had a delightful time.'

And he triumphs immodestly, eager to elevate his impotence to the rank of a privilege. . . .

No, nothing bothered me. What could happen to bother me, as we say, for we have long substituted the moderate for the tragic word. Bother serves for all purposes. The cash is low in the till? It's a bother. A friend, whom we loved, dies, his death is a bother to us. 'It's a bother that your leg plagues you so. . . .' Our language diminishes the phrase since . . . since the 'bother' of the war — more exactly since a day in December 1941 when rings of the bell and blows on the door informed us that a man, the master of this house, had to get up at six in the morning and leave his bed for the camp at Compiègne. Since then, what that was really a bother could happen to this man and to me? A ring at the bell still afflicts me, to a lesser degree, with nervous shock, a twitch of the mouth and the corner of the eye, of the shoulder raised to the ear. Will one never get over it? Yet many women who suffered the same experience at the same time change so as to obliterate these reflexes. . . . But I . . . I'm too old to get over it. . . .

Twenty years ago, certainly thirty, my resilient physical constitution would have already eliminated the various starts associated with the sound of the bell. Twenty years ago, certainly thirty, I should soon have ceased to interpret in sinister fashion the sound of strange voices, the noise of nailed boots and of the bell, the lighter sound of the steps of the man who goes downstairs, his small suitcase in his hand. . . . Once they had left, he and the twelve hundred of that batch, they immediately became like the nameless dead. Not a word, not a letter, no longer anything to tell us that they were still alive. . . .

The tenacity, the ingenuity of the women to some extent ameliorated their lot. Their basically feminine, conservative role overcame various obstacles. The women I saw at their work were of the very best type. Bloodhounds, virtuosos in rescue work, in the daily domestic miracle. Now and again one would have a good cry, then take up the trail again; for her prisoner's parcel she needed the half-slab of chocolate, sugar, the pair of socks, all the antidotes to thin soup, cold, dysentery, lice.

This is the first time that I've written pages which revive the time whose consequences developed into the perfect and classical nightmare of absence. . . .

'Madame, I'm going to do some errands. If anyone rings, Madame need not bother to open the door. So much the worse, they'll be back soon enough. If anyone kicks at the door it will be the Little Milkman.'

The Little Milkman is three years old. He is a child who has taken a dislike to milk. When he's made up his mind not to drink a drop he climbs up here, carrying his quarter-litre of milk by the handle, and we make an exchange. He has full liberty to kick away at the door. Next year he will be big enough to ring.

Nightmare of absence. . . . What did I have in mind to write on the subject of the nightmare of absence? Certainly nothing very urgent. I can always recapture what I want to say about it since it is, I believe, indelible.

The silence expands around me. When I am alone, my apartment relaxes. It stretches itself and cracks its old joints. In fine dry weather it contracts, retracts, becomes immaterial, the daylight shows under all its doors, between its every hinge and joint. It invites the wind from outside and entrusts my papers to it, they go skimming off to the other end of the room. I shan't unwind my cocoon of bedclothes for their sake. Greedy for air, I am a coward when it comes to cold.

On Saturdays and Sundays the garden is inexplicably deserted until midday. But a child's whistle suffices to breach this quasi-divine peace. At the time of the Occupation we did not find the explosions, gunfire and other rackets disturbing. But we did find execrable certain jolly sounds which marked the visits of the occupying forces to the rue de Chabanais close by. There were also — profound terror, agitation of our hearts — the cries and appeals of a night when the enemy took away the Jewish children of the district and their mothers, separated the Jewish husbands from their wives, and caged the men in one van, the women and children, sorted out, in two other vans. . . . Can I compare my own nightmare of absence to such separations as these? I do not dare, since my own came to an end at the moment when my absent one, set free, staggering on roads glazed with frost, arrived at the station at Compiègne and the train, reached the Métro and the Palais-Royal, and stripped himself to the skin on the second-floor landing so as to abandon, with his clothes, the grosser of the swarming souvenirs he had brought back from Compiègne. As well as being thin, I had never before seen in a man such non-human colouring, the greenish-white of cheeks and forehead, the orange of the edges of the eyelids, the grey of the lips. . . .

This traveller, exhausted by such a short journey, told me that, called to an office at the camp at the same time as two other detainees, one elderly, one very young, he heard, after the brief announcement of liberation, the soft sound of a fall : the two others released had fainted in perfect unison. They had to be dragged out to be given their liberty. The younger one hung on my husband's steps as far as the station and never stopped stammering, the whole way : 'You know, it isn't true. They say that, that we're free, but it's not true. Just you see, once we're at the station they'll pick us up again. . . .'

The silence over the garden recalls, even in winter, that summer morning in 1940 that blessed the avenues of elms, the flowering rose-trees, the lawns blue with their sprinkled dew, the quadrangle of the Palais-Royal soon to be emptied of its peaceful inhabitants by the heat, and above all by the imminence of something other than the dog-days. . . . In the morning shade a man was cleaning out his bird-cages, replenishing the water and seed and squeezing lettuce leaves and segments of fruit between the bars. When certain moments of a fine day become too beautiful, a human being stops his work or his play, reveres whatever is silent or that sings around him, purifies himself unconsciously by contact with that which heaven and earth and the city dispenses to him — unless, forewarned, he mourns them in advance. Perhaps that is how it was with the man busy with his cages, now savouring the solitude and peace of the deserted garden, now motionless, a bundle of millet in his idle hands.

It was then that a civilian entered the garden. He seemed surprised to find there only chattering sparrows, pigeons indulging in their amorous gurgling, a communal dog who was called — is still called — Kiki, and the man with the cages whom he accosted with a quite theatrical ease and courtesy.

'You seem to be very happily occupied, monsieur.'

'It's early, monsieur. The garden attendants are having breakfast. If they caught me washing out my cages outside the arcades, what wouldn't they do to me ! But just now I've peace and tranquillity.'

These last words seemed to make an impression on the sociable civilian.

'Peace and tranquillity. . . .' he repeated. 'Monsieur, don't you know that the German armies are in Paris?'

The man with the cages merely gave him a glance over his shoulder.

'I know what you're saying, monsieur. But I don't have to believe it. I shall wait till they reach here to tell me themselves.'

'Monsieur, I've just come from the place de l'Opéra, where the German troops, even as I speak to you. . . .'

'It's true that you're speaking to me, monsieur, but you must allow me to point out to you that I haven't asked you anything.'

The civilian moved away two paces and then, essaying a jest himself :

'No doubt, monsieur, you consider this event devoid of interest?'

'Monsieur, my chief concern, this day as on other days, is to look after my canaries. Remember, my canaries are Saxons, monsieur. . . . Saxons!'

The civilian stopped short, contemplating the beautiful enclosure of stone and verdure, listening to the silence broken less by distant clamour than by the song of the Saxon canaries.

'Are the inhabitants of the Palais-Royal,' he eventually said, 'as serene at this moment as yourself, monsieur?'

'All of them, monsieur,' replied the man with the cages. 'You'd think they were my brothers.'

'To judge from the appearance of the Palais-Royal, your brothers are . . . away?'

'Not at all, monsieur. It's just that they're having a lie-in today.'

The civilian frowned, searched for a biting retort which did not come to hand, and decided to move off. Left alone, the native of the Palais-Royal cast a glance at the carved windows, closed for the most part on apartments left empty by the exodus, and resumed his task. But noticing that the civilian departed slowly and circumspectly, he began to whistle a little tune — a gay little tune, naturally.

Thus it was that, in its urbane, sly, stubborn fashion, the Palais-Royal began its resistance and prepared to sustain it. What 'resistance', what war can I speak about other than those I have witnessed? I can hardly any longer leave this window corner in the heart, the very heart, of Paris. It was from there, after all, that I saw Paris sink into suffering, darken with grief and humiliation, but also, each day, increasingly resist. . . .

I enjoy declaring, repeating, that our Palais-Royal, even before the war, was a little province, adorned with a charm and homogeneity that the provinces themselves lack. From a handful of inhabitants the war created a coterie of friends.

Like the other districts of Paris, the Palais-Royal had its *maquis*. It held its hidden parachutists, its Englishmen sheltered in risk and silence, its protected Jews, its children rescued from a stern fate, its defaulters. . . . Did it not also have its black market? And why not? Isn't it a fact that the black marketeer, more discreet at giving than selling, provisioned for many a month a man to whom the German laws denied the right to live, and who never emerged from his suburban hide-out?

To mock, resist, evade, to slacken the torturing bonds, to thwart the spies. . . . The embroideress used to sleep on a narrow mattress in her shop so as to give those who had 'fallen from the sky' the use of a diminutive dwelling on the Left Bank. Quite near me the elegant shadow of a Russian neighbour, thrown on the sand of the garden, would replicate itself at night in singularly masculine outlines. . . . This was the time when, through the arched windows of the *entresol*, the hidden soldiers breathed the night air, the scent of lawns, and smoked seated between the horned shadows of two cats.

Who did not offer his cellar, his house, his bed? A woman who lived in one of the attics suggested to a Jew who was a dear friend of mine — his service record of '14-18 did not save him from the camp at Compiègne — 'If they come to take you away, run to my room, it's not bolted, and go on, hurry, don't be ashamed, snuggle up with me in my bed! You can be sure they won't think of looking for you there!'

This close tacit understanding lasted as long as was necessary. The occupying forces invaded our royal garden only in small numbers, except for rare idle groups to which a civilian would

stumblingly announce: 'Here is the cradle of the French Revolution. . . .', except in pairs — a green soldier, a grey mouse — who
conversed in gestures on the benches. Entering from the place
du Théâtre-Français they shuffled, dragging their heavy boots,
in front of the group of little shops and made their exit without
delay by the passage du Perron. 'Melancholisch. . . .' The unani-
mous rejection emanating from every stone, every passer-by,
every woman seated by her perambulator, pushed them out. An
intense, compact rejection, a rejection that was blind and deaf,
and dumb, a refusal to acknowledge the presence of the invader,
to read Paul Chack's poster and the other dishonourable
announcements, a mental regurgitation opposed to the propaganda waged by the newspapers and the wireless waves. . . . A
refusal to smile, to be seduced, to be terrorized. All that offered
itself insidiously, or made use of violence, Paris rejected equally.
Let us caress with a happy hand its still-open wounds, its upset
pillars, its subsided pavements: its wounds apart, it emerges from
all this intact.

Two

Fifteen hundred days. A thousand days and then more than five hundred on top of that. As many days and nights as it takes for a child to be born, grow, speak, become an intelligent and ravishing human being; days sufficient for mature blooming creatures to descend, in frightening numbers, into the grave. In fifteen hundred days of war and oppression, of organized destruction, may not a people abandon even hope itself? Our own astonished its tormentors and defied the devilish caprices they thought so humorous.

Humbly, I am one of those who did nothing but wait. Prolonged over four years, waiting found an opportunity to elevate itself a little above a mere passive exercise. If nothing could remove me from here, enable me to sleep elsewhere, banish me from here for twenty-four hours, it was because suffering and happiness were borne better here than anywhere else in the world. Sustained by a hunted companion, then deprived of that same companion when in prison, I took my place in the ranks of the host of women who waited. To wait in Paris was to drink from the spring itself, however bitter. Maybe a born provincial draws on a special faith in Paris, in the light of which it is easier to support the foreign menace, to receive and transmit the imponderables of a beleaguered capital, to adapt oneself to nightly bombardment, to assimilate a war-laden atmosphere, darkened and corrupted by war, to admire the child, to admire the man, the woman of Paris, mocking the crude propaganda posters. . . .

Courage and bravado kept the incorruptible townsfolk going; yet winter followed winter, the dismal summers roasted our arbours from July on. After which it happened that some light dawned in our hearts, some news was heralded in the air. Straining an ear did we not hear an even stifled rumbling propagated by the quaking earth? No. We were still in the troubled times of contradictory rumours, clandestine radios, whispered denials. But Paris was already swarming with hidden men, invisible allies, with enemies haunted by insomnia who no longer had time to sleep, while our stripped forests cast their shadow over their camouflaged trucks. . . .

Then voices, our own, were raised, shouting aloud the names they had only whispered the day before : Leclerc, Koenig. . . . In the final hours the great captains lost their names, were called gloriously '*They*'.

'*They* have reached Anthony ! . . . *They* have taken the heights at Châtillon. . . . No, *they* are still fighting. . . . *They* are repairing the road to let the tanks through. . . . *They* are nearly here. . . . *They* are here. . . .'

From every window meagre poorly-dyed flags, cut and sewn in advance in darkness and danger, wave like foliage along the rue Vivienne. . . . I can't see any farther on account of my leg. But when the night rose like dawn, a glow towards the east denoted the Hôtel de Ville, its lights, its crowd, its armies, the new colour of the soldiers. . . .

How strange it is, how poignant, a street that laughs and sings, that weeps too ! For so long Paris had neither laughed nor cried publicly, freely. . . .

Gunfire and carillons fly over the dark garden whose windows, that used to be shuttered each night, are all open together, pouring light into the quadrangle. Every window sings the *Marseillaise*, at every window, wide open, black arms stretch out against a gold background. . . .

Happy were those, that night, who did not restrain their frenzy. Happy were those who wept, laughed, cheered, flung up their arms, embraced strangers, took each other's arm and sang, marching forward at random, dancing, carrying lights, waving flags with the tricolour, with stars, with two straight and two diagonal lines. . . . Happy the unfettered, the children, the elderly, the curly blondes, hurled at last as if by order into full celebration, flinging themselves in waves on their rescuers ! Happy those who were beside themselves !

What quiet. . . . If it weren't for the night-bird of a printer who does his printing on the ground floor, the nights would be even quieter, quieter than the days. During the recent time of the nocturnal fusillades, the snipers on the roof wouldn't give up; they ran all round the courtyard and shots were interspersed with warning shouts: 'Don't shoot, it's me! — Shoot, I can see him, he's behind the chimney!' These scalp-hunters were not, alas, from Tarascon. One, who calmly blazed away in the rue Vivienne, and who was caught, had eleven hundred thousand francs on him. . . .

The shots, reverberating from wall to wall in the garden, exploded with dramatic effect. The great difficulty was in keeping back a bit from one's windows. Your inhabitant of the Palais-Royal spends part of his time leaning out of an open window, or at the threshold of his shop. My exhausted traveller, who used to sleep here and there like a chimney-swallow, extracted from me a solemn promise never to lean out to watch the nightly fusillades: 'Those people are dangerous,' he'd tell me. 'Their aim is so bad.'

He would make his way in the evening from attic to attic, in our district or in the Étoile.

For eighteen months he experienced in these places the discomfort of heat, the suffering of cold, quietly enjoying the contrast of the one and the other with his memories of the camp and resisting the friendly overtures made to him by the Palais-Royal.

'Do you know how to climb down a knotted rope?' Mme K . . . the bookseller asked him point-blank. 'If you're forewarned it's easy enough, you tie a knotted rope to your window, you come down in front of the door of my shop which I'll leave ajar, and I've put you out a cushion and a small lamp behind the big Gustave Dorés. . . . But don't let the cat get out.'

Another neighbour, the one who traces with a needle on canvas the blue ribbons and bouquets of roses that are unaffected by war, came with her mouse-like step, with even fewer words, to hand over a key to my nightly evictee.

'It's the one to the back of my shop,' she said. 'You'd better keep it on you all the time, monsieur.'

This was at about the time when Germans — the elegiac sort, amateurs of art and beauty — used to saunter in our garden. One of them, plump and tightly-belted, a Commandant Lust or Lutz, used to try to strike up acquaintance with the shopkeepers in their glass compartments, where trade dreams and dozes, hardly awake even at the hours when the Banque de France is buzzing with people. . . .

'I love,' declared the Commandant Lust or Lutz in good French, 'only three things in the world : birds of paradise, love-stories and *objets d'art.*'

As for love-stories, he bought *Spurs and Riding Crops, Flagellation, The Empress of Patent Leather*, and other reputable works.

With a mulishness that she tolerated with difficulty, he insisted on visiting my embroideress of roses and blue ribbons, who also sells antiques. She was barely able to hide her impatient claws behind the most impertinent politeness. As soon as she heard the sound of the footsteps of the lover of art and birds under the empty arcades she would redden with irritation. One day when I was chatting with her she detected the enemy's approach, leapt to her feet, and began working at her door-handle, one of those weighty objects bequeathed to us by successive revolutions that are part boomerang, part truncheon and part axe. I noticed that my embroideress unscrewed it, then returned it, undone, to its place.

The bulky Lust or Lutz darkened the minute shop with his square shape, gave a rigid salute, and inquired about each object. My neighbour, suddenly voluble, took the words from his mouth and the curios from his hands.

'The candlestick? I've just this moment sold it, monsieur, see, I'll remove the label. . . . The little chair? Oh monsieur, it's not genuine, just a bad copy, a connoisseur wouldn't be taken in. I'm sorry, monsieur, the opaline lamp is not for sale, it's been left here for repair. . . .'

She bewildered him like a tomtit attacking a pillaging jay. He gave up, made a heavy about-turn towards the door, and was obliged to open it himself. To which end he grasped the door-handle — one half of which remained in his grip, while the other flew off under the arcade.

The object, in the grasp of a German soldier, became him like a weapon, and standing stuck there in front of my embroideress he seemed to have come to knock her down.

'Oh,' he said in confusion, 'it's broken. . . . I'm sorry.' The tradeswoman was all smiles.

'Yes, monsieur, you've broken it. Don't apologize, monsieur, it's not worth bothering about. No, no, monsieur, we'll get it mended ourselves. . . . We'll have it repaired . . . together with everything else. *Au revoir*, monsieur.'

Right up to the end of the war the angry tomtit's attitude remained the same. And so did that of the other sedentary sparrows of the Palais-Royal. Marvellously imprudent, cheeky, irreverent, insistent on their miserable 'rights', they never forget wisdom and the instinct for duping their conquerors.

During the Occupation this royal palace was a stronghold of pinched adventurous old men, of disrespectful children, of shop-keepers without goods, of derisive adolescent girls, pure Parisian types whom the occupying forces never really understood.

During a sudden silence, thick as a mist, I've just heard fall on a nearby table the petals of a rose which also only waited to be alone before shedding its blossom.

Someone has rung. As Pauline says, they'll be back. Nevertheless, one of these days I'd like to change this electric jingling for a bell, a real one, shaped like a black convolvulus, who would shake her bronze leg within her skirt when her braided cord was pulled.

The air, disturbed by the ring of the bell, has settled down again while I made my way back, by my favourite paths, to the past. It's time — since I've just finished, first a short story, second, a little article, a discreet advertisement for a fountain-pen manufacturer — it's time to lose myself in the most selfish daydreams, a mental exercise which must do for me till the end of my days (my horoscope threatens me with longevity). This cursed fractured leg, the cause of my arthritis, has spoiled all my plans. Before then, I expected to grow old like the roan mare, elderly, tired and resolute, of which we used to say: 'Come next winter we'll pension her off, she's earned it.' But winter would come and the roan mare was still between the shafts. The winter came to an end; just from the sound of the mare trumpeting shrilly in the stable, we knew that the return of the fine weather would see her once more out on the roads with us, climbing the gradients with stepping gait, stopping to browse with her worn teeth on the new shoots. She did not like to rest.

I shouldn't have needed as much begging as she did to accept my retirement and my grazing, for I have loved — with a most ill-requited love — rest, and even sloth. But I should have stayed longer in harness, retained my taste for the road. An accident and its consequences have settled my fate. I don't complain that it offers me the pleasure of staying put, whereas that of the young and healthy is to go out. My fate demands only resignation — not that it's easy — and harmony between past and present. I have devoted a little time to assimilating the recent past, in the shape of 'war' and 'memories of Compiègne', which I wanted to absorb, then reject and bring up. But the released prisoner gave me no help and answered every question with a disarming patience: 'I've forgotten. . . . It wasn't so bad. . . .'

It may well be that he suffered in another way, once he was back with us. For, barred from ordinary existence, from his pleasures and recreations, banned from entertainments like a punished schoolboy, from restaurants as if he were a leper, from all work as if he were a mental defective, I wonder if he did not prefer the bloodlessness of Compiègne to the eighteen months that followed his 'liberation'. The existence of a Jew, during the Occupation, depended on a kind of insane bureaucracy, complicated by violet symbols imprinted with a rubber stamp, a sign in the shape of a star applied to the left flank, by brutalities worthy of Doctor Goudron and Professor Plume,* by a methodical and always heavily menacing interference. During the last eighteen

* Sadistic characters in a Grand Guignol drama. (Tr.)

months he whom I call my best friend would leave our roof every night to go and sleep, here, there, everywhere, his peaceful sleep of the condemned.

I marvel that I am capable of putting into writing the memories evoked by the ringing of a bell. It's just that one tires of everything, even of keeping silent. I care for nothing of what the war years bequeathed to me. Not even the trying passivity, devoted less to deceiving the occupying forces than to inspiring optimism among the occupied, since optimism is a matter of contagion. Sombre, dark, dissimulating, fuming, presenting a smiling mask, dry-eyed, I yearned, like everyone else, for the return of a time, before the war, that we used to find just bearable before having experienced what was to follow. Among other earthly blessings I longed for the freedom it would grant me to relish my sadness. 'Oh, when everything's all right again I'll let myself go, I'll cry in buckets. . . .' That's what one says at the time.

Three

It is usual to exclude the public from the garden when it snows. The snow is shut in. It becomes free to assume its snowy colours, to know that it is pink when the sun rises, blue along the zones of shadow, coppery beneath the setting sun.

In former years, up to 1943, I used to see, winter and summer, the woman who leaned up against the gate. I've already spoken of this woman, who had imparted to me that supreme confidence, the anguished appeal to another person:

'My name is Renée and I'm from the Cher.'

She owed her charm of manner to an exceptionally healthy appearance, for she was not beautiful. Her well-turned leg projected from her very short skirt. There was no obvious make-up to indicate her profession; the rare promenaders of the Palais-Royal, lovers of twilight and the parallel shadows of the colonnade, seemed to set little store on facial attractions.

During the year 1942, Renée, from the Cher, disappeared. In 1943 a woman propped against the gate made me a furtive gesture and I did not immediately recognize her.

'What, is it you, Madame Renée?'

'Yes,' she said. 'That is, it is and it isn't.'

She changed feet, rested crookedly on one leg: 'I've been in Munich. And at other places as well. *They* picked me up.'

She spoke in a low tone, defiantly turning from side to side her new face of an old woman.

'Yes, in Munich. In a restaurant at first, where *they* made me work as a waitress. But *they* made me carry boiling-hot dishes the whole time, from on the stove, pots with nothing to hold them by. Look at my fingers, they're like clams. I can hardly sew, me who used to sew so beautifully. . . . No, the backs of my hands, that's something else, that's because *they* put me on to winding wool, but there it was women who were in charge of us.

They said I didn't work fast enough and those marks you see there are from their nails. After that I was in prison. . . .'

She changed feet and spoke more quietly.

'It's unbelievable, what went on in prison. They left a young girl for eighteen months without the least ray of light. . . . I must be off, it smells too much of mignonette round here. . . . I'll tell you some other time about my foot, why I limp. . . .'

And limping, she made off rapidly and melted into the distance beneath the quiet geometry of the arcades, extended by the evening to infinity. I never again encountered the passer-by whose country of election was the Palais-Royal, and who clung with both hands to the gate to pour out to me whatever she felt brooked no delay:

'There's never a man comes into my room. For what I have to do with men Paris is big enough.'

She fell silent, then began again:

'I've got a bowl of goldfish in my room. To put under the bowl I've embroidered a round doily in a poppy design. It's really sweet.'

One day she said with pride:

'I've one brother, I brought him up on my own. With the money I made here. I was well rewarded, he married a school-teacher. Of course, she doesn't know I exist.'

On days of snow she would gaze at the garden as if this forbidden white rectangle were the symbol of an inaccessible freedom. I had promised her a book, which would have been fittingly placed in the ruined hands of this daughter of the night. My former books took shape mostly at night, between ten o'clock and three in the morning. This fruitful nocturnal labour — the indulgence of a writer relieved of telephone calls, friendly visits, or anyone's concern — continues with difficulty after the age of sixty. As age advances it's not a bad idea to grant insomnia its rights, but it's risky to hope for it to be productive. Nowadays, I can indulge in reading novels, tales of travel, and that kind of light agreeable study that consists of returning to books one has already read.

Only journalism, ogre that battens on regular rations at fixed hours, constrains to its nightly service the scrag-end of old scribblers. But journalism is a breathless occupation. Even when I was young I was never able to adapt my slow rhythm to the pace of the great dailies.

The obsession with overdue copy, with lines to be delivered between midnight and two in the morning, has for long held the same place in my dreams as the 'examination dream'. It sometimes comes back to me still, alternating with the ineluctable obligation to sing 'Les Huguenots' on the stage of the Opéra. With this difference, that the dream about the article is accompanied by neither pity nor reprieve, whereas at the Opéra I hope to conceal my deficiencies by an articulation drowned by the orchestra and plenty of expression. . . . From the height of the journalistic fantasy there spill several scalding words from the typographical glossary, such as : 'Two o'clock strikes at one fifty-five', and I wake up. . . .

In the middle of the Great War I made my début in dramatic criticism in the *Éclair*, engaged by its editor, René Wertheimer, a scholarly Jew, amicable and paternal. This winter's work seemed hard to me, because it was. The night, the war, the rain, the snow. I put asbestos insoles in my shoes, which thereby became too tight. The last underground train did not wait for me, and I was living in Auteuil. Sometimes Wertheimer, around half past one in the morning, on dress-rehearsal nights, would notice my fatigue and suggest with pretended indifference : 'If you'll give me another three-quarters of an hour, I'll take you on your way, I've got my old rattletrap.' I would wait.

At that time the *Éclair* was housed in one of the old buildings in the centre of Paris. These are so enormous that one can never explore them completely. I recall seeing Wertheimer descend from the attics, where he had discovered a charming pastel, a portrait of a young woman. The oval setting, the rose in the corsage and the blue ribbon in the hair dated from the eighteenth century. O unfathomable, inexhaustible Paris. . . .

The old-style editorial office naturally contained a long green table, a baccarat table of the gloomiest kind. A bomb from a zeppelin that destroyed a building nearby tumbled us all out of our chairs one night, but the house remained standing. Didn't you turn up there once, Francis Carco, so young in your uniform? I can see your tawny bird's-nester's eye. . . . If my stay at the *Éclair* has not left any more striking memories, it's because the war took first place. Its heavy-laden cloud darkens a long train of tortuous months, in which we trace our recollections more and more imperfectly. At every turning-point some error looms up or takes wing, an unintended falsehood, a hoary thirty-year-old truth which shirks the facts and respects appearances.

But as for that which dates from before '14-18 and will never return, what can bring that to mind if not my own especial and well-attuned reflections — and collections of such frivolous old magazines as *Gil Blas*? . . . Who will tell us whether the publication of Liane de Pougy's novel, *L'Insaisissable*, in 1898, caused a stir? The newspapers' society gossip carried news of the demi-monde to the distant provinces, detailed the decor of Mme Liane de Vries: brocaded ceiling, appliqué curtains, period chaises-longues and, on the drawing-room mantelpiece, a clockwork rabbit. Nineteen hundred. . . . the Exhibition? Yes, but above all the list of guests who attended the luncheons given by the Comte de Fels 'in his smart apartment in the avenue Mac-Mahon'. . . .

Suddenly it was no longer a matter of so many pleasures. One no longer read, heard, printed the names of Félisque Faure, of Nini Toutcourt; women no longer had the same names, the same breasts, the same buttocks, the demi-mondaines stopped getting up late, drinking frothy chocolate in bed while toying with a small dog, pouring half a litre of expensive perfume into their baths.

They say that everything comes round again. . . . Yes. Except what we consider as too agreeable, what we regret and blush at regretting. All at once the old frivolous journals contained nothing but men's names and politics. Public opinion became greatly concerned with the editors, proprietors, founders and financiers of newspapers. Some of these were friends of mine. If, for instance, I conjure up Gustave Téry's beaming countenance, founder of *L'Oeuvre*, a violent polemist masked by his plumpness,

I see beside him his editor-in-chief, Robert de Jouvenel, blond, brilliant, a hard worker who drove himself in nonchalant fashion and died from overwork. If I forage in my recollections, the burly bulbous-eyed Charles Humbert, bellicose editor of the *Journal* — 'Guns! Munitions!' — the great blustering Charles fades before the strange man who took his place, F-I. Mouton, plump and vague, muttering in the midst of his fair and greying fuzzy hair, who announced trenchant decisions in a hesitant tone. He had built himself a modest domicile somewhere in Paris and managed to get back to his château in the Île-de-France only at the weekends. I once had occasion to visit his Parisian pied-à-terre, furnished chiefly with a vast lacquered bed of the period of Louis XVI with canopy, hangings and festoons, and by a study of a nude young man in which the painter Sarreluys had carried a love of anatomical detail to a pitch I could not decently express.

The '14-18 war over, the daily papers tended to escape from those buildings where the sombre atmosphere of a provincial lawyer's lingered on under shell-moulded ceilings, in fine salons disfigured by accumulations of papers, divided into offices, cushioned with double doors in imitation leather. Bow windows and low tables, leather armchairs and rubber carpets improved the febrile, ink-spotted obscurity. The newspapers demanded refectories like convents and penitentiaries, bars like liners, office-boys uniformed like huntsmen or cinema ushers, tables topped with bevelled glass like clinics.

They also wanted, as editorial chiefs, 'striking personalities', as they were called. . . . The one the pleiad of great editors-in-chief took most account of, the crack-hand, groomed, polished, trained in fencing and the use of words, was known to me only through conjugal endosmosis.* And that is not the best way to find out. At the same time I took on the job of literary editor at the *Matin*, making my own weekly contribution to *Contes et Nouvelles*. René Maizeroy, from whom I took over, handed down to me, together with his duties, a great quantity of hair-grips, the tell-tale framework of his Mayol toupet, which he had strewn

---

* Colette is referring here to her second husband, Henri de Jouvenel, an editor-in-chief of the *Matin*. (Tr.)

all over his office and which gleamed like little fishes, caught in the strands of the carpet, stuck in the corners of drawers. . . .

It was already the period of decline for a certain type of journalism, which owed its brilliance to star reporters, valiant and stubborn war-horses. Hedeman interviewed abroad crowned heads and statesmen from the height of his old hat and ready-made overcoat. Naudeau was a young man, Helsey was being born. . . . The photographic reporters did without sleep or food; Roger Mathieu and I, storming the train bringing Queen Marie from Rumania, clung to the bars of the royal coach — God, how frightened I was of the track speeding beneath me! — Vallier, of the *Matin*, conducted his little personal inquiry into the Landru affair, leaped over the walls of the Gambais house, passed through keyholes. . . .

'Well, Vallier,' Jouvenel would say, 'what have you discovered?'

'Damn all, sir!'

He rummaged in his pockets; his hair, twisted into ram's horns, danced over his eyes. . . .

'I've discovered nothing, more or less . . . except. . . .'

He prolonged the pleasure, exploring his pockets. . . .

'Out with it, Vallier, out with it!' Jouvenel said.

'Except . . . a . . . tooth. . . .'

And he suddenly brandished, with voice and gesture, a human molar with long yellow roots. . . .

'. . . and a . . . Ah! Here it is! A finger-tip. . . .'

And Vallier would lay his macabre finds on the desk with a mocking air. . . .

'Disgusting! Dung-beetle! Get that out of my sight!'

The dung-beetle would feign bitterness.

'One can't bring back a thigh-bone just like that,' he would say in an injured tone.

He was secretly jealous of the concise phrases of Felix Fénéon, who could splash a news-item with humour in three lines. One day when the chandelier at the Opéra fell into the auditorium — without, incidentally, claiming more than one victim — Vallier announced the news the next day under this headline:

CRASH! THIRTY THOUSAND KILOS ON A CARETAKER'S HEAD!

He was censured in high places, for the headline, in large letters, caught the eye. Whereas, for instance, a lower-case typography concealed one of Felix Fénéon's masterpieces; the day when a mountebank, a sword-swallower, was killed with a revolver-shot by a husband he had been deceiving, Fénéon summarized the drama: 'The sword-swallower who couldn't digest bullets'.*

It happened on rare occasions that I would find myself with them at these morning conferences when I had nothing to do, in an ever-thickening cloud of smoke, among men whose characters I can still discern. Hedeman, a genius at reporting police news, who never had the time to buy a warm overcoat. He died somewhere in the Balkans, from an excess of cold. My good friend, Roger Mathieu, died early and untimely. He scorned his body and all prudence even going so far, for over twenty-four hours once, as to sausage himself in an enormous drainpipe of a rolled-up carpet, whence he photographed at arm's length the session of I don't know what secret conference. Fine fellows, ill-paid, decked with the frivolity of gay warriors. . . . Where is Tardieu, of the *Écho de Paris*, with the golden, rather too gilded, beard? He loved those pleasures that morality censures, but did not sacrifice his professional duties to them. His predilection drew him to young and handsome policemen.

'Why, Tardieu?'

'Because, at the same time as I satisfy my personal conception of eroticism, I have, when one of these caryatids yields to me, the anarchical satisfaction — granted, the illusion — of undermining one of the foundations of society. . . .'

Tardieu marked the end of that line of journalists who could be seen at work in cafés. The greatest of these was Mendès, who, amid the tumult of the *Napolitain*, simultaneously dealt with his dramatic criticism, short stories, verses, and his romantic serial, *La Maison de la Vieille*.

Didn't the management of the *Journal* take it into its head to

* A play on words. *Pruneau* can mean either a prune or a bullet. (Tr.)

reprimand Mendès for spinning out his lines, the lines being reckoned to his credit without deductions for the blank spaces? Catulle had a ready answer. The next day he afflicted one of his heroes with a mystical crisis, plonked him down under the balcony of his beloved, and had him murmur, from beginning to end . . . the litanies of the Virgin:

> Star of the morning,
> Refuge of fisher-folk,
> Ivory tower. . . .

This took up all or most of the five columns of the *feuilleton* and Fernand Xau, founder-editor of the *Journal*, said not another word.

At that period there was no dearth of men who, already elderly, did not hesitate to appear lighthearted. The spectacle of their roguishness was not always cheering. But they, at least, were cheered by it. They were addicts of the pun, and even of mystification. By stages — I should say, in shifts — they grew melancholy. The melancholy and the little light accent of Capus ended up in Feydeau's hypochondria and the black humour of Jules Dépaquit, inseparable from the steps of Montmartre. Everyone cannot be an Adrien Hébrard.

Two editors-in-chief, as well as a third, called permanent editor-in-chief, were none too many for the *Matin*, a powerful newspaper, and ostentatious in its buildings and its external activities such as subscriptions, official contributions and sporting endowments. Anxiety for its popularity did not prevent it, internally, from experiencing bursts of economy, as sudden as they were unnecessary. An invisible hand cut in two the watery green sheets of paper allotted for public use, everywhere suppressed balls of string, ink, and every kind of envelope in the offices. Before long there was an outcry, envelopes and bits of string and blotting-paper made a hesitant reappearance, preparing the ground for the next wave of restrictions. . . .

The fortnightly turnabout had, among other advantages, that

of keeping going a little cat-and-dog war between the two editors-in-chief : Henry de Jouvenel and Stéphane Lauzanne, who since. . . . Between Jean Sapène, 'commercial director of all the *Matin*'s services' and René Schoeller (who was later to control the great Hachette enterprise), who took to quarrelling nearly every day in the most violent manner, so that the smaller fry at the *Matin* used to bet on the outcome of all their set-tos.

Stéphane Lauzanne, learning from Charles Sauerwein — around 1909 — that I was to contribute a weekly story to the *Matin*, laid down his pen :

'If this person joins the *Journal*, I'm leaving straight away.'

'Straight away seems to me very emphatic,' retorted Charles Sauerwein. 'Do you know her?"

Stéphane Lauzanne blushed for the first time in his life.

'I ! I know that circus performer, that. . . .'

Charles Sauerwein, who was well-disposed towards me, held out his hand to Lauzanne :

'Goodbye, old friend, I say goodbye because Colette's first short story appears tomorrow. . . .'

Doubtless Stéphane Lauzanne took the necessary steps never to run into me. I happened to see him but once, walking quickly, 'behind his forehead' as Sauerwein would say. From the point of view of actual slander, we went little further than to call him *'Et alors'*, because of his ready resort to these two words, out of context and out of syntax, in many a paragraph and even at the beginning of his leading articles.

It may seem strange that I had no contact with the little despot who ruled over the *Matin*, I mean M. Maurice Bunau-Varilla. Endowed with great rapidity of movement, he would cross like magic the gap between his car and the entrance to the Maison Rouge, never halting on the broad pavement of the boulevard Poissonière. A sure instinct seems to counsel the great ones of this world to escape the crowd.

As tall as three apples, 'Monsieur Varilla' displayed the robustness of little men, lost neither a hair of his beard nor an inch of his little height, nor the bright red of his complexion. He closely resembled a theatrical columnist — Georges Boyer — similarly bearded, short, despotic, who used to make as much noise during the intervals at rehearsals as a cockchafer trapped behind a window-pane, and whom Louis Schneider called 'the drum-major of the lice'.

Of this man, whose striking name, Varilla, means in Spanish a little stick, I knew only that in aiming at majesty he achieved tyranny, and that he sponsored commercially certain pharmaceutical products. The entire staff of the *Matin* served as his field of experiment. From chief editors to typographers, he flooded the establishment with mycolisine, then synthol, to restrict myself to just two panaceas. Germaine Beaumont, the malicious seraph who insisted on brightening my hours of journalistic bureaucracy with her presence, came to see me one day all damp with one of the two products that a vigilant propaganda showered on the stairs. During an influenza season Henry de Jouvenel once arrived home in a frightfully distraught state, uttered with difficulty: 'Varilla . . . my colisine, half a litre . . .' and fainted. For three days he succumbed to bed and fever. Varilla kept in touch with him by direct wire, each time affirming that only the massive dose had dispelled a crisis which would have proved fatal. Later the proprietor of the *Matin* affirmed that synthol, administered in hair lotion, restored greying hair to its original colour. He practised what he preached, 'thanks to which,' said Jouvenel, who harboured a resentment towards the institutional pharmacopoeia, 'we knew that the original colour of Varilla's hair was a pleasant, lightly salmon-coloured, pink.'

I never recall this period of my life without a golden gleam, without an echo of gentle laughter to endear it to me: the laughter, the fine-spun hair of Germaine Beaumont. To this great writer, so much like a little blonde girl, I owe precious hours and unforgettable days on holiday in Brittany. I see her still, at the precipitous edge of a smuggler's track, leaning over with hand outstretched to pick up a large slate-coloured snake that hissed in her face like a goose. A charming St George, her honey-coloured hair along her cheeks, she found it altogether natural to overcome the dragon with the forked tongue.

Together, we spent more than one September in Britanny,

in the foam of the equinoctial tides, writing, gathering shrimps and mulberries, cutting out for ourselves decent nightgowns in flowered cretonne, bought at the haberdasher's in Saint-Coulomb. Germaine Beaumont sometimes wrote her letters in verse, 'because it's easier', as she used to say. We talked while sewing. I could have listened endlessly to the utterance that brought to a too-small mouth the flower of a clear and ornate spirit, discerningly whimsical, which judged forthrightly and gaily. She is the best memory of my pilgrimage through the great newspapers, during which so many things and persons changed, even the code of masculine beauty. . . . What waistcoats! I can still see Jacques Liouville's in hairy ponyskin, done up at the back. . . . 'Mama,' exclaimed a little girl, 'look at the gentleman whose stomach is showing!' And what cravats! Cravats of rice straw woven with little turquoise designs, shirtfronts in Chantilly on a changing taffeta background, sailor-knotted ties in antelope-skin, in hand-knitted chenille. . . . May I never see God if I lie. A great deal of Anglomania was necessary to cope with these outbursts of individuality.

Still quite distracted by the war, women forgot to point out to the men that a garment which attracts attention is a blameworthy garment. In the corridors of the great newspapers the female element abounded, seemingly devoted to watching and waiting. The freest, the most expert, kept a morning look-out between half past eleven and one o'clock. On the cane chair, on the moleskin of the imitation leather armchair, they awaited the passage of replete ministers, of slovenly parliamentarians, of aloof bankers. Some had their petitions at hand, others, idle and empty-handed, were none the less prepared. . . .

It's difficult now to make the political atmosphere of the *Matin*, at the zenith of its circulation and influence, appear credible. To do so, I should have had to have participated in it by inclination and to have been initially accepted. Was the aversion that politics always aroused in me visible in my face, since in my presence the spiteful warmth of these discussions subsided or even expired? I was shown an indulgence, a kindness, that could not have been bettered for the village idiot. This gave me even greater esteem for 'these gentlemen' and their offhand way of using the telephone : 'Drop in at the paper for a minute, old boy. . . .' 'I'm on my way,' would answer the interlocutor, who was none other than the President du Conseil, the Ministre des 'Affaires', the Excellence of a neighbouring country. . . . At the *Matin* the 'old pal', once more an ordinary mortal, would use the maximum of arrogance in meeting glances, in turning up his otter-skin collar, in not looking at anyone in the lift, but expected neither anonymity nor secrecy.

Personally, I recall with neither pleasure nor profit that busy, echoing, red-painted hall, outside the offices, where the feminine element was not lacking. Patiently, submissively, they camped on the vast lobby staircases, notable for their ostrich 'weepers', their scarves with which to catch hold of the passer-by, their insistent petitioners' perfumes. The experts backed their guess. They could distinguish between the fine fellow in a hurry, the common or garden Deputy, the stockbrokers; they recognized the 'big bugs', laden with riches and financial burdens, the Louis-Louis, the Daniel, both of them Dreyfuses. At the passage of these over-whelming financial powers they kept a straight face and did not stoop to little grimaces.

They could have taught me, those women, that the rich man is not a spendthrift who is always changing motor-cars, an indus-trialist with large profits. I wend my way — not too precipitately — towards the end of a life devoid of contact with the rich man, but that is not his fault nor mine, it's just that we had little to say to each other. The dealer in gold, wheat, ships, once encoun-tered, could do no better for me than to try to make me believe that he was like other men, the one by purchasing rare books, the other by writing articles and memoirs. A third loved the country, took my advice on planting persimmons, copied a recipe for an iced drink — half champagne, half claret, a large sprig of mint to refresh it all. They came down to my level. . . .

Yet none could alter the picture, worthy of Épinal, that I constructed of the rich man and his boundless riches. I ended by believing, having heard so often from their own lips the words, 'I can't,' 'It's not possible,' 'It's too dear. . . .' that they were exhibiting dissimulation or reticence when in fact they were at grips with such forces as time, distance, hostility, illness. . . .

I should be sorry if the distortion I inflicted on them were entirely obliterated. For if so, what would have become of the sybaritic resemblance of one of them to Balzac's Rigou? I mean by this the subtle and complex man whom masculine friendship and feminine flattery addressed by his first name, Daniel, the only one, in fact, in whom I recognized the attitudes of possession. He excelled in adding to his assets, multiplying possessions of every kind. An ardent appetite attracted Daniel towards succulence, not excluding that of women, from whom he bred a stock of fine children. His hand expertly weighed *objets d'art* and fruits, pictures — which he liked small and famous — stroked a horse's neck. 'Qua-li-ty . . .' he used to say rather greedily, 'qua-li-ty. . . .'

He put precept into practice. Beneath an unprotected shabby body he had fitted a new Rolls-Royce chassis so as to get about smoothly without attracting attention. In cold weather he would don an ample cloak which had nothing to do with fashion and sport, but whose layered vicuna melted in the hand. Wearing a Louis XI hat, pulled down well over the ears, he would leap into his camouflaged Rolls, passing by a miniature pavilion that he sometimes lent us. He would throw us a morose farewell gesture, portraying a Daniel irritated at having to leave his country house, his cup of coffee served in the garden, his antique spit from which chickens hung. . . .

One day when I saw him passing, alone and withdrawn in the corner of his motor-car, I ventured to opine that, instead of going forth to battle on the 'terra incognita' whose extent and mortal conflicts were beyond my imagining, Daniel would have preferred a hundred times to stay at home. . . . 'What do you know about it?' someone said. 'Is Daniel the man to reveal to you where he finds most relaxation?'

Balzac has invented everything, and the Balzacian character I mentioned certainly had fewer secrets than Daniel. Rigou, a peasant avid for secret delights, who insisted on fine hay for his fodder, a well-shaped rose beside his place at table, a warmed, freshly-sheeted bed and, between the sheets, a rosy servant-girl, that Rigou did not know how to smile. Only for Daniel, laden with those burdens of worry and expense under which men succumb, only for Daniel was there reserved the art of appearing lighthearted.

It was on the rough gravel of the 'terra incognita' that he would encounter his redoubtable namesake, he whom his friends of the *Matin* and elsewhere called Louis-Louis, a gentile Christian name as suitable to his bulk as a tulle cravat to a rhinoceros. A striking face, whose extreme and impressive strength of outline were unforgettable. He seemed slow, yet moved with ease and speed, concealed his gaze behind louvred eyelids, his caustic wit beneath an entirely affected hesitation.

I should still be wondering what he found in my company, had I not realized that he enjoyed being criticized. The lion's pleasure in enduring the fly, probably. . . . This likeable friend often came to the *Matin* at the end of the day. Seeing him appear, I knew that, floor by floor, he had visited Maurice Bunau-Varilla, then Henry de Jouvenel. . . . He brought to me, from the editorial offices, a strangely formal manner:

'My dear friend, may I hope to take you to dinner this evening at Maillabuau's?'

I would assure him that his hopes were fulfilled and inquire:

'Is Jouvenel dining with us?'

'No. Varilla's keeping him. Besides, I'm not so keen on dining with such a fine gentleman. He knows I'm taking you out. I've warned him.'

I would be ready in a moment and we'd leave. Sometimes I would linger to rebuke him for his overcoat of ancient date and its marks of antiquity. He'd finger the whitened lapel, the somewhat shiny sleeve, lower his heavy eyelids and answer wittily:

'Don't you see, dear friend, this is not just an overcoat, but a levite, *the* levite. . . .'*

'Well then, buy a new levite!'

He lifted his myopic gaze to tease me. . . .

'There aren't any new levites. A new levite wouldn't be a levite at all.'

* A play on words. *Lévite* = Levite or a frock-coat. (Tr.)

More than the dinners — excellent ones — at Maillabuau I enjoyed the lunches taken with Louis-Louis in his office in the rue de la Banque. Encouraged by the proximity of my home he would insist on my joining him at midday. A gloomy office, a small table, on which appeared the good cooking of a Parisian concierge : an omelette and a veal cutlet with a very agreeable Chablis.

'A workman's humble meal,' Louis-Louis would say.

What was I doing there, tête-à-tête with a V.I.P.? I can tell you, I was never bored there. On one occasion I was intrigued by a hundred little drawers, from top to bottom of one wall; they contained grains of wheat. I thought naïvely that day that I was about to 'understand' Louis-Louis, comparing him with a wholesaler dealer in cereals, perfectly capable as well of lifting and loading on his shoulder a hundredweight of grain. I was not deceived for long. He only wanted to question me, just enough to provoke my impatience, and to furnish me with anecdotes in which he played a part that I might criticize. Were they true or false? The point was that they introduced a pseudo-romanticism into our conversation and, for his part, a deceptive and racial humility that were contradicted by the sweeping gesture, the threatening fist, a sombre and superb tone of voice and a turn of phrase that brought a rapid rejoiner. One day, when — for the last time — Gustave Téry invited me to one of these masculine lunches, not unwelcome to either the men or myself, Louis-Louis, beset by political intrigues and a parliamentary candidate, arrived last in a suit that was visibly new and just as visibly dove-pink. I allowed myself, eyeing him up and down, a barely sincere whistle of admiration. . . .

'My dear friend,' replied Louis-Louis forthwith, 'it's suits like this that enable me to convince my voters in the Lozère that they've a unique opportunity to elect a man of fashion.'

He bought a magnificent town house on the Left Bank, one of those great houses where life retreats, provided with gardens of evergreen foliage, shaven lawns to which one no longer knows how to distribute their vital moisture, nimble ivy that refuses to die under any dispensation. Louis-Louis seemed to me, at first, a little embarrassed at such a fine purchase. One of the first visits I paid there took place after dinner. Staircases, flights of steps, terraces, unfinished salons; staircases . . . the plaster was still wet.

'I am going to show you what I like best in this house,' said Louis-Louis.

He threw open a door, brusquely lit up a white room. He sat down on a narrow bed, grasped a plait of hair, which he employed to lift and brandish before us the face of a very young girl, fresh and blooming from sleep.

'My daughter,' he said.

'But Louis,' I protested, 'you'll frighten her!'

'Frighten her? Do you think I have nervous children? They're used to it.'

And, in fact, the long calm eyelids barely lifted over two blue eyes, and the young girl returned to the depths of her dreams. Her father behaved likewise to a brown-haired little lad who complained a little, laughed a lot, asked the time and did not hear the answer.

The heavy confident paw that grasped and flung back these infant heads balanced its weight of paternal pride and despotism. This is how the wild animal behaves, which plays and roughly handles its offspring at will. This image is the best I retain of Louis-Louis, the most familial and the least human.

At the *Matin* a critical and unfailing eye used to observe people and things. Charles Sauerwein, news-editor, was a shrewd man who died too early, and my good friend and adviser. He showed himself severe towards the 'office mice', furtive women whom he would compare to the crêpe-rigged privateers of cemeteries. Consequential, rather cocky, a little the distinguished prefect of police, he preserved a lighthearted misanthropy which served to protect him from no small danger: those male dinner-parties, the bane of wives, political and private blow-outs, a guzzling freemasonry. . . . The Commission's luncheon, the weekly dinner of the Group, the monthly banquet of the Left of the Vivarais. . . . The choicest vintages used to wash down the murky sauces in the gloomy temples of La Villette or Les Halles; the tall silhouette of Maginot, a bottle of Richebourg under either arm, would climb a crooked little staircase. . . .

I only glimpsed these feasts, no one wanted my presence there. Grave quadragenarians, brisk sexagenarians, how many so-called 'public men' made a dangerous habit of that most French of qualities, *gourmandise*, of their knowledge of local wines, of produce of the soil, of time-honoured recipes? Under low ceilings an inn-keeper would act as accomplice, piously closing the door on their 'private room' as if to conceal them. In fact, they concealed themselves. Plenty, when it comes late in a man's life, remains somewhat furtive. It rejoices but does not honour.

It is a dangerous period that the public man embarks on when he emerges from his initial obscurity. He finds therein the illusion of a general acquiescence. He tends to satisfy, in artless fashion, those schoolboy appetites that linger with him after the age of forty. Should he totter, his country is indignant: 'He had it coming to him, that one!' He had to have everything, like so many of those who were born poor. He had to have that ribbon, that estate, those white cattle on those green fields: 'Just this million, the last . . . just this sinecure . . . this ravishing woman. I've only to stretch out my hand. . . .'

He had not realized that it would be so hard to refuse what is available to the mature man who has inherited from his youth only the sour smell of poverty. He had not foreseen that a loaded table, cigars, the barrel of expensive wine, the dining-car, the raised hats, the petitioners, might be the prime movers of a voluptuous dishonour.

'What d'you think, I'm writing a continuous novel,' Kessel confided between two aeroplane flights.

'Bravo!'

'That is, I mean it to be continuous. It isn't yet. And then, I compress my manuscript more than usual. I disembowel myself, I smother myself . . . I produce surprises for myself. You know what I mean, I make a fool of myself,' he said with his gentle smile.

I cheat to the same end but in a different way, by numbering my pages *bis, ter, quater*. . . . An expert and exhausted worker, our lamented Henri Duvernois, used to calculate the length of his manuscripts with unfailing precision.

'Nothing easier, so many times so much makes so much. My good woman,' he'd say to me, 'what are you reckoning up there, muttering to yourself and pencilling in a corner of the page? *I* can work that out for you, by length, by weight, in *europe*, in *didot*, in *grattenèze*. . . .'

Credulous as usual, I believed that the word *grattenèze*, invented by him, belonged to the technical vocabulary of typography. When Duvernois undeceived me, I appropriated the word for the exclusive use of the Cat, who according as to whether she was, or was not, disposed to scratch her divine '*nèze*' against the box hedges clipped *en brosse* thereby qualified as *grattenèze* or *antigrattenèze*. Foolish pleasures are the most enduring; now and then the primeval *grattenèze* reappeared, with his vaguely gothic architecture, spiked with cat's claws.

Our Duvernois, to my astonishment, used to work at a lacquer table as large as a skating-rink, and just as slippery, in the black water of which I thought to see the reflections of pine-trees, birches, a flight of cranes, a frozen shoal of fish.

'How can you work on a lake?' I would ask.

He pursed his reticent prelate's mouth.

'Not too badly at all, my good woman, not too badly. I'm so tired of reality. . . . I find everything that's unreal pleasant, even useful. I've seen Ophelia floating by, as recently as yesterday.'

But from his habit of rubbing the underside of his forearms I understood that the beautiful table made his elbows cold. It's to Henri Duvernois that I owe the restful habit of using blue-coloured paper.

'Give up white paper, my good woman, it rasps the retina. Choose either mauve, pink or sea-green. Leave that rather melancholy yellow to me, blue suits you so well. Ask at Gaubert's, in the rue du Jour, for the tinted imitation Japanese paper they cut for lawyers.'

Although I was not enrolled at the Bar, the blue legal paper stayed with me for a long time, then I lost it.

'I haven't any more,' Gaubert told me. 'I could have it made for you if you were to take a *cuve* — go on, have a *cuve*!' But I resigned myself to another blue when Gaubert told me that a *cuve* meant twenty-five or thirty thousand kilos. . . .

Writers are not, for the most part, very good at securing professional comfort. Carco plants his lamp at his right side, inconveniently casting the shadow of his right arm on the paper, loses patience and blasphemes. Kessel aspires to work in the Midi, in the open air, dazed by the light, stung by the flies, driven away by the mistral, and confronted in his labours by a relentless 'view' of sea, sky and sunset. . . . And in the distance, for a bonus, the Alps. It's pretty presumptuous to measure oneself against a panorama. Quite naked, pierced with stings, Kessel comes out of it with honour.

I was often curious enough to inquire of them in what favoured spot, in what set-up, so-and-so worked, the young and the worn-out, the well-off and the poor. But these are topics which invade an author's privacy. It's bad enough as it is to have to explain the connections between our hygiene and our work. 'Oh, no! Never after meals. . . . No, no, no spirits, I have to be careful of congestion. Mind you, at a certain age. . . .' Would we make more fuss over a disease of the bladder?

I have refrained till now from vilifying congestion. A difficult page, the end of a novel, are often the better for a hotly-spiced meal, an exceptionally well-filled glass. Congestion then becomes synonymous with inspiration. A quickened pulse, a stormy and transient contentment, are profitable to us. Provided we do not delay, provided we hurry from table-cloth to work-bench without sparing a moment for digestion, a fig for prudence. What, we shan't fall nose to page, struck down by the search for an adjective and by plethora! Which of us, nowadays, guzzles and stuffs himself even half-full?

We are what we are: irascible, finical, nice enough at heart so long as we're left undisturbed in the heated disorder appropriate to inspiration, the errant slipper, the old dress, the late hour or even the dawn; we even sacrifice our private discipline to an older and more personal order of things: 'When will Monsieur — or Madame — remove his papers from *my* table so that I can lay *my* cloth?' For we are timid with our servants; it is so rare for us not to lose all their respect from living with them.

From time to time a novelist evades his fate, finds himself exceptionally well-provided with cash. He thinks to find reward and surcease in the temple he raises to himself: reinforced concrete, a balconied Arnaga, an improved manor house. . . . Some calculated collector's pleasure may also be involved. But the newly-rich either ruins himself or becomes discouraged. He will do wisely to fall back on the daily travail of composition, even if it entails amusing himself with modest little distractions.

Someone has rung. I am not so helpless that I cannot, pushing back the bed-table that straddles my divan, go and open the door. But I don't want any visitors. I'm ill today. To be ill is no excuse, no real impediment. Am I to die without having reached the limits of my various capacities? What was the length of my jump, my supreme endurance in swimming? What were my capacities in drinking, eating, making love? I don't know. I wasn't curious about it. I shouldn't have been picked up, exhausted and victorious, on any race-track. Joseph Caillaux used to say that the habit of sniffing the cup and looking at it twice before draining it came to us — it was he who said 'us' — from a sound heritage, and that it helped to make us live longer. He said further that persons 'like ourselves', who manage their affairs without calculation, have a marked distaste for the formula: 'Will you bet that . . . ?', and that they only make wagers in secret, in silence, and sullenly.

But, paradoxically, my 'cousin' — a cousin of the Casimir Périers, themselves cousins of the Jouvenels — cherished and quoted a phrase of Gordon Bennett's which breathed the quintessential spirit of all rivalry: 'The best way to triumph over one's adversary is to survive him.'

To live, to survive. . . . After so many years of war these words possess immense importance. The will to survive is so alive in us women, and the lust for physical victory is so female! When they notice it, our men can't get over seeing us so ferocious. Hardly had he left the camp, restored in health, though still constrained to the nightly hide-out, than my companion was already reincorporating the sentiments we call 'human' but which — and with good reason! — I've never heard called 'feminine'. I belong to that sex which is supposed to be capable of cutting an enemy into pieces, so long as a tiny mouse, passing nearby, does not demoralize its fury. (But what of those, on the contrary, like me, who are not afraid of mice?) It is very probable that ferocity is our accustomed climate. Nevertheless, I am shocked by masculine moderation. Men whom the war has gashed and injured, on whom it has exercised the whims of its arbitrary cruelty, it is we, nevertheless, who astound you, we with our vengeful fires, our murderous laughter, our insatiable malice, our antics — like negresses — around the stake.

One day in 1942 a German came to see me. This was during the period when I was living alone, and in such apprehension! The Berlin journalist had called on the aid and assistance of a French 'colleague' whom I do not name as he is in prison. When I think of this passing Berliner, I think each time of the executioner Laffont, for both of them boasted a passionate love of flowers. My colleague who introduced him left me in no ignorance that the German journalist was 'ruining himself' (*sic*) in fresh flowers. A certain florist of the Victor Hugo *quartier* made no bones of the fact that, every day, fifty thousand francs' worth of orchids went to adorn Laffont's 'salons'. As if to prove that the love of flowers can be tainted by a monster, Gilles de Rais used to kiss and comfort, before the final end, the child whose throat he had just cut, half through, half only, just half to begin with. . . .

As for the German horticulturist, it may be that he transformed into a guilty spectacle the contemplation of a petal, of a fresh floral throat, of a calyx wherein he sought the semblance of a lip, a sex, a wound. . . . I sometimes think of that German, very dark, dressed in black. I have forgotten his face. His overall appearance, in clothes and features, was dark and gloomy. I should not have liked this sombre individual to contemplate a flower in my presence. When it issues from certain beings on whom dishonour lies ill-defined but flagrant, we do not care for admiration to be bestowed on delicate objects and very beautiful children.

It was a postcard — if I may so put it — which rang just now. My mistrust drove me to investigate and to pick it up from under the door of the ante-room. It is all decorated with multicoloured *centavos*, with *correo de sereo* and comes from Guatemala. A postcard rarely fails to reach its goal. This one had been searching it out for two months. For two months its trajectory slowly brought nearer to me its cheerful Guatemalan news, to inform me that 'my brother-in-law's family is adorable', that 'the volcano of Agua is planted like a magnificent image against the pure blue of the sky', that 'the climate is delightful'. I arrive at the essential phrase, which unpremeditatedly holds ajar the double doors of a sentence : 'A hummingbird has come into my room while I'm writing to you. How he glittered, and how I wished I could have shown him to you !' My correspondent need hardly regret anything. Ruby-headed, marvellously green, having quenched its thirst at a flower, not knowing whether it has drunk it dry, the hummingbird has passed my way.

It came from that South America whence I had already garnered that which is dismayed by neither time nor distance, notably the hummingbird too small to be afraid of man, the mother elephant interposing her flank between the javelins and her little one until she fell dying; an inexplicably *sweet* spring of water and a recipe with whose aid Mme Ida Pfeiffer braved every malignant fever, 'even those of Sumatra', drank the waters where poisonous creeper and gigantic snake macerated together, slept under the tropical skies and healed her wounds. It is comforting today to know that the gentle and intrepid traveller completed a world tour on two occasions, alone, took with her neither quinine nor dressings ('my baggage weighs around ten pounds in all'), and railed against the savages only for the sins they committed against decency of vestment.

I give here the recipe for the sizzling fire-water. But I fear that our young girls, with their precociously galvanized palates, may find it a little tame. . . .

'Take half a glass of good strong *eau-de-vie* (brandy), with a small teaspoonful of finely powdered red Cayenne pepper, and six small spoonfuls of white cane sugar. Mix all together until the sugar is properly dissolved and leave to stand for four or five hours. Then one begins to take two teaspoonfuls of this medicine every hour from the time the fever sets in until one has drunk the lot. Before taking the medicine it is necessary to shake it up each time.'

What do *I* think of it? I'm waiting to have the *fevers*. Up to now I have only had the *fever*. I'm also waiting till I possess all at one time cane sugar, good brandy, and Cayenne pepper which shall have lost none of its potency. I accord this last more credit than the spirit. The spirit is an article of faith. But the pepper, the genuine pepper, the lively fire, salutary for the kidneys, trust yourself to it without fear. One glacial spring evening, in Tunis, as I was wandering about with a fever brought on by hail, cold, and the murky water of the port, I encountered a thin man who addressed me by name despite the darkness; I recognized Federico Madrazo, known as Coco, a good painter and better musician. I did not conceal from him my miserable state of health.

'One thing or the other,' he said. 'Either you've caught syphilis by drinking from a dirty glass . . . it's only an hypothesis, dear friend . . . or else what you need is not to go back to your hotel — watch out for the dangerous pale loin of veal *jardinière* — but to dine with me on couscous at some Armenians I know, by virtue of which you will be cured by tomorrow morning.'

I fell in with the latter course and, in an inn as green as a green pimento, green as a glazed jug, two bare brown arms served us with a couscous which would have satisfied eight persons — at least, so I thought before I saw melt away, between the two of us, the granular Fousi-yama, rich in morsels of meat, Malaga grapes, sweet onions, young artichokes. . . . Neither wine nor water on the green table; on our plates the most fiery of peppers, the *sauce forte* which has never inflamed occidental palates. . . . I panted. The fine perspiration released by the honest peppers beaded my face and I begged for a swallow, just one, of cold water. . . . 'Don't make an exhibition of yourself,' said Madrazo severely. 'One doesn't drink when eating couscous.'

He shaped me pellets of breadcrumbs, as one might fatten a fowl, and the fire of the couscous abated. That of the fever also. Madrazo saw me back to my hotel, not before having paid a bill of some eight to ten francs for the two of us. O times, O places. . . . The least colour made me feel I was in the Orient. I bought crudely synthetic perfumes, but the merchant, in carpet-slippers, fez and gandoura, wore on his ear a little bunch of jonquils and jasmine, moist with a spray of water, and he swore to me that the perfume was distilled only from flowers, and I believed him. What don't I owe to my credulity? As they say in my natal province : 'If I believe, the evil is not great, afterwards I can always stop believing.' But first impressions are always pleasing. I've believed in travel for a thousand kilometres of railway line, and I believe in solitude when I shut the door of my room behind me.

Four

What would a stranger who arrived unexpectedly think of me? But I don't entertain without notice, and not strangers. Today my workcouch is strewn with photographs . . . which would spoil my appetite if I were to eat in front of them.

Andre Lecerf, the graphologist, is at present studying the handwriting of the sexually abnormal: passive homosexuals, morbid onanists (it was Paul Massin who used to say that 'distinguished onanist' might pass for as flattering as 'numismatist attached to the Collège de France') and other unassuming monsters, lovers of the shadow, inclined towards assassination or suicide. One part of this mass of material comes from Germany; if it is not the most instructive, we may take it to be the most unhappy, as it deserves. I can only interpret it graphologically, the text is in a foreign language. But nothing escapes its essence, and this is very true of writing. The scandalous curve of a letter, the arabesque as revelatory as a cry, an insane affectation in crossing the *t*, a spiral, a curve — what imprudence. . . . Which corresponds to the obsession, the delight, of wearing pink suspenders beneath a navvy's corduroy trousers? Which reveals a shameful mortification, a geometry of deliberately incised wounds, kept open daily? An abyss of sadness opens up on contemplating the photographs of half-naked men burdened — with an eye to what joys? — with empty female brassières. Empty. If it were a matter of simulating, by padding, the advantages of the opposite sex, if it were a matter of the strange but admissible jealousy inspired in a man by the decked torso of a woman, the

> *Seins elastiques et légers,*
> *Seins de la belle sans rivale,*

the shadow would be less heavy. But no, they are empty, put to another purpose, these twin pockets of satin or tulle, flattened like the flowers in a herbal, flaccid, inexplicable. . . .

In contemplating these little unnatural crimes, I deduce only sadness. How sad it all is, those lacy garments on hairy black thighs, those hairy thickets round a shapeless sex, those pink rococo garters round a pebbly kneecap. . . . And those wretched faces of imitation men, those female figures fit to be thrown away, those abortive essays at forehead, chin and skull. . . .

Their love-life is even sadder. For they have their romance, their aspirations, their disaster. Some have at their disposal, to introduce sensuality or sentiment into their lives, a bare hour of night, a fringe of shadow, a narrow and restricted space. Their field of operations may not transgress that limit, that corner, that alcove, beyond which there is an accusing streetlamp, a lighted road. . . . One more step ruins their illusion, their hope — I won't add their security, for they have found no place for security in their existence.

How many hesitations does their appearance represent? Here is a . . . a . . . yes, a woman. . . . No, for her straw-hat is a man's straw-hat. But a ribbon tied prettily round the crown brings realization. That hair is too long for a woman with short hair, even more so for a man. The ready-made jacket is ordinary, badly cut, the waistcoat not up to much. . . . But beneath the waistcoat a starched shirtfront forms one piece with a collar and tie, the whole device done up at the back with a stud. No linen beneath this, but underclothes in cotton tulle with baby-ribbons in the trimmings; but there's a short pair of male underpants; there are women's suspenders, long enough to hold up a man's stockings; in short, a pell-mell disorder of vestments which assumes a tragic significance, a confusion, a kind of mix-up of the two sexes. . . . My name is Arthur — no, I'm called Emily — Sir, I forbid you to follow me — Madame, may I see you on your way? The series of photographic contradictions concludes with a pitiful nudity, a vain portrayal of hermaphroditism, in its infantile state. . . . Where are you, graceful son-cum-daughter of Aphrodite and Hermes who sleeps at the Louvre, creature perfect in your totality, promised to us in dream? You exist nowhere in reality. Marcel Proust, and Hélène Picard who did not read Marcel Proust, both knew that there is little difference to be seen, initially, between a pretty woman and a beautiful adolescent boy in bed :

> *Les cheveux sur les cils, comme une femme au lit,*
> *Et, le gars, il abuse un peu trop de son style.* . . .

Barbette, adorned with as many feathers and attractions as Mistinguett herself, was the supreme example of a playful ambiguity, an exquisite source of demoralization among the masses. None of us was entirely taken in by her. We acknowledged loudly enough the tribute we paid to her deception, and the more innocent among us would say, composedly, that what they applauded, petticoated or otherwise, was the acrobat, the bird, the way she soared. But they lied. I once saw two photographs at one of Barbette's devotees — devotion was permitted by fashion — one radiant in a geyser of plumes, artfully, half-naked — O, that beautiful knee, nonetheless virile! — the other portraying the gymnast reduced to essentials, bare-headed, a little bald, a pair of underpants screening the hidden sex — a severe working get-up, the minimum of extent and weight, the right framework to support the exuberant superstructure. And yet I found the lithe virile appearance, the mysterious statue of Barbette-the-man, more disturbing, more deceptive, than the despairing apotheosis of Barbette-the-woman.

The science of graphology is a bitter one. Lecerf derives his revelations from the depths of horror, by interpreting a little zigzag design, an abortive downstroke, a musketeer's hat capping the capital F's. . . . That stroke like a knot in a whip speaks the same language, stoops to the same avowals, as the hidden pink suspender, as Masoch's torture cord; or as the cascade of ribbons, fond adornment of the 'proud externals', so little external, alas, as to be hardly worth emphasizing. . . .

By an association of ideas it comes back to me that in the Bois de Boulogne, a good twenty-five years ago, spring's exuberance stimulated an eccentric, harmless save in one respect. He used to take in even the keepers in that, according to them, he was dressed 'in the latest style', in a bordered black jacket, black-and-white hound's-tooth trousers and a bowler hat — not to mention the fancy waistcoat in garnet-red velvet, the shirtfront and necktie, and the yellow gloves; 'in fact,' as a burly keeper informed me, 'a man of the best circles, up and about at ten-thirty in the morning. . . . He played only inoffensive little tricks and was quick to clear off, the bugger. . . . Once he left a poor lady and her daughter in my lap. . . . The poor lady wanted to lodge a complaint, if you please. . . . It was just as well her little daughter had enough sense for two. . . . "But Mama," she said, "I tell you I didn't see anything!" I got rid of this fine lady by telling her that it was a matter for the Commissariat de Boulogne, that settled her. All the same, as for my man, we ended up on bad terms. I must explain to you that my wife and I had agreed on a little Hou-Hou when I was outside and I wanted her. What d'you think I discovered, ma'am? My man of the world had appropriated my signal and came to shout Hou-Hou outside my lodge! My wife would go outside all unsuspecting or lean out of the window, and this gentleman would take advantage of it to give her an eyeful! Ah, that was the end of things between us!'

'Did you have him arrested?'

'No. But I lost my temper. I told him: "Don't let me catch you around here any more. Go and do that in the Bois de Vincennes!" '

A bibliophile friend called today. He took out of his pocket a small old volume, the binding of which retained a pleasant faded pink colour. He held it a little beyond my reach, half opened it so that I might hear the sound as of new banknotes made by its laid pages, untainted by any chemical washing; he showed me — from a distance — an engraved frontispiece, the gilt of the coat-of-arms still bright on the plates, then put it all back in his pocket. Before leaving he whispered the price of his acquisition — as much, or thereabouts, as a property in Touraine might have cost in the old days. I feel that I did not show myself sufficiently overcome by admiration. The next time. . . .

The next time I'll let him down again. There's no deceiving oneself; I don't see anything in bibliophilia beyond the pleasing feel, the fine page-setting, the impressive style of printing, the odour evocative of cellar or ancient herbal. The next time, my bibliophile friend will once more be unable to resist showing me his find. For him, after all, I am part of his family, though unworthy and only distantly related : I am a writer. He grants me a much-curtailed right of inspection. For my part, if I welcome him somewhat coldly, I acknowledge that he represents the aristocracy of an intrinsically elevated taste. It was therefore wrong of me to mortify him by not being sufficiently welcoming, I who favour the curio devoid of genealogy, if not of mystery, and even old photographs provided they don't reproduce, multiplied by an inexplicable fashion, the features of Emile Ollivier. . . .*

'Madame, it's those two. Madame knows them, those two who come a long way. . . .'

'But I didn't hear anyone ring.'

'Madame knows well enough that those two don't ring. They knock, or they scratch. . . .'

Let them enter, those two. They bring me their strange odour, their stories as good as hunting anecdotes. I've known them from the beginnings of the black market but they won't give their names. Before the Liberation they were wont to tell me calmly : 'What d'you think, three times on the road the aeroplanes came down over us. Three times we threw ourselves in the ditch with our bellies in the water. . . .'

A sedentary, my ears love to listen to these adventurers, the man and the woman. I once asked them : 'Weren't you frightened?' The man said nothing. The woman fixed her intrepid gaze on me and answered : 'Yes.' Her cupidity made a heroine out of her; why not? The black market is an activity that bristles with dangers. While I was thinking : 'Twenty francs the egg. . . .

* A politician, who became *Président du Conseil*. (Tr.)

Two hundred francs the rabbit . . . the bitch ! . . .' the bitch was including in their cost the water in the ditch, so many kilometres, the burst tyre, the peril that throbbed in the air, then fell from the skies, and answered me *in petto* : 'Twenty francs an egg, that's right. And it'll go higher still, you wait till next time. . . .' I've no grudge against this deadbeat man, this fierce woman. They extort from me, as well as money, a complacent smile. I should like to know more about this black-market pioneer. It's difficult. She confronts me with an incredible unpretentiousness. The time of her departures for remote parts, for dangers, for haggling ?

'Oh ! Any old time. Three o'clock in the morning. . . .'

'By lorry ?'

'Not always, there's times when the lorry's no good.'

'What then ? . . .'

'The bike. But sometimes the bikes are spotted, and then again, how much can you carry on a bike ? Next to nothing. . . . It's a nuisance, you waste time, the stuff goes bad. . . .'

What gravity, what formality, to judge from these words. . . . The couple, still young, possess the avidity, the dash, the poetry, of pirates. They name neither villages nor accomplices, but they retain an enjoyment for certain aspects of the life they lead. . . .

'We went two days and two nights without food once. . . .' says the man.

'Yes,' says the woman, 'but when we got there. . . .'

I essay a 'Where ?' which subsides without echo and my interlocutor skilfully avoids it :

'When we got there, what did they dish us out for a snack ! They'd really put on a spread for us. . . . Bread still warm, salt pork, a pot of fresh cream, butter that was still bubbling, coffee of course : and shortbread to soak in it. . . .'

'You're forgetting the chicken broth ! . . .'

'So what, and the two hours we slept in a real feather-bed. . . . I don't forget everything. . . .'

The way they exchange a glance, a greedy smile, these two associates manage to push their complicity as far as that of lovers.

What was I saying just now in connection with Emile Ollivier when 'those two' arrived, so impressive in virtue of their bulk, the shadows they cast, their significant smell of crates, of chicken-straw, of mock-camembert? I was complaining about the strange posthumous and photographic popularity of Emile Ollivier, three of whose portraits by Disderi my mother kept for herself. . . . 'Did you know him, Mama?' — 'I? Not at all.' 'Why is he here, then?' — 'I don't know at all.' — 'Then let's throw these post-cards away.' — 'No, no, they're not in your way, are they? Leave them alone. . . .'

No doubt, if I had a good look in my box of photographs, I should find an Emile Ollivier. 'And that one there, who's that?' my daughter would ask me — 'That's Emile Ollivier.' — 'Did you know him? — 'Of course not! How old do you think I am, then?' — 'Then shall we throw it out?' — 'No, no,' I shall cry, stretching out my hand to protect two, ten, fifty yellowed effigies . . . which are linked with my unreasoning fidelity and the memories we never get rid of when they have spent half a century in our shadow. Some drawers, which I'm not very proud of, so far from becoming empty, fill to overflowing; one of mine boasts a massive German knife-cum-dagger, brought back from a nest of German ruins where a charming American soldier plucked it like a daisy. . . . Dignimont has just given me once more an album of cross-stitch tapestries dating from the Second Empire, with — as suggested patterns — a griffon terrier in tears on a tombstone, a ten of hearts, a rosebud seen from in front, from the side, and in three-quarter view. . . .

'I hang on to them because I haven't given them away.'

That occurs to me, from time to time, in connection with the glass marbles at the heart of which there coils the rainbow-coloured serpent, or when I look at a gold bracelet, a clasp, a silk scarf, an illustrated book, which have kept me company for so many years. 'I ought to give it away; someone would derive an entirely new pleasure from it, a genuine pleasure. . . . Oh! No, no, I don't want to, I'll keep it.' Then I think it over and scold myself: 'The reaction of a magpie, a squirrel, a dormouse — the last two, at least, only hoard their winter nourishment —

a miser's response, a constriction of the possessive instinct, diminution of the object possessed. . . .' Shall I invoke art, the great standby? Apart from what may have contributed to the painted colour, a well-loved text, a sonority, a shape, art has scarcely governed my life. It's not nice to have to drive oneself to be generous. A shallow wisdom murmurs in my ear that the glass marbles would be suitable for children, the silk scarf for a young neck, the small jewel would adorn an adolescent breast. Shall I give them away? Let us give them, let us profit from the moment when I still cherish what I want to give away. Let us make this effort, do this favour, come on now, let me give rein to this gesture, let me be torn a little on the thorn of regret. . . . But I soon come to myself and part merely with a fistful of coins, share only my ration of food. . . . Is it so hard, then, to dispense with a coloured marble, the trinket that catches the light, a strand of gold? I have devoted as much time to understanding that my ruthlessness was false as to growing old. If I give away the toys of old age, if I turn and empty the casket, the drawer, I discover that I no longer cling to anything and that all that was necessary to prove this to me was to cast these worthless relics to the wind. That the visible and the tangible exist only so that a blaze of colour, a cool touch, a style, should delude me as to their actual presence and efficacity, whereas they are really a spasm of appetites that are already defunct.

The attempts I make suffice to edify me. Already I have given as presents the coloured sphere, the little jewel, even the book. And I have waited, in vain, to suffer for it. Did I then love them so little, so poorly? Maybe. Then I must be prudent, that is niggardly, with what I used to dote on. I continue, without further and better inquiry: 'Oh, no! I shan't give it away, I'll keep it. . . .'

I'd kept Sido's blue dress till now, her little short bodice, all gathered and drawn together by pleats at the back, under the breasts, beneath the arms. . . . Only the skirt bloomed widely, embroidered with white chain-stitch garlands. Oh, no! I don't want to give it away, I'll keep it. . . . And it will do to cover the binding of the manuscript of *Sido*. That's certainly a graceful thought. In that way the blue dress will still clothe Sido. In that way the manuscript, on imitation Japanese vellum in three different blues, is well protected, bound by the hand of an old binder, masterly. That is very good. A little too good. It is art. It goes beyond piety, the cosy jumble of crumpled souvenirs: I am no longer so sure that I'm still fond of it. But my best friend, a bibliophile and amateur of fine bindings, is so pleased. . . . One must give, decidedly, and give all. Misia even gave a rival the husband she loved. A test which is not unique. A good many of us have tried it, profiting from a troubled, quasi-fatal moment when the rival touches her apogee of innocence, of beauty, of unreason, and begs us to yield in her favour. That is all that is needed for us to carry out what we call 'a beautiful gesture of renunciation', which won't afford us the least pity or shadow of consideration.

Or else we must hang on to everything and restrain our fine impulses, which risk sharing out our stray possessions. . . . All that becomes remote and absurd. . . . Yes, one must keep everything, that's the truth. But I allowed the departure for the long unalterable sleep of that old sylph with wings matted by rain, my brother, without his having handed over to me what he alone held, our ancient possessions, our ritual songs, the topography of our natal village, the names of the departed commended in the sermon every Sunday: 'The Church commends to your prayers the souls of Edouard de Lacour, Clémence de Lacour, Pauline Beauchêne and Fernand Bourgneuf; of Claude Brunet, Geneviève Gonnot, Toussaint Gounot, Irène and Octavie de Vathaire, Jacques Corneau, Marguerite Danjean, Adolphe Gressien, Laure Desleau, the widow Mallet, Prix Thillière, Paul Gentil, Estelle Reboulleau, Jean-Baptiste Glaumot. . . .' After Jean-Baptiste Glaumot I see no more than a misty file of humble dead. An insubstantial patrimony of words, of images, was lost with this amazing brother, who hoarded only time past. Our few treasures lay undistributed in the old sylph's room, on the sixth floor. A white wooden wardrobe and the cast-iron wash-basin defined the exact and severe condition of our past. . . .

The remainder, more tangible and doubtless less precious, was
frequently stolen from me. I have been robbed of books, letters,
small pictures in their frames, the excommunications, in red ink,
that Erik Satie scattered as a rosebush does its flowers. That's
what comes of not believing in locks, nothing of mine is shut
away. Where is the little light gold dollar which we cherished like
a pastille, the bracelet of chestnut hair, finely plaited, cool,
exactly the temperature of a snake? Where has that string of
branched, bristling, red coral faded away, which resembled I
don't know what choleric crustacean? I search. Foot- and finger-
prints are by now effaced. One should keep a watch on everything, or else burn everything. . . .

I know of women who say: 'Oh, me, I keep everything. I
can't remember ever having destroyed a paper.' What frightful
archives. . . . One of these, a literary woman, and charming,
reproaches me gently — there are gentle literary women — for
always having maintained silence about the 'major encounters'
of my life, all — she says — that one feels 'throbbing behind a
curtain spread by your own hands, the great experiences that
have been landmarks on your way. . .' But who thinks them so
great? Close, dear friend, the credits you so generously open for
me; I am, from poverty, a bad payer. And then, my dear, I did
once try to elevate my memoirs to the plane of complete confidence. . . . In a large account-book, devoid of any accounts,
ruled in blue with vertical lines, in red with vertical columns,
what emerged deserved instant obliteration, smelled of gossip, of
botching. So I confined myself, thenceforward, to more or less
amorous histories. . . . 'One tells of a lover and is silent about the
rest.'

Let's keep everything, out of respect for the ways employed by
dispersal and return. A little frame in flecked yellow thuja wood
hangs on my wall, and I don't think it will budge from there
as long as I live. It desperately threw itself in my path in order
to meet up with me again. This dates from the time when I was
a regular visitor at the Sunday market, the so-called Flea Market.
Nearly every Sunday I scoured the fortifications of Saint-Ouen,
their terraces, their culs-de-sac, their banks of worn grass. The

tricksters there required no stocks other than three half walnut-shells and a jet bead — 'Where is it then, that little black bead?' — the smoking basins of oil, standing on three-legged stoves, crisped the garfish and the slice of bacon — 'bacon five sous, real bacon!' *Objets d'art* and kitchen utensils succeeded each other in a strange and seasonal fashion. One month there would be an abundance of glove-stretchers and sugar-tongs, which gave way to walking-sticks with knobs of ivory and silver, precious canes with tassels of plaited leather. The following month a funereal abundance of second-hand top-hats was rife. Then there were fine sheets of hemstitched Friesian linen, altar-cloths, damask curtains which had retained their youth in the chill shade of a Second-Empire salon. . . .

Coveting a set of fine sheets, knocked down to Germaine Beaumont at ten francs the pair, I praised the attractions and advantages of the Flea Market so highly that one fine Sunday Charlotte Lyses insisted on accompanying me. She was bored there and made me give short shrift to the rickety furniture, the knives without handles, the handles without knives and aphonic phonographs. In the time it took her to acquire a little chain in smoked crystals I exchanged a greeting with le Barbu — I did not know what his other name might be — seated on the ground among his luxury articles on a sheet of oilcloth.

'And now, quick, the Métro, I've seen enough,' declared Lyses. 'Are you coming, Colette? Colette, what is it you're looking at?'

To tell the truth, I wasn't looking at anything. I had just fallen into one of those mental states which confound the past and the present, the false and the real, where we wait passively to regain control of them and of ourselves.

'You've got a lorgnette, Lyses, would you mind trying to read what's written — it's nearly worn away — on the back of that little thuja frame there?'

'Does it interest you? I can see, that is, I can only just see. . . . I see "Adèle, Sophie Landay, or Landoy, née Châtenay!" . . . . and something else. . . . "Châtenay . . . children, never forget. . . ." The ink is so pale. . . .'

But I didn't need any more help:

' "My children," I recited, "never forget your worthy and virtuous mother." It is signed Eugène Landoy. The miniature painter was named Foulard; his signature is on the left of the miniature with the date 1830. The ivory layer is split from top to bottom, a crack as fine as a hair. . . .'

It was the portrait of my maternal grandmother, Mme Eugène Landoy, née Sophie Châtenay. A portrait stolen from me, gone astray for thirty years, for thirty years struggling towards me, by what paths on earth or beneath it. . . . Le Barbu, responsive to the strange family setting, asked me only fifty francs. 'It's like a play,' was his comment. A connoisseur, Charlotte Lyses shared his opinion.

The miniature represents a young woman with a trilobed coiffure — a large bun on top, a bunch of curls, like chipolatas, on either temple. She smiles, well content — to my mind — to have regained the corner of my mantelpiece. She died young, and deceived twenty times by her husband; all I know about her is her premature death and her silence as a betrayed wife — the essentials, in fact. All that is very far away. . . .

What interests me is the last journey of this painted lady. The thieving hand, the abduction, the halting-places, the obscure places, other unscrupulous hands, the interminable waiting until, perhaps, she despaired. . . . I love to see her at peace in my home. No doubt, before having betrayed her twenty times, her husband, a shade 'coloured', had been seduced by the pallor of that Parisienne of the boulevard Bonne-Nouvelle. . . .

Five

'*Have they been looking after you? You haven't been bored today?*'

My best friend, how can you think that I might have been bored? Why, the sky alone is distraction enough. I'm always aware of those cardinal points whence the clouds flow that resemble Victor Hugo and Henri Rochefort, the wind that settles the rain, the sun that burns the double curtain, the hail so harsh to the rose-bushes. The moon enters my room at will, advances at a cat's pace, extends a white paw to attack my bed: she is satisfied with waking me, she at once loses heart and climbs down again. At the time when she is at the full I rediscover her at dawn, all pale and bare, straying in a chill region of the sky. Returning to its slumbers, the last bat slashes her with a zigzag stroke.

At the day's end my youngest neighbours have a charming way of feeding my more or less stagnant curiosity. They haul up here their finest products, a pair of nine-month-old twins, fresh and downy as two peaches from the same branch; a little boy, thoughtful and distinguished, who, at three, plays with the most difficult words, such as: stalactites, ornithorhyncus, trochilidae (I teach him them so that he may astound his father); the Little Milkman comes to sing me his latest song and to introduce his fifteen-month-old sister called La Carrée, since she is such a fine girl that she bursts in her skin like a well-stuffed sack of coffee; Anatole, Mme Laure's parrot, leaves his home in the *entresol* — formerly my *entresol* — grants me a few minutes of his frigid courtesy, his judicial gaze and his relentless resemblance to Offenbach.

Sometimes, at night, it's the unknown man who sets out to divert me, calling me to the telephone. It is two or four o'clock in the morning. . . . He asks if it is I, really I, and I assure him it is. Then he says: 'I shit on you,' and hangs up again — too soon, for I should like to question him about his mysterious ailment, the motives for his insomnia, to discover whether, having nocturnally shat on me, he can fall back on his bed to sleep there, at last happy and released. As it happens, he is discreet, only wakes me at long intervals, and utters only that, shall I say, essential word.

There are so many of them, those who stay awake despite themselves. Last year, for a long time, the foul-mouthed Unknown tormented a young girl. He would ring her up but did not speak to her. He breathed a long gasping breath in her ear, a sort of great wild beast's panting, a hateful 'haaahh' which made the little fool very frightened. She decked out this punctual summons with pompous names. She detected in it an infernal sigh, an implacable obsessional will. For it takes little to banish reality and probability from a young girl's life.

I have had other nocturnal callers. For the timid human creature needs to 'say something to someone', even if in the coarsest terms. A man's voice sometimes asks me to listen to a serenade which begins as follows:

> *Poil au bec de gaz*
> *Mon cul sur la commode,*
> *Poil au chandelier,*
> *Mon cul sur l'escalier. . . .*

I admit that these words are of doubtful merit, and that they attribute an improbable hairiness to items of furniture. But what a fine baritone voice!

None of this is very serious. No nocturnal episode has seriously disturbed my nights since the ring at the bell, the hobnailed boots, since the coarse whispering voices, since . . . well, since.

When the stubborn will to live and to manifest ourselves one to the other, the absent one and myself, began to stab sharply, like needle-pricks, at the obscurity of the camp, the massive obstacle which separated us, there was at first a piece of squared paper torn from a notebook, hardly bigger than a Métro ticket,

covered with a writing unused to being so minute and cramped.
I thought of the greasy paper which used to line Vautrin's wig, of
the few lines destined to save Lucien de Rubempré. I thought of
all those curtailed messages, compelled to choose only between
words of encouragement and words of menace; I thought of
Gordon Pym when he deciphered a fragment of a letter where
there gleamed the terrible words : '. . . blood. Stay hidden. Your
life depends on it.'

I have preserved these lines, the first to arrive from the camp
at Compiègne, which stood for communication, life, the return
of hope. I also keep a list, which reached me later on. No doubt
it was compiled in one of those moments when the name and
the savour of the foodstuffs mentioned arouse some delirium in
famished prisoners. A list, a litany rather, which demanded, if I
could entrust them to a safe channel — thank you, Dr
Breitmann! — butter, jam, sugar, and, above all, like a burning
refrain, above all 'bread, in the name of Heaven, bread!' And
I could not restrain an agonized smile on seeing that the word
bacon, the not-to-be-found BACON, was written in capital
letters. . . .

They also begged, those who were there, for the help of
alcohol, dreamed of condiments and seasoning before and after
the solitary soup, barely disturbed by vegetables, between two
infusions tasting of boiled hay. Questions and answers, separated
by long silences, confiscated, gone astray, did not make a
dialogue. Uncertainty still reigned over those first batches, those
massive round-ups, and the jailers themselves seemed inexperi-
enced. No routine, no procedure for ordering the brutalities, to
endow them with the character they assumed later of a prescrip-
tive ferocity, an organized anti-Semitism.

But the thermometer, after the 1st January 1942, began to
fall. Eight — ten — twelve degrees below zero; — fourteen on
the chill plain of Compiègne. And the word 'deportation' took
a larger and larger place in the forecasts and the news; and there
were many of us women who stood aghast, to learn that
what had seemed to us the worst was about to become worse
still.

Inability to help a loved one is the bitterest of disappointments. We savoured it, ate it, drank it. It left its mark everywhere, made us vindictive, unjust. A little gilded horse, in Capo di Monte porcelain, still suffers at times for my past misery. He it is, his burnished gold rump that the first light drew out of shadow, and even in the shadow he bore the weight of my unrelenting gaze. Today he asks me to be reasonable for a moment, to reaccord him, exorcized, his essence as a very nice little horse on whose gold dwells the first ray of sunlight, the last of moonlight. We were alone, he and I, in the masterless house, and from my bed I gathered, from his bright golden cruppers, an impossible hypnosis. . . .

Six

Il ne vous atteint pas, l'affreux cri des sirènes,
Dans les bars de cristal, éclatants perroquets,
Frivoles favoris des sombres capitaines.

Now she is dead, she who scattered verses like these with a grand air of display and indifference. Running, she would abandon them if one of the blue parakeets called out, if the sparrow tapped with his beak on the window, if the bar of chocolate was cooking too quickly. I find it unbelievable that she is dead and it will take me a long time to grasp it. I cannot even confront such a vivid friend with a still image, were it even that of her peaceful sleep.

A life as pure as hers cannot fail to appear mysterious. It isn't easy to read within the crystal sphere. Chastity, pride, poverty — she lived on these three heights. She spent her last years on the fourth floor, where she lived in the rue d'Alleray, solitary for some quarter of a century. A neighbour, a child, an obliging tradesman carried the essentials up to her eyrie, well-orientated, furnished entirely with leftovers, light furniture, blue opalines, pious images, Second-Empire night-lights, many blue trinkets.

Hélène Picard's last journeys were only from the rue d'Alleray to the St Antoine Hospital, then from the rue d'Alleray to the pretty Château du Val, near Saint-Germain, a pleasant family convalescent home run by the Légion d'Honneur. The trips she made to be with me in the summer I don't count as journeys, although she never engaged in them without agitation, without losing a suitcase, bringing something useless, forgetting the indispensable, enjoying some contretemps, distressed at having to leave Paris just when the Foire aux Puces of the Fourteenth of July enlivens the square des Arts-et-Métiers. Once settled deep in the country, she would take root there with a unique strength and eagerness. Her poesy gained from everything, ennobled everything. That is the privilege of those who are born to sing. . . .

Her parakeets were also blue. When, at the beginning of the war, millet and canary-seed became scarce, Hélène put the blue birds out of her heart and gave them to an enthusiast who was better able to supply them with seed. . . . If I had to reckon up her renouncements, carried out with a nun's lightness of heart, I should be bound to forget some. Plagued by a serious bone disease — shortly before my own arthritis set in, never to leave me again — Hélène Picard also renounced the visits we used to exchange so happily, our conversations in the blue room where this ascetic gourmande filtered her coffee as no one else could, cooked — like no one else — a little stew of pork that was our *plat de résistance*. I would bring the millefeuilles she liked, and creamy éclairs from Flammang's.

It was hardly a matter of number or rhythm or even literature in our intimate conversation. Our correspondence was marked by less reserve. Hélène, endowed with an aptitude for keen and faithful criticism, enthused for or against a new work, judged it with an angelic severity. Traces of poetic abundance were scattered around her. Often one of her mornings would suffice to strew the blue room. The morning light would ripen a poem for this daughter of sunny Ariège, who went early to bed and woke with the parakeets. She rose at dawn, percolated her coffee, wielded the broom, abandoned furniture-cleaning for strophes, and her adventurous writing impatiently laid its spiky antennae on little bits of paper, on the back of the gas bill and the dairy account. With what arabesques, what rhymes, she would illustrate a catalogue of electrical appliances which came to the poet's hand at the tumultuous moment when a poem insists on being born. . . .

'Have you been working, Hélène?'

'Splendidly! But I've mislaid what I wrote. It's not important!'

What fine disdain, what pride, what modesty. . . . She would use a barely dry poem to wrap up the slice of cake, the triangle of mountain cheese, harder than a roof-tile, that she slipped into my bag.

'I hope you've kept a copy of it.'

She would pirouette on her little feet, agile and dancing. She laughed in mock heroism:

'No! I can make some more!'

And I would admire this rich undisciplined woman with the wonder of a thrifty prosodist.

When she did not have the time to write to me she would send a packet containing a bouquet of her latest verses. One December 31st I received *Songe*, with these words: 'Happy New Year and all my love, Hélène.' We never delayed writing to each other for long. At times her letters consisted of pages on a sharply critical note, at times of spontaneous messages, reports that might have emanated from a schoolgirl of genius, sealed with a charming domestic humility: 'Today I'm quite taken up with laundering my big embroidered muslin curtains, the ones that bathe my little drawing-room in a calm snowy light. . . . My jam has come out splendidly. As much strawberry as cherry, then a little more of greengage later on, I can reckon on sixty pots for my ant-like meals. . . . I can look forward to a fine winter's gormandizing. . . .'

I can no longer recall the year our friendship began. I remember that Hélène Picard, separated from her husband — a former sub-prefect, himself something of a poet — arrived in Paris, there to enjoy her poverty and independence; she took the same fierce pleasure in the one as in the other. Still young, very pretty, pale and dark like a daughter of the Midi, eyes sparkling, her chief beauty derived from her proud, fine, sensitive nose.

The enlargement of a snapshot by Henri Laval is a magnificent portrait of Hélène at around the age of fifty. A perfect nose, a sturdy warrior's neck, hair in a devil's tangle, the corner of the mouth parallel to the angle of the eye. What a good likeness, how ironical, assured, impressive! The first time that she came into my office at the *Matin*, Hélène was adorned — following her rather gipsy tastes which Paris never completely tamed — with little pearled combs, cabochon necklaces, écru lace, and her long hair covered her ears with shell-like curls. The sacrifice of her hair soon after cost her some misgivings, regrets, tears even; but she thereby acquired a charming bohemian air, an abundant foliage of curls. Sprightly, frugal, spontaneous, embodying in all her actions the pleasant manners, kindliness and meticulousness of provincial France, it was not difficult to believe her when she assured us that a slender monthly allowance was wealth enough for her. To convince me, she would itemize her budget, counting on her fingers. The attractiveness that goes with childlike women did not desert her in maturity.

She would bolt her door to embark on the washing and ironing of an exemplary housewife and forget, at night, the key left outside. These gay confident caprices, the love of idling and laughter, were only temporary, gave way to a fundamental unsociability. If the bell rang, Hélène would approach the door silently — the door that a blow with one's fist would have driven in — and listen: 'Who rang?' she would cry. Then she might add: 'Madame Picard is not in,' careless that her meridional *a*'s, clear and short, gave her the lie. . . .

Our friendship once established, Hélène Picard used to join our little colony which the dog-days exiled to the Breton coast, and which included Francis Carco and his first wife, the Leopold Marchands, Germaine Beaumont, and two or three children of Henri de Jouvenel's of different beds. . . . To all of them I was most grateful for being far younger than myself, for loving the sea, bathing, silence, gaiety. . . . Hélène Picard seemed the youngest, intoxicated by the sea she knew so little. She leaped about in the waves like a child having a dip, turned pale, her teeth chattered, she would cover her girlish bosom with her hands as with a shell, and take shelter on the warm sand or in a dell of dry close-cropped thyme.

Carco sometimes teased her rather cruelly. But she bore his attacks with a sort of gratitude. Léopold Marchand would invent stories of pirates for her which she listened to, quite taken in. Germaine Beaumont, from her vantage point as a twenty-five-year-old, showered her with so-called practical advice. We allowed ourselves, in our contact with Hélène, a familiarity that she did not attempt to restrain.

But one of these shameless individuals might pick up a stray page of manuscript, striped with verses, read, stop laughing, gaze incredulously at our 'little Hélène', busy with marbles or a medicine-ball too heavy for her delicate wrists; the page would pass from hand to hand and its passage would give rise to admiration, respect, the silent promise to treat 'our Hélène' as she deserved. . . . Not for anything in the world would she tolerate these signs of our reverence for long. But she could not prevent us from being haunted by a verse from her lasting light :

> *Houleuse fille blanche offerte aux matelots!*

Leopold Marchand would declaim on the beach, bare feet in the foam. . . .

> *. . . Que ne puis-je suspendre*
> *Mon coeur, comme une merle, au cou du rossignol!*

would sigh Germaine Beaumont.

How can I separate from those Breton summers the memory of certain of Hélène Picard's verses, fed by an unformulated sensuality, a secret incandescence which the poet did not deign to explain. . . . The Brittany that I lost, the fragment of Armorica that melted away in my imprudent hands, is at least preserved for me in Hélène's verses !

> *Domaine forestier, ensoleillé d'automne,*
> *Arbres, secrètement sur la mer entr'ouverts . . . . .*
> . . . .
> *Le sol sentait le fruit, l'eau morte, la Bretagne,*
> *L'herbe amère . . .*
> . . . .
> *Le chevrefeuille errait dans l'ombre incriminée . . .*

She gave us matter for thought in stranger lyricisms. The last collection Hélène Picard published she entitled *Pour un Mauvais Garçon*. The seventy poems contained in the volume have the style of voluptuous riddles. Their dazzle, their plastic richness, as much as their gilded shadows, seem to veil a name, to mask an individual. . . . What mystic might not apply himself to discern therein the signs of a phenomenon of possession? This volume, wholly seized with mystery, seems under a spell, illuminated by second sight, thrown, like a malefic flower, at some young, accursed face of flesh. In it Baudelaire, barely astonished, encounters the heroes of Carco's novels, and sometimes their tangy vocabulary. . . .

As for the readers of *Pour un Mauvais Garçon*, I know some who remained dazzled and uncertain, who could come to no conclusion regarding the most singular avatar that an unbridled yet chaste poetry could authorize. To avoid the temptation of tarnishing the poet's purity among so many hovels, pistols, absinthes, furnished rooms and yellow eiderdowns, whistle blasts and bluish blades, it is only necessary to read, or re-read, in *Sabbat*, the contempt held by Hélène Picard all her life for the avid kind of female consumer whom she calls 'Madame how often'.

Printed in an edition of seven hundred, this surprising poem was a prompt commercial failure which its publisher, André Delpeuch, does not seem to have survived. I had the good fortune to rescue a few volumes of *Pour un Mauvais Garçon*, besides the one the author gave me. We are far here from the earlier works of Hélène Picard, from the *Instant éternel* crowned by the *Académie*, from *Nous n'irons plus au Bois*. . . . Where are the fountains and the moist moonlight, the muffled piano, everything that sobs and tinkles, so crystalline, in *Province et Capucines*? Where the most audacious verse — still so *jeune fille* — of the *Instant éternel*:

> *Je l'aimais tant qu'il me semblait l'avoir volé!*

The fires of a personal hell glow in *Pour un Mauvais Garçon*. Berlioz might have called the strange still squall bearing away the hallucinated Hélène Picard '*Le voyage de Mephisto*'. But the poet decided that her Tempter should wear a checked cap and red pouch without his seductive powers being in any way thereby diminished. Thus he drags his blissful and tormented prey across a Baudelarian glory of pure-eyed demons and half-damned guardian angels. . . . What can we say? And what is there to fear?

Nothing. We have here the magic of poetry, mirages, in short whatever comes most easily to a poet. Whatever, as a privileged confidante, I might interpret for the benefit of the strict and misleading truth I shall suppress. The truth never prevented Hélène from going to sleep every night in her small bed covered in the Virgin's colours. It was there, boarding her flying carpet, that she would run the gauntlet of the 'dens', cross the 'vile' thresholds, stroke the perfumed necks of the *mauvais garçons*; there it was that she would wake at first light, at the first cry from the chattering parakeets. . . .

She would have nothing to do with licentious books. Did she read much? The latter part of her life she shunned everything, even reading. Everything, except love and the expression of love. From what reverie flowed these lines, thrown on to a sheet of blue paper:

'At times you bend me like the vine which one begins to harvest and which resists. . . . At times you stretch me on the ground like a layer of ripe leaves and you lie down sighing on this shepherd's litter. . . .'

These grand divagations, these grand dissipations, amount to nothing, nothing but Poetry. Poetry alone possesses, seizes, lets fall, distributes to her eternal champions that which human love scatters so parsimoniously among its creatures.

Exuberant to a degree, Hélène, in conversation, seemed to have no secrets. But another aspect was that of solitude. One could hardly catch her unawares save at brief and furtive intervals, and when she allowed herself to plunge into deep reverie. What fierceness then on those so Latin features, moulded, recast by the expression of a mysterious fury. . . . Calmness would follow, as if from prudence, to extinguish this flame: 'Don't pay any attention, Colette! This is when I frighten children!' And her flinty eyes would regain their benevolent sparkle.

What were the targets of this mysterious anger, this launching of fluid and arrows? She was always brusque in her judgments, and ingenuously misogynous. Ingenuously, too, she would rejoice, as a savage, as an artist, in the charm emanating from some handsome passing plumber; she could say, in praise of a well-mannered man: 'He's almost as attractive as a delivery boy.' She might also say: 'That splendid butcher! Just look how attractive he is! And his crest of golden curls!' Her connoisseur's eulogy carried weight, a good peasant humour, the serenity of those who are capable of contemplating, face to face, the admirable and virile miracle that they esteem above all. Entirely, almost passionately, feminine, this literate Hélène would fall silent, embarrassed, when the talk around her was of homosexual perversions. She refused to concede that they might even exist. In connection with two women, who played the couple and whom we were judging without harshness, Hélène cried: 'No, no, it's ugly! Or it's only a joke. They're pretending, they're ridiculous.' One of us pointed out to her that the opposite sex was not exempt from or disdainful of analogous distractions. Hélène calmed down: 'Between boys, that's all right.' And when we protested in our turn, she could not or would not explain further. Again, in her masterpiece, *Pour un Mauvais Garçon*, the expression of her amorous fervour sometimes astonishes us when she speaks to the 'Unknown', her insubstantial lover:

> *Comme tu sens la fille et la nuit et la haie,*
> *Et peut-être, parfois, le bel enfant de choeur. . . .*

The august and impassioned scorn which is exhaled by such verses — she even goes so far as to call the idolized and disparaged lover *'ma chérie'* — scandalized even Carco:
'Hélène, Hélène, what you've written is outrageous!'
Hélène would give a wry smile and the poem would resume its enigmatic course under her hand:

> *Fais voir tes yeux dorés, dans cette fin de jour,*
> *Donne ta peau qui sent la rose at la vanille. . . .*
> *Et ton sourire, enfant, et ta main, pauvre fille,*
> *Tu es né sous le signe infame de l'amour.*

It is apparent that her mood, like the tone of her letters, darkened during her convalescence at the pretty Château du Val. Vain summer, unhelpful shade; I visit there a Hélène who is intolerant, rebellious as a student, irreverent towards the aged, even if they are ornamental, imposing former magistrates, still-young lieutenant-colonels, and she is bored at table. . . . She can stand it no longer, abandons the rheumatic Romeo with his two sticks, makes her escape, and returns to her small Parisian dwelling, where at least the dog-days are white and blue, where her window-ledge houses, between a clump of nasturtiums and the promises of a gladiolus, a minute kitchen-garden of garlic, thyme and parsley. But nothing now can prevent a baleful shadow from advancing towards her little by little, tarnishing her healthy rosy pallor, her tuberous pink. The attack was not confined to the bony damage, the very serious decalcification.

From what date did she resolve, overcome by aversion for the blood shed by animals, no longer to consume their flesh? Hélène did not tell me. She never gave herself away. Her bohemian subtlety easily outdid our own. The sudden and complete suspension of her meat diet, effected like an unimportant whim, threw her off balance, hastened the end. She, of course, disguised it as gourmandise, sang the virtues and fresh savour of raw mushrooms, pink radishes, leeks *en vinaigrette*, praised the feasts of salads, fruits, of cress with lemon. One day when I asked Hélène for her neglected succulent pork stew, she made an involuntary gesture of withdrawal: 'Forgive me, Colette, but *I can no longer* touch pork. . . .' Perhaps we, her friends, were not vigilant, not discerning enough, to track down and combat this mystical kind of revulsion. Only Professor Moreau knew a secret of which she was only partly aware. She allowed him to treat her for the deforming disease which began by bowing one tibia, then the other, then. . . .

'I have just,' she wrote to me, 'I have just had more than five hundred francs' worth of bolts fixed to my door. I am convinced, I am *morally* certain, that someone has been getting in.' She began to believe that someone was diverting her mail. She would trust only the *poste restante*. . . . Again she wrote: 'If I were not attached to this house by so many bonds, I should leave it, I have proof I am being spied on. But it would be the same, or worse, anywhere else. . . .'

Was this menacing cloud to grow even thicker? Hélène Picard had her remissions, she had not yet entirely lost her sense of the comic, her fresh mockery: 'My father and stepmother came from Foix to pay me a visit and I didn't know what to say to them. One interview every quarter of a century, that doesn't encourage conversation. They left eventually, leaving me . . . a little box of dry cakes.'

Prose, for her, was facile and of no account; her rapid sloping writing covered page after page in a few minutes. The invasive alexandrine gave rise to discarded material, thrust forward with insect feet, with pointed mandibles. . . . Active, sensitive, joyous writing which transmitted to me so many affectionate messages and childlike appeals for help: 'Help me, my own Colette! Once again I'm without any blue paper! Once again the ink at my stationer's has been diluted with the milky way! See how the nibs of my latest "sergeant-major" pen, brutalized by my . . . adjutant's fist, are crossed like the beak of the bird which is called — naturally! — the cross-beak. . . .'

That elegant sharp handwriting; its immateriality troubled me when the poet made use of it for her more glutinous verse, verse both winged and dense, burdened as if with a weight of flesh:

> *Toi qui fus ma bête et ma fleur,*
> *Et la jungle de ma caresse . . .*
>
> ....
>
> *Cette bassesse sourde, amoureuse et pâmée . . .*
>
> ....
>
> *Chaque fois que mes yeux s'abîmaient dans tes yeux,*
> *L'inceste nous frôlait de sa patte animale . . .*
>
> ....
>
> *Ton silence insolent, ta paresse légère,*
> *Et ton coeur pavoise, ô chaland des faubourgs!*
>
> ....

And this unlooked for threat, brutal rather than amorous :

Tu ne quitteras plus les hontes triomphales,
Qu'inventa, cette nuit, mon vieux démon charnel.

We falter over these two sombre lines, sensual and reticent, suited to the temperature which prevails in *Pour un Mauvais Garçon.* If it were a matter of another poet, I should have said that, when she wrote them, Hélène Picard had reached the age of authority, which often coincides with the stage of amorous exigence. But I should vouch that her 'season in hell' was not linked with any dishonourable gehenna. Let us rather entrust ourselves to the verbal freshness that abounds from her pen :

J'étais comme le vent incertain qui balance
Une rose narquoise à la porte d'un bal. . . .

The direct threat of the war seems to have passed over the fragile roof of the rue d'Alleray without disturbing her who slept among the blue opalines and the great curtains of embroidered tulle. She believed only in those perils conjured from the past. From her flowered window-frame she followed the coloured trajectories in the sky and listened with a serene spirit to the gunfire, the chromatic alert. Only death could have interrupted the 'rosary of rhyme' strewn at each breath around Hélène Picard. Though she did not stir again, the remainder of her existence was a progressive and concerted evasion. This courageous woman flees, this vivid presence loses its substance; the wanderer, the habituée of remote suburbs, of colourful markets, little shops with gates and bell-pulls, grows static. . . . Worse still, she is fading away. She still suffers a benign ray of sunlight to touch her : the regard of an unknown, of a small local shopkeeper, of an errand-boy, these she admits in the darkness of a corridor, through a door she half opens. . . . She seems to be afraid of melting like rime in the warmth of affectionate commiseration. . . . I could wish not to have experienced the moment when the enemy's strength bore her down, bowed her to lean on two sticks, cast earthward that brown golden gaze enamoured of all that was elevated, winged, celestial; nevertheless, an ardent affection must attest that a poet died in hospital, in 1945, as one died in 1830.

Save for destitution, which she was spared, a cruel romanticism surrounded Hélène's ending; the hospital reduced to one communal ward (she had been discovered unconscious in her home and hurriedly removed), the prompt twilight of a winter's day, a coming and going of anonymous passers-by. Hélène died in such a setting, mute, evasive, terribly attached to her solitude. She died, and I think of her. How many friends have passed away whom I can call friends? Very few. Very few, thank God. How can one gauge friendship, save by its jewel-like rarity? When death intervenes, with its constancy of regret and its illumination, we can think: 'I loved truly.' The fine sentiment that risks being corrupted by physical illness, embittered old age, is restored by death to its pristine and faithful condition. . . . So that I can cherish Hélène anew without fear, severely, according to the example she used to set. For it was she who decided that our friendship had grown to become a bond which separation stretches but does not break, which is tested by its strength in absence, and which forms its judgments with uncompromising freedom. How many times have I heard Hélène abandon her scrupulous provincial protocol to emerge — the heel-thrust of the great diver — ablaze with paradox and arbitrariness, to comment gaily on some domestic crime. . . . I remember confessing to her some action I could have wished not to have committed, for which I reproached myself: 'Enough of these stories!' cried Hélène. 'For once you've been capable of a little greatness!'

It was this Hélène who lived in secret beneath the spangled cloak of Mme Hélène Picard, laureate in 1907 of a jury of women, as literate as they were *mondaines. Femina* boosted her to the level of the Baronne de Baye and Daniel Lesueur, not very far from a dinner photographed at Mme de Pierrebourg's, alias Claude Ferval. *Je sais tout* commemorated Hélène in evening dress, black tulle and jet, her hair in a coil round her forehead. Seated in a photographer's armchair, she holds, so as to bear witness to her literary status, a large open album. . . .

I've no other means now of being with her than to talk to myself about her. My husband hardly had more than a glimpse of her. She welcomed him from the height of our long friendship, with a circumspect gentleness which conferred on the presence of this best friend beside me a character, shall I say episodic, which he has been able to resent in silence. Our friends find it difficult enough to like our friends.

Seven

I've done no work today. Writing is often wasteful. If I counted the pages I've torn up, of how many volumes am I the author? Lucie Delarue-Mardrus, who has also just died, had the good fortune to attack all her work with an overwhelming dash. Rheumatism twisted this valiant performer in every direction and put her on the rack. I found her ever ready to pour out verse and prose, speak in public, study Latin, model in wax, string a melody on a five-lined stave. . . . She enjoyed correcting my texts, without malice, when she thought they required it. 'I expect you're very proud,' she wrote to me from Château-Gontier, 'because you've stuck the word *anatife** in your latest book to astound us. Well, too bad for you, but you must say *invectiver contre* and *tâcher à.* . . .'

I could wish that she were still among us, busy lecturing to me. I thought of her when I was writing the word *pholade*.† She would have reprimanded me for it in her child's voice, looking down from the height of her little head with its great slow eyes, its artless and turned-up nose which pulled her lip upwards. . . .

'Aren't you ever short of subjects for novels?' I once asked her.

'I've over a hundred, over two hundred, three hundred,' she replied. 'Do you want any? I'll give you as many as you like. Come and see my new apartment. Come and see my carved candles. Come and see my models for a puppet theatre. . . .'

We separated and all was silence between us for months. It was not our fault.

She, too, had cut her abundant brown hair, the thick tresses that she wore for so long braided round her head. My hair, a metre fifty-eight long, the silver straw which wreathed the

* Barnacle.
† A mollusc — the piddock or stone-borer. (Tr.)

forehead of the Amazon, what a harvest reaped by whim, by fashion. . . . At least the widow of the Duc de Morny, around 1867, had strewn her hair on her husband's coffin, and her gesture, heralded by the sound of horns, preserved an air of loving sacrifice. . . .

'Oh, how I wish people would shut up about my mother's sacrifice,' grumbled Mathilde, known as Missy, the Duke's youngest daughter. 'For two years she pestered my father to let her wear her hair short and he strictly forbade her. She certainly got away with it!'

They are very various, the guilty pleasures of widows.

'A black veil, and underneath a monkey's smile,' as my mother used to say.

It has grown late, without my having noticed it. It is the hour which is often said to be particularly long and gloomy for elderly lonely persons. Yet two hours, three hours are to me like moments, so long as a relative indolence comes to my aid. Working, the time drags, the quarters of an hour are chewed with difficulty, like hunks of coarse bread eaten without drinking or salivating. This afternoon I had a quiet day, passed in idling and suffering. Near me, in the blue of the evening, there still gleams the watch with the golden dial which I call my cardiac watch because, hanging by its ring from a nail as slender as a pin, the beating of my heart makes it oscillate gently. It measures out my life but it is I who keep it going. If I forget to wind it even for one day, it will fall silent, overtaken by death. Who could repair it? It is old, the skilled craftsmen who could have looked after it are dead too. I can see that, one of these days, I shall have to see it acquire the melancholy status of an *objet d'art*. . . .

Behind the frosted glass that takes the place — poorly — of a wall between the two rooms I inhabit a yellow glow has just lit up. Now it's time all at once to suffer less, to make up one's face rather better, to listen to the telephone, a premonitory clashing of plates, and rings at the bell which excite only defiance, mockery and hilarity. On some days I go so far as to say, inwardly: 'Sh . . . on all these bells, but *now*!' But these are out-bursts of irreverence that do not last. . . .

I had barred my door, this afternoon, in honour of a visitor who had come from her suburb at considerable inconvenience, a little woman of about sixty, rather dumpy, dressed in rusty black. She is a 'home clairvoyant'; a rather timid clairvoyant who must be frightened by the phantoms she conjures up. It was our first encounter and she immediately warned me honestly:

'You know, madame, I don't always *see*. When I don't *see*, I prefer to say so right away, right? My *clientèle* consists mainly of people who can't get about, so I can come back again. Do you want me to ask you questions or shall I just tell you what I see?'

I preferred to abandon myself to her clairvoyance and she removed her gloves from hands worn by housework. For a quarter of an hour no dazzling light was shone on either my past or my present. Illness, vexations, estrangements, successes, removals — the small change of prophecy poured out and my little clairvoy-ant excused herself like a singer who feels out of voice. I was sorry for her, I could have wished to prompt her. . . . I offered her a hot infusion. She thanked me with a kindly tentative look from her eyes, bluish and bulging as were those of the celebrated and defunct Elise, 'the woman with the candle'. For a moment she leaned forward, appearing to look for something on the carpet.

'Have you dropped your glove?'

She did not reply but went on looking:

'Ah!' she said, 'it's a cat.'

'What?'

'It's a cat.'

'You see a cat?'

'Yes, it's just gone under your chair and mine. For a moment I said to myself: "What can that be?" It's a cat.'

'Why not a tomcat?'

She made a gesture of ignorance.

'I don't know, madame. "A cat" is what they tell me.'

'What's she like?'

'Oh, she's not very pretty ! . . . I mean she's not like those fine big long-haired cats. . . . She's grey all over.'

'Can you see her now?'

'Yes. There's no problem, she's there all the time. She doesn't want to leave you. You mean everything to her.'

'Can you see her move about?'

'Certainly. She comes and goes, she walks around. She does what she likes because she's dead.'

'Do you know how long she's been dead?'

'No.'

She corrected herself, adding immediately :

'It's four years now.'

'But you just said you knew nothing about it.'

'I didn't know anything, *someone* has just told me.'

'Is it a voice you hear?'

The honest seer gave me an imploring look :

'Yes. . . . No, it's not an ordinary voice, I don't hear any words, but I grasp the meaning. . . . I'm not very good at explaining myself. . . .'

She would accept only a modest sum and I let her go. I told my best friend about her visit when he got back and our discussion thereon, as can be imagined, centred on the presence of the Cat, the Last Cat, the one of whom we used to say : 'What the Cat doesn't know isn't worth knowing.' If her soul, got up to look 'grey all over', still haunts our dwelling four years after death, visible only to eyes sensitive to the invisible, then it's because we have remained worthy of her. We shan't forget those consoling words : 'She does what she likes, because she's dead.' And I shall take care never to summon the humble seer again for fear of learning from her lips that the Cat, this time, has left us for good.

I don't recall ever in my life having consulted more than four or five persons gifted with second sight. But it pleases me to recognize that their diverse gifts are able to disconcert our human sight. If the future — my own — had ever made me curious, I might have sought more frequent meetings with these exceptional persons.

My first contact with the occult came about when, at her request, I accompanied one of those young women who are feminine to the point of shunning anything masculine, including therein men themselves. A wounded dove, a wilting flower, incited by the vogue for *Aphrodite* and the *Chansons de Bilitis* to certain moral indiscretions. Unknown to her Myrtocleia, this sensitive Rhodis requested my reassuring presence at a 'highly born' Russian's, named Saphira, whose gaze, according to her, 'pierced' the future and the past, not to mention the present.

Reality revealed an elderly man, made up and reeking of perfume. His clients, if any of them remain, cannot have forgotten his very beautiful eyes, whose pupils were surrounded by two concentric rings of velvet blue. 'Don't leave me alone with him, I'm frightened!' said Rhodis. I did as she wished and we awaited the oracle — not for long. The soothsayer bent his great height over the young woman and said abruptly:

'Beware! You're going to a man! Beware! There is danger. I tell you, there is danger!'

The effect of this prediction was unforeseen. Rhodis got up and with the air of a woman who has just had her bottom pinched in the Métro, burst forth with:

'Why, monsieur! But not at all! It's a slander, monsieur! I won't allow you. . . .'

I think, red as she was, that she would have left without paying if Saphira had not demanded a sizeable fee, as befitted a Russian of noble origin.

The very next day a gossiping, slanderous, fearful, curious little world squawked the news: Rhodis had just run off with a handsome young man. Myrto made herself ridiculous by pursuing the heterosexual couple, fired off a couple of unskilful revolver shots, and everything settled down.

Who can give me the key to Saphira? How is one to disentangle, from a mass of tinsel, banality and Slav origins, from a name borrowed from the Kabbala, from make-up, large rings, a wasp-waisted frock-coat whatever he could lay claim to of authentic lucidity and sorcery, to use the word I find most satisfactory? Who will enlighten me on a reader of cards, who used to be called 'the good wife of the rue de Chazelles?' She seemed, one day, very intrigued herself by what the tarot cards showed and repeated, as if her client could have done something about it: 'See, there is a person who is a long way away, a child rather, thirteen or fourteen years old, who is moving about a lot. But what can he hope to achieve by moving about so much? I can't see. . . . But someone ought to tell him not to create such a disturbance!'

Three days later the young man 'a long way away', who went riding on horseback every day, fell and was confined to bed for three months. The fanatic client did not wait three months to return to the rue de Chazelles, where the seer rewarded her with nothing but senseless remarks. Repetition is as valueless to clairvoyants as to poisonous snakes. Strange ability to uncover what is hidden or to furnish venom, when both are exhausted by repetition. It is this exhaustion that makes for deceit. A medium counterfeits, a clairvoyant improvises, for fear of proving inferior to their genuine gift.

Only Elise and the 'sleeping woman', both of the rue Caulaincourt, rent the veil of the future, and with assured hands. But then the sleeper died, worn out and cadaverous from the slumbers demanded of her. The astounding 'woman with the candle', Elise, underwent an eclipse which desolated the faithful:

'Do you know what, Elise can't *see* any more! It's a calamity!'

'Impossible! What's happened to her?'

'She's taken up with a curé and all at once she can't see any more in the candle.'

A joyful verbal publicity announced the restoration of the wonder-working:

'You know, she's not with the curé any more. All of a sudden she can see again in the candle!'

For many years Elise, with the end of a kitchen-knife, exploited the candle that her clients used to bring between skin and chemise, and that she held, inclined and lighted, over a plate. Peremptory, foul-mouthed, capricious as a wild ass, Elise would speak, or not speak. She would open the door of her small apartment herself. 'Is Madame Elise at home?' A look — the pop-eyed glaucous gaze that seemed overcome by myopia — and Elise would reply: 'No!' or, more gently, 'Go ahead, come in.'

She scraped the melting wax that spilled from the lighted candle. She teased the wick, which became long and black. She wandered incoercible among unexpected deaths, hidden illnesses, accused events which would remain dormant and disguised for years to come. If her client, sometimes taken aback, did not implore her silence she would continue to overflow with whining and coarse expressions, with 'You don't half give me a headache!' or 'I don't care a fuck for any of that!', with details of a barely believable crudity and infallibility (fact):

'A fine marriage. Yes, there'll be a marriage. But as for children, that's another matter. No kids.'

'Why, madame Elise?'

'Because the young man has poor spunk.'

I soften the expressions. . . .

I once had the good fortune to hear Elise — every great artiste has his moment of triumph — amble through four years of the future, describing accurately, naming misfortunes, announcing an imminent drama 'in a country beyond the sea. . . .' (Chevandier de Valdrôme was assassinated by his cook in Casablanca), the inheritance that would follow, the financial problems:

'Ah, what lawsuits there's going to be! For three million, no more, no less, there now, that'll teach him, that one, to buy so many foreign bonds! It's the same with this young girl, they're off for a spree at the spas, much good that'll do them! She'll get hold of his three millions in the end, but can she hang on to them, eh? Three, four years and then, in the can! She's had it all right, she's had it.'

She smiled into space, above the plateful of congealing wax.

'They don't know anything about it, not them.'

Suddenly, at the height of her prophetic fire, she would fall silent, yawn noisily, press her forehead, and wipe her swollen eyes with a corner of her apron. Painfully she would return to earth among us. . . .

I was introduced to her, at the beginning of the '14-18 war, by Mme Paul Iribe, the first of that name. This beautiful young woman, Jeanne Dirys, intelligent but without talent, tried her hand in the theatre, in business and in marriage with incorrigibly bad luck. Accustomed to Elise's infallibility, she often made an appearance at the rue Caulaincourt, as she might have visited an opium den. But opium lies sometimes, and Elise fuddled her with the truth. Far from employing the wily modes of information to which minor soothsayers resort, Elise refused to know the names of her clients, the names of countries and towns, or portraits. She wore her mystery entire, her waggish humour, the disordered knowledge she had of our destinies, her brief charity: 'When I'm talking to someone I predict everything, except death,' she used to say. She would add, with a disdain clothed in frankness: 'They'll stand anything but that.'

Whom else should I think about, peaceful and solitary, if not the transients of my life, those passers-by whose illegible but firm outline permits neither explanation nor forgetfulness?

The sleeping woman of the rue Caulaincourt was far from the level, the everyday level, of Elise. She was a poor little grub with a face the colour of a blanched salad, barely alive between two slumbers. Asleep, she fell at once into an invalid posture, twisted over to one side like some of the children at Berck, her neck all crooked. To get her to speak it was necessary to hold one of her soft, boneless, inexpressive hands. Apart from the oracles in her little girl's voice, her appearance and her touch frightened the timid. But the dismaying unvarnished future truth had chosen to pass through that wretched body, and pass it did, unpityingly. It wandered therein, blocked by islets, held up at every turn of its course, slowly disgorged, mingled with the crackle and smell of the onions that one could hear frying in a small adjacent kitchen.

Eight

As well as the need to see only a very few faces, to hear a small number of voices, there takes shape, paradoxically, the need to decipher this fine masked design for which a pair of eyes, a solitary nose and mouth suffice. It's in the light of this thirst, this minimum of sociability, that I let anyone in. And then, the old politeness, learned and never forgotten, which insists on one salutation being answered by another, on the consent to a request. . . . The glazed door of the 'bull-pen' half opens, the stranger enters. . . . He has his purpose. His weapons are inquiry, the request for an article, simple curiosity, a business proposition. Since the war I know nothing of him or her, while they have an old stereotyped image of me. He tells me, she assures me, that a very important journal, due to 'come out' soon, would like to know. . . . They imagine that I could not forbear to burst forth on the world with an opinion on votes for women, the purge, the role of the young girl in the new order, reform of the theatre, the closing of restaurants, the questions of paper and housing. He asks, she begs, for an account of my literary projects. . . .

There they are, on the edge of the divan which I use for working and being ill, the divan-raft on which I've floated for so many years. They're seated on those small tapestry-work chairs which I enjoyed covering with an old design, which testify to a well-ordered solitude. And for a time allotted, fortunately by me, I am their prisoner. Appearing to find their presence natural, it is I who feel on trial. What can be more normal than to quake in the presence of the young? Maybe they too are inwardly uneasy. They think that I have some general ideas. It is not f-r me to inform them that I exist on those funds of frivolity that come to the aid of the long-lived. That a time comes when one has to choose between bitterness, pessimism as it used to be called, and its opposite, and that my choice was made long since — or let us say, more accurately, that it is flaunted.

I have no other recourse, where they are concerned, than to stare at them. It's a difficult profession they've embarked on. The war has not taught them anything about it. Their ingenuousness shows through their offhand manner and it may well be that their assurance is as deceptive as my own. Not that it prevents them from having the great advantage of manipulating the question-mark, an aggressor's weapon. I can interrogate only their faces. What is the origin of that precocious wrinkle? Of that scar round the neck? Of that forlorn look in so young a person? Of that profound fatigue betrayed by frequent long respirations?

'Would it be tactless, madame, to. . . .'

Of course. Before the end of the sentence I know perfectly well that it will be tactless.

'And among your literary projects, madame, are you. . . .'

The speaker is twenty-two or twenty-three years old, with the volubility of an old stager, a blond curl that falls over his eyes. If I did not see his fountain-pen shaking I might take him for self-assurance personified. Plans, my lad? But of course. At sixty-three years of age, less a quarter, one still has plans. I've no lack of them. I plan to live a little longer yet, to continue to suffer in honourable fashion, that is without complaint or rancour, to rest my gaze on faces like yours — you look like my daughter a little bit — to laugh quietly to myself and also to laugh openly when there's cause, to love those who love me, to put in order what I shall leave behind me, the bank deposit as well as the drawer of old photographs, a little linen, the few letters. . . . But these plans are not for you. And I reply to you gravely, young man charged to investigate, responsible so young:

'My plans. . . . Hmm. . . . I don't want to talk about them for a few months. . . . No, no. . . . By that time possibly a volume of memoirs. . . . As for the novel. . . . Oh, no! I couldn't tell you anything about my method of working. . . .'

I keep a straight face. He makes a note. I add a few hesitant words, a gesture, behind which he may choose to descry an expanse of great thoughts. . . . There, it's over. He goes off with a piece of American chocolate I've given him making a bulge in his cheek. He leaves by the wrong door — Pauline has gone out — he enters a little shower-room and apologizes to it, he enters the glacial little room with a glass ceiling which lets in the rain, wanders into the lavatory in the hall, tries to close behind him the front-door which only obeys a password — in short he's gone and I am left to ponder on what that young hanger-on calls my method of work. 'Perhaps you might have among your notes, madame. . . .'

He seemed to find it quite natural that I should have a method of work, and even that I might wish to keep it secret. He himself certainly has one . . . I should have interviewed *him*. . . .

Among my notes. . . . What notes? I shan't leave a single one behind me. Oh, I've tried! Everything I wrote down became as sad as the skin of a dead frog, sad as a plan for a novel. On the strength of those writers who do make notes, I had made notes on a sheet of paper, and lost the paper. So I bought a notebook, American style, and lost the notebook, after which I felt free, forgetful, and willing to answer for my forgetfulness.

Not a note, not a notebook, not the least little scrawled indication. Whence, then, were derived my anonymous heroes? The first of them all, that Renaud whom Claudine married, is inconsistency itself. This ripe seducer, born of the imagination of a young woman still girlish enough to believe in ripe seducers, I had no sooner created him than I took a dislike to him, and as soon as he gave me the chance I killed him off. His death gave me the feeling of having attained a kind of literary puberty, a foretaste of those delights allowed to the praying mantis.

But the Maxime of *La Vagabonde*, the Jean of *L'Entrave*, were hardly any better. Neither of these two transcends the level of the male extra. Not knowing how to deal with my own inadequacies I condemned them to idleness and allotted them as fields of action only the bed or the divan. Sensuality is no career for an honest man. I did not venture again to depict lovers devoid of scruples.

With Farou, of *La Seconde*, I felt rather more at ease and my fine fellow was less artificial. Cosily ensconced between wife and mistress, Farou leans against both, acquiring a little life from two female rivals who do not hate each other. Who have not hated each other. Who will not hate each other. Who grow old with a high opinion of each other, without ever completely forgetting the contempt they had nursed for the man's peculiar cowardice. . . . So-called *roman à clef*, how you tempt us! How you incite our pen, not to deny, but to establish the sentimental truth which binds two women and their tolerable unhappiness in the service of one man!

Young man, I should have answered you: 'Yes, I have met Chéri. We have all met Chéri, endowed with his meteoric characteristics.' Perhaps you wished, young man, vaguely disturbed, to go into what you privately call 'the story of a gigolo'. The word ages gracelessly, evokes I don't know what nervous tic. Why not 'diabolo'? Why should a young demon not boast a name as amiable and charged with menace as himself? The story of a diabolo. . . .

Oh yes, I've met Chéri, more than once, just as I've met other temptations. To every woman her own trouble, and the comparison she makes of it with different troubles. No doubt I shan't make myself well understood if I say that, for me, Chéri has a symphonic value. His mutism conveys the disintegrating power of music, borrows disorder from instrumental and, especially, vocal timbres. A voice — such a voice! — that rose from an Italian tenor, ugly, old and fat. . . . Another voice which emanated, very improbably, from a Prussian singer named, barring orthographic error, Von zür Mühlen, a worn, feeble, almost exhausted voice which sang very rarely in Paris around 1900; after an hour's concert he would dismiss a red-eyed audience. The career of a great neurotic artist is brief; this one began to detect, in every gathering of music-lovers, a man or woman with the evil eye and every time he would refuse to sing or stop in the middle.

The link between Chéri and music appears less close when Chéri sings out of tune. If he sang in tune, his charm — using the word charm here in its malefic sense — would be definable, even admissible. I do Chéri the honour of comparing him to music only because the latter is the delectable agent of all melancholy. Potent, incomplete, Chéri is *par excellence* the one who can make a well-informed woman, orientated towards precise goals, lose her great gusty laughter, her gaiety and assurance. From the moment when she realizes that Chéri, even in subjection, is not a case of appetite alone, that, though useless, he is yet irreplaceable, that a glow, an expression, a feature, mysterious as an indecipherable signature, are affixed to him, generic and tenacious, she still has time to accept or decline the danger.

I could not wholeheartedly affirm that the Chéri, the '*fils Peloux*', of my novel resembled anyone. But I should lie if I said that he resembled no one. In the presence of such a young man, silent, grave, mistrustful, admired, I have thought: 'In tears he would be even more beautiful.' But I did not imagine that I should be able to make him shed these tears. He whom, in my novel, I call 'the inaccessible bearer of light', whom I endow with 'an illiterate majesty', keeps us at a distance, even after our embrace, with an unspoken *noli me tangere*, by subsiding into a silence which is, perhaps, a premature mourning for his own beauty. Chéri is no more capable of eloquence than of laughter. Attacked at his weak points by his audacious partner, it is by silence that he regains his arrogance.

I speak of him with an authority that I do not mistake for infallibility.

Thus it was that I patiently dealt with the various queries of the fair-haired reporter. If people talk to me about Chéri and his fate, or about Sido, I exhibit competence and complacency. I know where my best work as a writer is to be found.

At one point it seemed to me that the young reporter overstepped the bounds of his mission. 'Madame, did Chéri . . .' — he blushed, which made him look three or four years younger — '. . . did Chéri ever exist?' He realized that, even for a journalist in 1945, the question was rather pointed. It's of no importance to establish whether, in some place or other, a very old young man, now bent and grey, escaped the suicide I inflicted on Chéri. But it pleases me that my youth of obscure birth, with the melancholy of a very handsome man which constrains him, finally, to a barren purity, should have influenced a wide public, if only by tickling their curiosity.

It once happened, in the course of a lecture tour, that I arrived at a spa where I was welcomed to the station by an unexpected chattering and charming group of young girls who had spontaneously delegated themselves to meet me. Speaking at the tops of their voices and all at once, they eagerly imparted a great secret:

'Madame, we've got Chéri! Yes, madame, we've had Chéri in person for some days now. We're mad about him! Anyway, if you come to tea with us — oh do! oh do! — you'll see him go by, it's his time for tennis, you'll recognize him right away, it's Chéri himself!'

Naturally I did as they wished and I saw their Chéri, who was certainly not mine, or Léa's. If I kept silent, it was not from admiration. But that everyone should model Chéri in their own fashion, isn't that just what I wanted?

He received more than praise, the 'naughty child' whom I laid on Léa's bosom. Men were hard on him, especially those whose youth had departed. Those most affected by the great evil of age showered me from above with words of severe and disinterested disapproval:

'What can you be thinking of, my dear,' said one of them, 'to want to draw our attention to a type as exceptional, not to say improbable, as your Chéri? And those people, those whores, those. . . .'

Instead of reacting like a chestnut in the fire, I kept quiet. I acknowledged that virtuous masculine incompetence might treat a lover devastated by a unique love as a 'pale gigolo', and a 'leech-like queer'. For the first time in my life I felt morally certain of having written a novel for which I need neither blush nor doubt, a novel whose appearance massed partisans and critics round it.

And I was able to put on airs in obtaining my reward from women alone, when Chéri became a success. Here I evoke the phalanx of 'Léas', masked combatants, invincible, bare of face and breast. . . . They had an indescribable way of recognizing each other, of applauding me and becoming my friends, of showing their fealty in a look, a squeeze of the hand. The most beautiful, the closest also to her total ruin, once wordlessly cried to me the 'Ah yes, yes!' with which Balzac scorched the lips of Veronique Greslin, lover of a Chéri as young and culpable. . . . Another, full-blown, like a rose crumpled under the weight of a happiness whose hours were numbered, profited from a solitary moment to tell me 'all' in three words rendered disarming by a smile, a sigh:

'Ah, the swine. . . .'

She departed. She wore a blue mohair dress, like Léa, a leaden blue that went very well with her grey-blue goura's crest,* and thanks to her long skirt no one noticed that her ankles were swollen. . . .

See how the visit of this young sprig of a journalist has taken me back with his determination to talk to me of plans and future! Who will succeed him on the edge of my boat?

Come in, it's the appointed time, you whom I call my idleness and my recreation. Come in, just a few. Come in, you who scratch at my door to spare me the shock, the alarm of the bell, you whom I do not name, whom I do not describe, whom I do not despise, whom I respect. Come in with your rubber boots or your fine tailor-made costume, your woollen scarf round a muzzle frozen by the wind of your bicycle. Don't be afraid of me, neither your name nor your story will be found in these pages. Come in, still braced and dazzled by music, you who have suffered melting snow and wintry blast to hear a fine concert. Come in, you who run in search, every day, for what you and yours need. Put down your inseparable basket, let's extol the clandestine slice of hake, veal chop or coffee; let's share the dirty trick of honest folk embroiled in the foul traffic, since one must eat. Come in, you who travel from the steppes of Neuilly for me, just for me!

Come in, my neighbour the poet, my neighbour the playwright, my neighbour the scenario-writer, my neighbour the

* The goura (Goura coronata) is a large crested pigeon of New Guinea and adjacent islands. (Tr.)

painter, come in all of you in a single personage — like a grey-hound, tall and mobile. You are like those shrimps of translucent agate, the colour of water save for the last little alga they've swallowed; one can see your alga inside you : a five-pointed star.

Come in pairs, my charming frock-coated doctors, exclaim how well I look; in exchange I'll let fall some brief remarks on your professional fatigue, unmatchable prescriptions, advice on régimes. Come in, yet another, turn round so that I may see your new dress, your lumber-jacket lined with real sheepskin. There slip in among you one or two men who always have an habitual air of jays surrounded by a flock of tits. It's because you're alive and still such as the war has fashioned you, prompt in decision, quick in talk, glad henceforward to contradict the opinions of the man you protected. . . .

Talk to me about the cinema, about painting. I'll read you the latest letter from the wives of the small farmers, alone on their flat Normandy earth, who struggle for their existence and that of their livestock, reduced almost to nothing, read in the snow the delicate tracks of the hen-stealing fox and his busy brush, deliver the cow at three o'clock in the morning in the great silence. Not a man on the farm, not a man to fork the litter, to saw the wood, tend the colic of the aged horse. . . . Two women, as solitary as if they were on a reef. . . . Let us admire and pity them; before you go, warm your little cold paws under my stuffed quilt. A moment more. . . . 'Let me tell you about. . . .' We know how to laugh, and very well. But just a word, the mention of a date, an anec-dote, and there reappears fleetingly on our faces the old expression of the women you were — destitute, hunted, partnerless. . . . If one of you here should be called to the telephone, she stops laughing, she coughs as if something had gone down the wrong way, she says in a feeble little voice : 'Oh dear, what can they want of me?' She, no more than I, likes the doorbell, the clock striking, loudspeakers, sirens. A whole family of sonorities has become hateful to us, since. . . .

Nine

Night, O Night, sighs the Arab chant, O thou Night once more. . . . When I embark on night in the name of rest and, if possible, sleep, she is already half-engaged in her course towards the limpidity of morning. We go to bed very late, my companion and I. But how to limit the length and seduction of these evenings that make us aware of the solidity, the substance, the silence of Paris? It is midnight, one o'clock, half past one. . . . Our routine eventually separates us, obedient to its rites. 'Yes, I've bolted the front-door.' But as the door doesn't hold fast. . . . Never mind, it's best to bolt it. 'If you don't feel well, give me a call.' I swear to do so. But this oath is only a codicil to a pre-existing convention which commands respect for a neighbour's sleep. Respect for this — to me — so surprising form of complete repose : the creature which, going to sleep at night, neither stirs nor opens its eyes till the following morning. Once I had to shake my best friend out of his long and deep slumber, from which he emerged with a start, and I had the time to observe on his forcibly reopened face that his startled awakening will doubtless always bear the date of December 12th, 1941. . . .

The door closed between us, I am free not to sleep, to wander around a little, to limp unconcealedly, to go and eat what's left of the marmalade. There's no noise to give me away, I've charmed the latches and hinges long since.

I hesitate to call those nights bad that the arthritis chooses to torment my leg and hip. There is, in the pain that comes in bursts or waves, an element of rhythm which I cannot entirely condemn, a flux and reflux whose autonomy grips the attention. What I call honourable suffering is my dialogue with the presence of this evil. Standing, it stops me from walking, but lying down I can hold my own against it. The proof lies in the absence from my bed-table of any analgesic or hypnotic drug. Pain, save for a few rare failures of my will, I've waited for you to withdraw from this limb you torment and you've withdrawn. You've not yet succeeded in making a morass of my awakening, my tongue bitter, my sleep clouded with pale and suspect marvels. . . .

It's not forbidden to read at night, when one is ill. But it's rather like being a spoilt child, seeking to shorten the night's darkness. Darkness or slumber, which is the most pressing? 'Have the maximum number of sunny hours', counsels hygiene. If this is to the detriment of the dark hours, I protest. The night has its various needs, and insomnia satisfies at least one of these if we do not insult it with great parade of lamp and book. Are we so tormented by remorse or grief that the shade becomes our enemy, and the night-bird can only tolerate a night wounded by a thousand lights? My mother used to tell me ('Off we go again,' as Lucie Delarue-Mardrus might have said. 'We're back to her mother already, her cat can't be far away!') with astonishment that my elder half-sister, when she was young, was infatuated with the night, during which she neither slept nor cried but 'thought' in her cradle. Her blank eyes, wide open, contemplated the darkness with a precocious air of vigilance and good humour, and as she grew up she remained faithful to the shadow.

The lamp relit at my bed-table, I reproach myself for having suppressed those points of light which — in the absence of the big moon — the small moon, Vesper, and the stars grant us after dark over Paris. A kind of dawn haloes the Conseil d'État, betrays beyond it the lighted regions of the city. In the beautiful blue-black tinges of my room a luminous wand attaches itself to the hands of a watch. Another, as I've said, climbs the cruppers of the little gilt horse. If I press the switch of my lamp my feeble landmarks, pensive, ranged like the lights of a village, will be eclipsed and the white slab of the book will shine out. . . . I prefer, visible through the gap of the half-open window, a green signal, another desk-lamp, suspended at the very end of the Galerie Montpensier. . . . When the pleasanter season of 'sleeping in the garden' arrives — and it is due — my starboard light will be seen, in its turn, by that other pilot-light down there. Grave guardians of my night. . . . It's from them that, immobile in the depths of

my obscurity, I asked for the *Story of the Sick Child*. Little by
little, they granted it to me. I invented the child and, for the rest,
I went from the green lantern to the golden rings that intertwine
when one is half-asleep. . . . What can no longer be worked out
as a novel can be managed for eighty pages.

Were it not for this arthritic illness, I should not have got to
know those who look after me. Before then, I'd never given a
thought to doctors. In the past, when I was ill, they used to trust
me. If I had influenza or bronchitis they would address me
politely over the telephone: 'Yes, yes, I see, you've been careless
again. Now you know as well as I do, my dear, what needs to be
done. . . . That's right, cupping-glasses at the back, poultices in
front . . . aspirin. . . . Fine! . . . Hot drinks can't do any
harm. . . . And ring me about your temperature this evening!'

Their seeming indifference was a tribute to my robustness.
But now, because of this increasingly handicapped and painful
limb, because of my age, they come without my sending for them
and insist on looking after me almost against my will. They have
determined, if not to cure me, at least that I shan't suffer any
more. They devote to this a private passion which fills me with
delight, not for any hope this may give me but as an index of
their affection. The long hollow needle, masterfully inserted in
the crease of the groin, the gold pin stuck in Chinese style into
the little toe, behind the heel or at the level of the kidneys, and
the 'rays' — I see in these the material emblems of a magic spell.
For real relief there's something much better, there is the spoken
word, the warm hand, the zeal of an individual who, full of his
science and overburdened with work, pretends when he is with
me to be idle, dawdles, turns the pages of a book, lingers, talks. . . .
Forehead against the window, he contemplates the garden of the
Palais-Royal, seems to forget me. . . . Delicious deception, his
back watches me, his neck listens to me, his care envelops me. O
great man who has remained generous, continue to hold my
hand, lay on my cheek your own rough cheek, shaven at dawn,
when you say goodbye. Ask me, as if you were greedy, for a cup
of coffee; thus you can feel sure that I shall do you credit and
that, after the treatment, a cup of coffee will save me from

transient giddiness or dizziness. And see how you love me enough to give me, if I beg for them, the drops, the pills, the lozenges that pain grasps at so eagerly and digests, exhausted, like an insect overcome by formalin vapour. See how you think to yourself: 'She really deserves this respite.' But I don't ask you for them. I reject them even. I've two small tubes here, one of gardenal, the other of dial, still unopened after thirty-four years. I had depended on them once to get rid of a female complaint which was like a good many female complaints. The two little poisons are still sealed. Their intact seal marked the beginning of my defiance, and the distinction I insist on making — I, who cannot face the dentist without a gum full of novocaine — between useful and unnecessary pain. I insist and you shrug your shoulders, you friends who lead me to believe that the medical profession is recruited from the saints. In these February days, when winter melts and becomes sunny, one of you, some man or woman, will come in:

'It's only twelve, I can spare a good half-hour. It's mild out, I'll take you in the car round the Île Saint-Louis. The forsythias are out in the flower market, the sparrows are running like rats among the pots of myrtle. . . . Let's go, let's go!'

Let's go! We'll go, here and there, to see Paris. We'll go alongside a hedge of barrows whose appearance, odour and greenery create an illusion of a food market. We'll go to gaze at the rainy mauve, the misty blue, created by paulownias about to blossom. We'll go to look at Hermes' window, for the sake of a purple and grey scarf, a broad old red-and-pink ribbon, a shimmering grouping on a violet background of the dormant fire of faded flowers, a cluster of golden jewels, scaly as fishes. . . . We'll go to the rue des Archives, where, at the centre of a quadrangle of narrow huddled arches, a Parisian tree, frail and enduring, glitters with buds like a jetting fountain with drops. . . .

We'll go. Meanwhile I drink in the sea breeze that mounts from the Seine; and beside me I sense the stirring, beneath the impressive medical exterior, of the precious gift to perceive and wordlessly to pity human suffering.

Tonight I dreamed that I was on horseback, with stirrups that were a little too long. The delightful swaying, the joy of galloping on a well-worn saddle, the pleasure of feeling a sensitive mouth with my light hand, my dream restored everything of which I had been long deprived. But the probing malignity of reality was not long in returning. I was made aware that I should have to dismount, in order to shorten my stirrups a notch. 'But if I get down, I shan't be able to get into the saddle again *because of my leg.*' An observation too judicious to be acceptable to the logic of a dream; I woke up.

When I dream — I dream but little — I very often delight in what my waking hours wisely deprive me of. If I were to regain the use of my leg, I should go to a boxing-match. I should go and sit in the front row at a wrestling bout. I should go to see a film of some great horse-race, I should go to share, with a muscled rhythm of legs or shoulders, the impact of the fists, the contraction of the loins, the gallop. . . . In dreams I do so.

A few, the choicest, dreams compile a miscellany of places unbeholden to reality, with its more tedious details. A dream occurred one night, then returned again, in such a way that, making my way at night towards a real place, I recognized the staircase of a house in the rue des Courcelles, and its wallpaper in raw jute. But my nights reveal it printed with lions of periwinkle blue, beset with oak balusters, with treads and hand-rails of oak; a forest of oaks, sacrificed to an 1890 staircase. . . . The periwinkle lions are pure creatures of dream, held fast in their oneiric alignment by the most authentic plinths and stylobates in the world. Periwinkle blue, rimmed with a grey-blue border, the mouth heraldically gaping, the tongue a marine helix. More or less upright, they have a heavy open forepaw. Rather English lions, in fact. How lucky that I can't draw. I'd stick them in my margins for you, faithful copies of non-existent figures. I take them for granted now, they serve as a firm link, an indispensable complement, to that pattern which is reality.

One of my colleagues, and not the least of them, has declared that I have no imagination. Now that's a fine state of affairs, if it's true. But what would he say to Mallarmé, quoted by Henri

Mondor? 'In the depth of the dream, perhaps, there strives the imagination of those who deny it its daytime flight. . . .' For sixty years I have peacefully scoured my countryside to flush out one more harvest, another cat or chicken, a twilight, a filial flower, another scent — if I had scoured *the* country, where would the nights and the dreams have strayed? A life slips by, work finishes and begins anew, an estate is mortgaged, crumbles to dust — a war, a love-affair, are born, come to nothing, another war — what's that, another war? Yes, one more. So I ask you, where is one to take one's stand, to find security? Whatever exists through sleep behaves exactly like the estates we frequent and survey in the waking state: 'Not bad at all; but the running water must fail in summer. And then, how to heat in winter a living-room nine yards by eleven! And then it's so inconvenient, that right of way, that path through the vines where our neighbours can walk by us whenever they like. . . .'

I do not have access to the periwinkle lions whenever I wish, nor do I desire it. In excess, I should be bored with my lilac beasts. Down with obsession. But it's to do with a staircase, a building, inhabited in vain for over three years. I had the fortune to add some lions, which themselves revealed to me a second courtyard, in depth, much deeper than the first, I mean than the real one. The lift, which, around 1901, used to stop below the top floor — my own — I repossessed, dealt with, fixed, during a quite severe attack of influenza which kept me feverish and secluded. Should I know better than to be pleased with it? The steel pillar that hoists the cage of the lift is bent. Because of this bend the whole works give a little jump to one side on reaching the last landing. That's the exact moment not to botch — hup, a little jump — getting off on to a narrow platform placed slantingly. Because if you do botch it, that little jump, my word. . . . Well, my word, I can't tell you what would happen since I've never missed it. But I know that I mustn't fail. Thanks to the benevolent presence of the purple lions, which climb simultaneously with my lift, I believe I shall never miss it — except once, a certain time, you can guess which.

However tame, and even insipid, my dreams may be, they

have the power to warm, to colour, to prise open the drowsy, listless flower of sleep. Too tame, they sometimes leave me bad-tempered on waking, irritable as a cat with a broken leg in plaster. And I get fed up with it eventually! And I want my leg! You all seem to find it natural for me to be in this state, that I should be not only 'laden with years and honours', as Laurent Tailhade says, but with pain and disability also. I'm fed up! A miracle, a miracle, by thunder! It's about time! There you are, my best friend, looking at me as if you weren't even worried about me. Upon my word!

'It's just,' he says, 'that I'm not. I trust you.'

With words like that, where does that leave me? I suppress my cries. I don't dare to betray this trust, once again I'm 'very well', I'm 'not at all ill'. Into the first ear held out to the telephone I shall let fall my great imitation of Edouard de La Gandara — don't I still seem to hear him when he used to ring me in the mornings?

'Good morning, dear friend, are you well? Yes, yes, I'm fine, I'm very happy, everything is going on splendidly. A friend is calling to show you the binding I've had done for one of your books, a dark blue and deep pink morocco. It's so marvellous, I never tire of admiring it, what a pleasure to see and touch it! I'm having some fruit sent to you, I only wish it were better. Take good care of yourself for those who love you, including me. . . . I hug you both. . . .'

Without ceasing to extol his life, Edouard de La Gandara left it at around eighty with solemn thanksgiving. He was the brother of the taciturn Antonio de La Gandara who painted Polaire as a young model, the Comtesse de Noailles in blue and silver, her sister, the Princesse de Chimay, in pink, Louise de Mornand crowned with feathers, and many another who, desirous of being painted, had to take sides, to be spirals by Boldini or stiff bamboos by Antonio de La Gandara. I have a bad photograph of him cut out of an illustrated magazine and I keep it, not because he was the well-known painter of his time, but simply because he was handsome. He must have been aware of this, yet he did not condescend to render commonplace, by making likeable, the rather palikere,* grave and haughty character of his entire magnificent person. Edouard, his brother, enamoured of all the arts, chose to be an antiquary. As far as furniture and curios went, he had a bold taste, for it takes a deal of audacity to impose the style of a recent epoch. Edouard de La Gandara's gentleness was afraid of nothing. He was one of the first to adopt the furniture of the Second Empire, the strong colours of their materials, their lasting gilding. . . .

My little writing-desk, with two doors and a flap, which I've moved around with and chipped about for over thirty years, came from him. I acquired this item of furniture, which its owner did not much like, for a nominal sum. 'Eduardo, what's wrong with this little writing-desk?' Eduardo lowered his eyes, hesitated : 'I find it slightly . . . slightly Directoire.' He could not have been more cautious in suspecting a fiancée of being a little . . . a little overripe. . . .

I imitate him badly. I lack the optimistic manner, the suave observance of happiness, which were so natural to him. His last present was an 1860 letter-rack with three compartments, encrusted with mother-of-pearl flowers, to which I've entrusted the care of a small museum of pictures whose disorder is only apparent. At first sight it is difficult to see the connection between a young woman in wide woollen trousers standing on the threshold of a Breton cottage, and a schooner stuck in the calm mirror of a Polynesian ocean before a horizon of flat islands. Nothing can account for a list of the services for Good Friday being clipped to the photograph of another young woman : the latter had too brief acclaim in the literary world : Claude Chauvière. The one a meek stay-at-home, the other a sea-rover, they both died, at a few years' interval, at the same age, Chauvière leaving a few novels and Renée Hamon two accounts of journeys to the Antipodes.

They were worth troubling to preserve; they were wont to say that I helped them, but I believe it was they who helped me. In view of the powerful writer's temperament that destroyed

* Greek: heroic, valorous. (Tr.)

Chauvière's frail organism, the thirst for the Pacific that salted the lips of Renée Hamon, I felt constrained to behave towards them in a manner worthy of them and of myself. 'Save me, madame, pick me up again!' wrote Chauvière to me. 'I've fallen down again!' A little later, Renée Hamon, trembling with inexperience: 'I'll never manage, I'll never manage! I've seen things that are too beautiful, I'll never manage to tell about them!' Can one give the waverer a leg-up without putting one's back to it? I put my back to it, with my whole weight. I smothered Chauvière with sufficient encouragement to bruise her all over. I pointed out to Renée Hamon that a book needs other ink than tears. When their mood changed I felt more lighthearted. 'Oh blessed day, madame,' exclaimed Chauvière, 'I'll have finished my novel in a week! It's made my hand hurt. I am a lion, madame! You can hear me roar a mile off.' Poor little lion, who coughed her last feeble roar one Good Friday. . . . She had wanted to be baptized, and I became her god-mother from July 2nd, 1928. The same day she received her first communion. She received it pale, glowing, almost fainting, so much so that her entire dress shook on her. '*In the chapel of Notre-Dame-sous-Terre, at the Monastère de l'Esvière, at Angers. . . .*' Towards the altar, towards that which is above the altar, she lifted her great eyes, on the point of tears.

Not lured on by me, but roused, spurred on, I found in them my own share of warmth. They would have plenty of time, later, to learn that one gives birth away from the flame, and with calculation.

The greater part of the poetry fell to the less cultured of the two. The little Breton from Auray covets neither literary renown nor the profits its brings — she would like a cutter. She comes from afar, as it is, and would like to return there, for ever. She'd like a cutter, and with the cutter to regain the distant seas, the continents crumbled into islands. The extraordinary thing is that she got them. A long while ago now, she might have been surprised at the bend of a Californian road, asleep in a blanket, her head on her bag, one arm between the spokes of her bicycle, with fifty francs in the pocket of her sailor's trousers — she might have been discovered at table, eating Tahitian pig on a leaf platter. In her feeling for solitude and her fatalism, she might be compared with Ida Pfeiffer, of vagabond memory. But patient, and Swiss as well, Ida Pfeiffer succeeded doubly in her undertakings. She did not possess those qualities, exaggerated in defeat, that ingenuity which led 'the little Hamon', in a Marquesan hut or riding the long swell among the native crew of a schooner — she worked her passage by scrubbing the decks and cooking the rice — to hope that she had at last found her inexhaustible country, unending reasons to exclaim, to weep with admiration, to place at the service of a poetic, a childlike lyricism, a great 'Ah!', a sob, an enveloping gesture. . . .

She described herself quite objectively : 'Tall as a hunting dog, rather low in the buttocks, but nice little breasts.' Add, to this brief and forceful portrait, a shock of crew-cut brown hair, a fine forehead, a proud regular profile. Tidy almost to obsession, the interior of her maisonette at la Trinité-sur-Mer shone, polished like her dream boat, until the day when she exchanged it for clinic and hospital beds.

'If I had any cash, I'd buy a cutter. . . . A sturdy cutter, lying well in the water, with its mainsail, its jib and its brutal boom. . . . A cutter with its cockpit where I could straddle my two legs and grasp the tiller with my two hands. Rough days in the monsoon or in the drizzle of the doldrums, watching the weather-sails and fetching to windward.' Thus the first pages of her book sing of boats and journeys, uniquely loved. If this Breton, devoted to Saint Anne, has received her reward, she sails eternally, cloud-rigged, there up above.

She leaves souvenirs which nearly all come from the other side of the globe, fabrics of bark and fibre, wood carved by knives, murmuring shells spotted like jaguars, photographs, besides those she gave me, where the sea is flat and calm at the edge of a torrent of vegetation. Beneath the dark verdure drowse Gauguin's models. A Maori young man and woman gallop on two horses. Horses and youths are naked, in flowery trappings. This Edenish image forms part of a film made by Renée Hamon in the Antipodes, which constituted one of the variations she tried to execute on the theme : 'If I could buy a cutter. . . .' Her legacy is that of a marine bibliophile; taste and care are rivals therein. But she had concealed from me, as several studies bear witness, that she could have been a painter. The little she left is in sober and scrupulous order, as ready for a voyage as to assume a grave and final immobility. The steadfast spirit had prepared for everything.

Ten

I've spoken about the ordered drawers I shall leave behind, and
the few letters my people will find therein. My best friend hasn't
yet recovered from his surprise when, having brushed aside a silk
scarf, the creased empty envelopes from the last post, a buried
address-book, my thimble, the two pairs of scissors and tapestry-
work mingled in superficial disorder, his search reveals a drawer
within which nothing clinks, dances, or strays. I haven't gone as
far as the drawer containing 'little bits of string no good for
anything' which Robert de Montesquiou claimed to have seen
at one of his female relatives'. But my domestic discipline had
already astonished — what am I saying, offended — Sido in the
old days. 'What cupboards. . . .' she would say. It wasn't a com-
pliment, but something that had to be said. She recognized none
of the personal and harmonious disorder of her own wardrobes,
flowery with dried petals, sprigs of citronella, silvery spiders
which she would shut in for a time so that they might destroy
the clothes moths. I'd run into her in the garden, one hand closed
on its mysterious contents: 'Let me by,' she would say, 'can't
you see I've got a fresh spider. . . .'

My companion, too, is almost offended by my well-ordered
accumulation of papers. He says that it doesn't go with the way
I look. He may be right. But it suits me, it's indispensable to the
need I feel not to be given short notice — you will understand
what notice I mean. To be precise, to be ready, to be in order,
it is all one. Georges Wague used to call me 'What's-the-time?' It
is time to put in an appearance, to be — under the dressing-
gown and woollen pyjamas — dressed, with chemise clean, feet
tidy, the rest also. And above all, no debts. I used to associate
with men for whom a debt was a joy, a victory, a stimulating
pretext for diplomacy, a state of victorious malice, and I could
never get used to it. So no debts, and tidy drawers. After which,

come what may. When one has not been bohemian in one's life-time, why falter at the end in what one most professes?

I am capable of whim only within order, or rather in classifica-tion. On the cardboard boxes in which I collect old photographs, it says: *Animals and friends. Beauty-spots and music-halls. Children and houses.*

The children, my own and those of two other women, are together as I had hoped for in their childhood. They are to be seen in the houses that were their ports of call and my own, and when one of them amuses himself still with the photograph drawer, his attention goes straight to the essentials, that is, to the setting.

'Ah, that's the little building that was knocked down to make a garage. . . . What a strange idea, instead of making the garage behind the barn. . . .'

'Why didn't you say so, then?'

He shrugs a shoulder: 'Much good that would have done. . . .' This one, the oldest, is an oldfashioned child, restrained and dis-couraged by the polite antagonism that reduced to a minimum the relation between father and son. . . .

'Those hazel trees, all the same. . . . Were they red hazel-nuts?'

'Filberts. . . .'

'Filberts, if you insist, you purist. . . .'

On the photograph the clump of filberts is invisible, since it was behind the small building. But the eyes of these former children — my God, the youngest of them is already over thirty — have a special way of exploring these old pictures and of savouring the past through the walls. A snapshot groups the three offspring of different maternal beds. They weren't very hand-some, but the photograph catches them at a moment when they resembled themselves almost tragically, the oldest in his worst imitation of Musset, hair wild, blond and salty, wild-eyed, charm-ing, irresponsible and affected. The second — thirteen years old — enclosed, inward-looking, is a brutal little poet who would have died rather than admit he was unhappy, that he was affectionate, rather than betray the least of his lyricisms. In this sturdy boy the pretty delicate nose, the fine, slightly receding chin, betray the mother's son.

With them is to be seen my daughter, in all the bloom of her seven years, flourishing, impenetrable. She used to walk barefoot on broken seashells and thorns; standing on rocky islets she would cry, 'On board!' and drag some driftwood to the shore, aided by a small Breton playmate over whom she tyrannized. Nothing else is revealed of her, save the nobility, the impatience visible in the photograph, of a seven-year-old body, momentarily immobilized and burning to hurl herself again into the interrupted frenzy.

The boys grew up without becoming over-intimate. One of them used to call me 'My dearest mother', the other addressed me as 'Madame'. Was it perhaps the latter who loved me the best? Since these portraits taken on the wing, on the Breton shore, one's never again seen them half-naked, scored by the porous rock and the salt, one's never again seen them all three together.

Eleven

How strange it is, a life removed from any kind of malice. No more benevolent lying, no more personal abuse. Never again to direct my steps in an unforeseen direction, hardly ever again to choose. . . . I have entered into dependence. 'You wanted someone to take you to the Galerie Charpentier? But you only had to say so! What, you felt like sitting on the *terrasse* of the little *bistrot* to eat oysters? Why didn't you say so? We could have telephoned for a car. . . .'

Impromptu, the pleasure might have had exactly the flavour of oysters on the *terrasse*, its salt, its fresh water, the taste of its glass of rather greenish white wine. . . . It might have had the dusty odour of an antique shop. Impromptu pleasure doesn't bother about a taxi. As it is, I have to account for myself: 'What, you aren't hungry? And why aren't you hungry? I'll go and find something for you. . . .' May I not, without causing too much fuss and bother, lack an appetite?

It could be a good occasion to lament that henceforward I've access only to the liberty of the imprisoned. I shan't do so, for the liberty of the imprisoned is vast and secret, but such an affirmation, if I published it, would gain little credence among the women I care about. They and I have known each other too long. Not that I lose interest in those of them who attributed to me the dangerous gift of persuasion. But I should say nothing to them touching the liberty of the imprisoned. On the contrary, I want to learn from them what they know about the other kind of prisoners, who did not all perish, thank God, before having seen their chains fall away and are now free men, free from everything save their wives. From fear of losing the last of youth a new feminine jealousy, less sexual than its predecessor, attacks noble objects and renders itself ugly thereby. It does not blush to show envy towards the affection that developed among fellow-prisoners in the camps where friendship was the only light, the sole warmth. This friendship, its gleam of tears and joy, its pure and virile bonds, dating from prison, is what more than one woman can hardly tolerate. She knows that a woman can succour without falling in love, but that the man who aids his fellow can hardly avoid becoming his friend. She listens to the tone of the dialogue between the two men, a *tutoiement* injurious, so she believes, to that of love. She takes stock, in her jealous style, and compares: 'It was with that man that he shared, *in there*, the bar of chocolate, the last piece of sugar, the bread. . . . It was with him that he made his miraculous escape. . . . For the sake of this man, who slept by his side, he gave up half his blanket. To me he has given only his life. . . .'

If these pages are published you will read therein, my wicked ungrateful woman, you will read therein, my fellow, that right up to the end jealous white-haired love prolongs the inestimable pain of loving.

The rack decorated with mother of pearl also holds within reach some family portraits, the greater part of whose number are four-footed. Animals who passed through my life and halted there too rarely, animals whose features and expression impose a wave of regret, of posthumous love. . . . I'm not altogether done with talking about animals. I've a lioness here. . . . The glossy postcard merely gives her name: Léa. That's how one treats famous personalities. She is lying beside a man who is talking to her, and on his arm she rests a paw that covers it, a heavy paw, trusting, friendly, palm upwards. One can make out the enormous pads of the fingers, and from these wide fleshy pads the white claws spring like stamens. Those who knew Léa will remember that she accepted her captivity without reproach. But I've no need of their honest testimony. I still know how to read what the face of a wild beast says. The pure gaze that Léa turns towards me tells me enough.

Her portrait lies next to those of animals who were happier, if not more resigned: my last bulldog, despairing at growing old, at growing deaf, at not hearing my voice so clearly, at seeing my features only through a mist. Perhaps she was afraid, seeing me so indistinctly, that I might be in process of dying gradually, and at night, each time I lit the lamp, I would surprise her sitting down, watching, holding me with a stare that blindness rendered bluish.

Thanks to the gifts received from domestic animals, I am finally done with egotism. That is why I call my latest, cat and tomcat, 'my last ones'. I hope to resist the temptation to hear about me the feline language with its hundred inflexions. And as for a bitch, its walks would now be too long for me. I submit to becoming bloated from inactivity as I've no choice, but I prefer my bulldog, with her wrestler's shoulders, to have the regimen that makes for a slender waist, an easy pace, a cool nose and a satisfied stomach. My last one shines in her departed beauty in an enormous glossy photograph, a cinema still taken during the making of *La Vagabonde*. This ephemeral film helped on no star's career. But the bulldog, Souci, if we had so wished, she and I, could have earned me a fortune. She appeared, photogenically black-and-white, ears pricked, wearing her ardent expression, her visible intelligence, tense with eagerness, and the public did not stint its applause. Afterwards she resumed her healthy regular existence, the worship she bore me, her ill-will towards the canine species, the little armchair she shared with the Cat. . . .

It may be that I shan't publish these pages. For this is the first time that I am writing as I please. It's a great novelty in the life and behaviour of a writer to cover pages whose fate is undecided. I've been writing for fifty-three years. For fifty-three years the material worries of life and commitments for fixed dates have regulated my work and my existence. 'I've promised my publisher. . . . It must be ready by November at latest. . . .' Novels, stories, serials, skilful enough treatments of truth and fiction, I've escaped from it all. But now the inability to get about, and the years, make it impossible for me to sin by fabrication any longer, and exclude me from any chance of romantic encounters. Henceforth, I possess only the images which unfold on the screen of my window, only the light of a sky or an eye, a constellation, the marvels enlarged by my magnifying-glass. So it is to the glory of God that I accumulate these sheets, devoid as they are of any deforming agreeable feature, of any dialogue between imaginary characters, of an arbitrary ending that kills, maims, separates. I abdicate from humbug. But they may be neither published nor completed. We shall see. For a start, I do without the interposed typewriter, which used to follow my pen at its own pace. Farewell to its flimsy paper, its pale or muddy inks. Later, if I have need of it, it will be time enough to resort to its honest aid. When I was young I used to fiddle when I was writing and I profited from my ignorance of design, as well as from my literary inexperience, to draw while writing. For instance, if I happened to hit on the word 'murmur' and to grope for the continuation of my phrase, this was the time to affix, under each of its equal sections, a little caterpillar's foot, one of those small sucker-feet which cling so tenaciously to a branch. At one end of the word I would depict the rather equine head of the caterpillar, at the other end the terminal tail, a ravishing appendix often formed of silky strands, like spun glass. Instead of the word murmur I had the caterpillar symbol, much prettier. And I'd dream of Alphonse Allais, who, finding in the country one of those brown, opulent, velvet-haired caterpillars which are the marvels of their species, would exclaim : 'Look, a bear. But Lord, how small it is, how small it is !'

Embellished with insects and butterflies, it seemed to me that my manuscripts did not take things seriously. I miss them. Those that survive are not so good. I'm more attached to the correspondence that I preserve in the same way as the photographs. Writing is a design, often a portrait, nearly always a revelation. That of the poets of the last half-century is entitled to its decorative motifs and I amuse myself with the significant graphisms of Henri de Régnier, Pierre Loüys, d'Annunzio, Madame de Noailles, curlicued, breaking like waves, coiled like viburnum tendrils. The messages of Robert de Montesquiou are calligraphic labyrinths, as are those of Léo Larguier. Wavy poetic gestures, tall leisurely-apposed letters, skilfully contrived margins — such letters are as enjoyable to leaf through as an album, and how can one forbear to smile when they make me recall that Annunzio mischievously used to call me 'Colettina' and 'my sister in St Francis of Assisi' ?

A uniformly pompous grace links together the large recurved arabesques of the poets, inflated, *appliqué*, witnesses to a slow toil where fantasy has become the theme. The politician denies himself this curvilinear licence, this vain but significant ornament, for he lacks the time and his thought is of the crowd. When I look at the incisive writing of Louis Barthou I seem to hear his voice, sharp, a little less nasal than Poincaré's but equally penetrating. The writing of Léon, Louis's brother, makes up for this, indulges in downstrokes and nonchalance because Léon was gay and sensual, and witty too. 'You should know that in 1898 I became a Mohammedan, simply to stop people from bothering me because of my several wives. Don't spread it. And come back soon from Morocco. It isn't true that *la patrie est en Tanger.* (Oh!)'

Philippe Berthelot, Sire of Cats, scrabbles at the paper with little strokes, scratches at Renan's 'stupidity', and signs with the figured imprint of a feline paw. And what a formula of greeting at the foot of one of his notes! 'A little rasp of the tongue, a purring while turning round on the leather of the seat of office. Ph.'

I enjoy this lightheartedness in men who were grave, I'm especially glad that they were pleased to laugh with me. Donnay's pranks appear on letter-cards in little improvised verses:

> O my adorable Colette
> With the violet-coloured eye,
> Every, every, every cat
> Applauds with its four paws
> The most becoming of cravats
> That bedecks their Mistress. . . .
> And the very old tomcat purrs.

'P.S. This isn't a quatrain.'

Gabriel Fauré, at a concert, does a pen-drawing, a very faithful caricature, of the composer Koechlin walking on his beard and sends it to me by *pneumatique*. I find my past enjoyable, illustrated by friends with whom I was frivolous. . . .

I have lost, or given away, a worried letter from Poincaré. He had just been elected to the Presidency and wrote to me that he would be unable to relax at the Elysée because of his much-loved cat: 'What may not happen to him in this great garden? I haven't yet had time to see if the gaps between the railings. . . .' The cat also wrote to me, in fine Italian hand.

The coarse witticism of a refined man: that's Lucien Guitry. A long, limp, agreeable letter, yet marked by vacillation: that's Drieu la Rochelle, after his novel *Blèche*. A small tidy hand-writing: 'Dear friend, do you happen to have in your possession a letter of mine, on dark blue paper if I'm not mistaken? Its rapturous tone, if my memory serves me right, worries me in case it might fall into hands less affectionate than your own. Would you mind returning it to me? Your Louis de Robert.' If I'm not mistaken. . . . If my memory serves me right. . . . I recall that I felt offended by so much caution and that, from sheer mischief, I kept the letter on dark blue paper. Less young, I should have shown myself less susceptible to the punctilious, refined and fragile author of the *Roman d'un Malade*.

The solitary example of the fine handwriting of a man at once cultured, audacious and restrained reminds me that Mendès was a man superior to his work and his life. His letter, too, is a fine one: it campaigns on behalf of a colleague. I couldn't say how it came into my hands, this letter not meant for me.

Another letter:

'Dearest Colette, today makes three months that I've been at Beaujon. I was kept here by force and I gave in. The brutal whirlpool of life mixes the good and the bad so powerfully. It was not for an ignoramus like me to resist. The magnificent devotion I've found at this hospital restores my will to live. Doctor Lion-Kinberg is determined to cure me, but. . . . They give me frightful injections into the lung. My little dog, who comes to see me twice a week, despises me because I'm ill. Perhaps he's right. It upsets me very much.'

That is. . . . Guess? No, you'll never guess. It's Polaire, at the

point of death.* It's Polaire, unknown, unappreciated, her gentleness, her handwriting that of the defeated who seems asleep under
the wind.

I don't want it to perish before I do, this epistolary past. I
bloom so readily in its warmth, it saddens me only when I have
to transfer from one file to the other the letters of a friend who
has left us. We'll keep this photograph of Pierre Louÿs's, I'm
going to stick it beneath the dedication of *Poétique* : 'To Madame
Colette Willy. Why? Why, to teach her to write!' He has a torn
collar, coarse thick hair, curls straightened with water, matted
like cassowary feathers, and the photograph is dated : 1896. I
was not so indulgent to love-letters. Born of the flame, the greater
part have already perished in the flame. A reasoned, reasonable
incineration for which I should not find it difficult to give
excellent motives. Love cast into letters, piously tied with a gold
thread, embalmed in sandalwood, is not free from the risk of
obsolescence, as I know only too well. Perhaps two centuries
might grant a reprieve? As it is. . . . 'Into the fire, you who've
destroyed me!' cries the hero of *Voyage où il vous plaira*, as he
burns his books. Myself neither lost nor saved, it's good to burn
the bushes that once were flowers, the dried herbs with the familiar perfume. Oh, it wasn't a matter of a grand auto-da-fé. Just
a modest burning of the stubble. . . .

I recall a woman I once used to know, one of those whom
the women of my generation knew only by her hair, resolutely
white at her latter end, belatedly, maliciously edifying. She used
to maintain that the preserved love-letter gives no one pleasure,
that it can give rise to a thousand irritations, and that, rather
than create posthumous difficulties, she had destroyed all her
own. . . .

'What, all of them?'

She winked her little old lady's eye, which still shone with the
colour of a great sapphire.

'No. I've kept one.'

'It must have been a very beautiful letter?'

---

* The actress who played the part of Claudine in the dramatization of
Colette's early novel, *Claudine à Paris*. As a publicity stunt, Willy, Colette's
first husband, used to take them about together dressed as schoolgirl twins.
(Tr.)

'For me. I know it by heart. Shall I tell it to you?'

She let her gaze, not devoid of majesty, wander over her well-kept gardens, her overflowing kitchen-gardens, her luminous sheets of water, and recited:

'The key will be hanging behind the shutter.'

'What's next?'

'That's all.'

She paused before adding:

'Believe me, it was enough.'

It is rare for a bacchante past her prime to refrain from extolling, and if necessary inventing, her sensual adventures. Yet I seemed to see on the cheeks of this one a surge of vainglorious red. A moment later, and once more she was all slander and malicious smiles and, God forgive me, I was imitating her. . . . But it's a style that hardly suits me, this affectation of frivolity about love. Love, bread and butter of my pen and my life! Whenever I sit down to speak ill of you, to disown or deny you, someone rings and the shock causes me to blink with the corner of an eye, to twitch a shoulder, a souvenir of the day when what I gained from you was taken away, that something that comforts me till the end of life. . . . I offer you my apologies, Love, victorious opponent, and to whatever name your final flowering may bear. . . .

Stirring in the moist air, the bud tells as much of the season and its progress as the flower it cradles. The explosive season is on its way, bringing its beneficent humidity. In the mornings, at dawn, the odour of mist fills my room. 'It's unhealthy,' says Pauline as she shuts the window. But I delight to feel the mucous membranes of my nose as moist as a dog's, not to have a struggle against the ageing dryness of the air.

Those who are healthy, or just young, are full of plans, and the theatres with old pieces brought up to date. Weekly magazines blossom, as numerous as the daisies on one of Dubout's lawns, and the art galleries send invitations to their private views to 'Monsieur Colette'. The stranger who has just telephoned pressed me to take on a lecture tour. . . . A tour! My word, they must think I'm still only fifty. It's a long time since my talks.

I've sent the two little farmers' wives, alone on their reef — paper being scarce everywhere — two great bundles of lined sheets, hieroglyphs rather than manuscripts, spattered with abbreviated words, with signposts in the form of stars, crosses, little snaky indicators like those along the roads. My memory, my eyes, will no longer need to refer to them on any platform. They will do to wrap up a piece of butter, a rabbit, a pair of sausages whenever a pig departs this life. . . . No regrets!

What a life for a woman, the lecture tour, after ordinary touring, and what a dismal task to travel alone — for, if not, what would become of the miserable pittance — to carry, alone, one's suitcase at arm's length, to defy hoarseness and to capture, single-handed, the sympathy of the public. This solitary expense of spirit, when I recall it, has not always taken first place in my more comic adventures. At La Rochelle the obscure alley labelled 'Artistes' Entrance' straddled a black streamlet and led into a glacial hall where, alone, seated at a white wooden table. . . . At Cannes, in hail and ice, I struggled alone against fever, decked with cupping-glasses, sitting on four injections of camphorated oil. At Aix, that same winter, so that I might change my travelling costume for my 'smart' dress, the coffee-room next to the cinema was placed at my disposal. I recapture the clear December, the mistral that threw icy needles and flakes of flint in my eyes. . . . The cold weather in the Midi is no joke.

Don't pity me, there was no occasion for whining, or even for boredom. At La Rochelle I missed the train for fun, because I couldn't tear myself away from a little shop under the arcades which sold — not to be found, even then — magnificent glass marbles, 'taws' stuffed with varicoloured spirals, as beautiful as the 'sulphurs' (I've still got them). In Avignon I rushed through my autograph session, after my 'chat', to hurry to Señor Rafael Paz y Ferrer in his house of marvels, brimming with mother of pearl, twisted glassware, rainbow-dripping chandeliers, pearled embroidery. At Hyères, seriously delayed by the stopping train, it happened that I 'lost' the hall where I was due to speak a few minutes later. I couldn't remember its name, I looked in vain for a poster. I ran as one runs in a nightmare, I couldn't find a car. . . . As you see, none of this is really sad, any more than I was really alone. Is one really alone, in cities and ports?

In what gloomy decrepit theatre was it, at the beginning of an hour of difficult campaigning, that I heard a great cry? Suddenly I saw a lady rise up, standing on an orchestra stall, who tucked up her skirts to her armpits, yapping: 'A mouse! A mouse!' While she was liberally displaying her . . . emotion, a man's voice announced: 'The lecture includes astronomical slides,' and I was not the last to laugh till I cried.

Traversing the centre of France, from La Roche-Guyon to Vichy, from Vichy to Ax-les-Thermes, by car to save time, I was assailed by a heat so ferocious that I took fright and told the driver to stop the car in the shade of a solitary tree. A moment to rush down the slope and I was sitting fully clothed in the little river that flowed down below there. I stayed there for a while, half-immersed, my linen skirt ballooning in the water round me, in a fish-soup of river bleak, crowned with the heavy green-black dragon-flies that haunt the sugary spikes of the meadow-sweet and the umbels of the pink hemp. . . .

At Marseilles, once, I found myself involved in an acrobatic turn, in an immense hall where everything bore the marks of the makeshift. A white wooden step-ladder led me, in full view of everyone, from the orchestra pit to the stage. From the stage a step-ladder reached the heights of a planking established in the flies, so that I might be visible from every point in the hall. Up there tottered a platform, a small table, a desk-lamp from which a flex descended towards the murky eddies below. . . . Hardly had I sat down than the lamp went out. . . . Amid laughter I saw a sort of kinkajou climb up who dealt with the lamp and descended again. He had just got down when the lamp went out again. . . .

The Marseilles public tends to oscillate between two extremes: tender familiarity and ferocity. I felt it swinging from one to the other. Perched over the void and holding the flex which threatened to drag down the lamp, I held out against vertigo. . . . Suddenly Marseilles, so highly strung, lost its temper. Then I had the idea of imposing, if not silence, at least attention. Pointing to the kinkajou mechanic, down below at the end of the wire, I cried: 'Shh! It bites!' And this phrase brought me a great reward of laughter, shouts and Phocacean objurgations whose intent was no longer dubious.

Was all that worth recalling? All the same, I do recall it. Where would I find tales of great deeds? I have never been anything of a pioneer. So leave me to my mice in Caën and my marbles in La Rochelle. I may not always be able to exclude from my painful memoirs and intermittent felicities the posthumous and frenetic life of the divided snake, the wriggling of the headless beetle. But it's quite enough, to enlighten me as to what it is that undoes me as if I were a young woman, it's quite enough — the ring at the door, the start of the shoulder, the quiver of an eyelid.

Twelve

It's Sunday. The garden is empty, empty my house. I've sent off my best friend to whatever pleases him. To what is moist, already turning green, is still bare. My daughter? Somewhere in occupied Germany, where she is collecting material for an impassioned dispatch. Or in a gloomy Parisian lair where she is writing a poem that she won't let me read. Or in her eyrie in Corrèze, planting her garden. She loves her ruin, where the ripe stonework flakes off and which she fills with roses and fruit-trees. She'll come back when she feels like seeing me, her gaze the colour of the shadow under a chestnut-tree and her mouth like a little pot of strawberries, as people used to say. She turns up unexpectedly and I issue some traditional bits of advice: 'Have you got a vest under your coat? Your skirt is too short. Watch out for the traffic. . . .' She laughs. We laugh. Perhaps our laughter, in some indefinable place, disturbs sleeping generations of mothers, who murmur in concert: 'Your skirt is too short. . . . Watch out. . . . Under your coat, have you got . . .', then subside and go back to sleep, having performed their maternal duty for the moment. Perhaps one, whom I once knew, sighs as she used to sigh in life: 'Ah! That little one. . . . My God, that little one. . . .' That little one was fifty-five.

The garden is empty. Empty the house, except for me. This almost daily apprenticeship in silence and hermit-like existence is far from unpleasant, and where nowadays could I find reasons for being miserable? This leg. . . . Yes, we know. Enough about this leg. We'll do without that. I am a normal old person, that is, one who is easily amused. Miserable old people are abnormal, sick or wicked. Sometimes they have the excuse of being frightfully oppressed by the generation they have engendered. Which is certainly not my case.

Worse still is the lot of the spruce survivor, stuck with the

Colette

heavy, over-palatable fruits that he gathered in his prime. He resorts to false aids, little pills, granules, a sadly too-physical culture, the weighing-machine and other beauty products. . . . His motto: 'I shall maintain' is not as good as mine: 'Taciturn but not serious.'

The solitude I cherish today seeks its despondency in the context of my past solitudes, which neither received nor sought support or saviour. Though I was in need of everything, I was unsubmissive to 'whosoever asks shall receive'. I did not ask.

In a confused period of the war, the last war, which disposed of our persons and our possessions, expelling many of us far from our home and work, I received a letter from Edouard Bourdet. With much precaution, circumlocution and subterfuge he tried to make me accept what he possessed in ready cash. I was so close to crying out of friendship that I replied in some such pathetic manner as: 'My God, how stupid you are!' But I had to promise him that, should the occasion arise, I would not seek any other creditor. Since then, still young, kind and handsome, he has been summoned to meet the overwhelming necessity. . . .

I've taken advantage of my solitude to sort out my papers. The rather testamentary nature of such a duty isn't enough to put me off. One of these days I shall attack the photographs, but that will be more for amusement. My photographic museum is so gay! No one represented therein casts a gloom on it, not even those to whom a somewhat secret memory might be attached. Does one discard the effigy when one has burnt the letter? Yes. . . . No. . . . All the same, one of these days. . . . Tomorrow. . . . And then I weaken, I waver, I shift the author of the burnt letter into the small group of good friends, I incorporate him therein, let's shuffle the mixture well. This is in no way a dismissal. Quite the contrary, the newly-admitted finds a place among the most worthy: Eugène Landoy, who poses with his faithful parrot, the composer Louis de Serres on a little cardboard horse, the procession of the children of Saint-Sauveur entering, for their prizegiving, the *bistrot* which used to place its 'ballroom' at the disposal of the primary schools. . . . A magnificent print: the portraits of M. and Mme Cornet, old employees of my father. The Douanier himself could not have set them better in their little garden in their Sunday best. And who keep them company in the same drawer? Why, La Duse, wearing her signature like a bandolier, poignant, misty and proud — a little malicious nonetheless, it was stronger than she. . . .

And then a young woman, all ringleted, a graceful young woman, ironic, lanky. . . . How I enjoyed the way she used to tell me about the best part of her life: 'I eloped with Maître Chéramy at the end of a dinner-party where I'd met him for the first time. Just as I was, in a moonlight spangled dress. . . . I didn't come back till eleven years later.' Charming, isn't it? (I made use of the episode in the second act of *Chéri*, Mme Peloux *dixit*.) To run away in a cab, perhaps in the rain, the beautiful moonlight dress getting soaked, the frozen young shoulders warmed in the embrace. . . . Perhaps I ought not to have written Maître Chéramy's name in full? Oh, never mind! I can afford to allow myself this small indulgence: to be veracious now and again. The woman was sufficiently beautiful, sufficiently elated, for the lover — I remember he wore large side-whiskers — to tremble with pride, if he hears me in his eternal rest.

I have here, in my disarray where nothing is mislaid, a collection of pretty faces in the style of the day before yesterday. Actresses? Yes, actresses. Famous? Yes. Who's this one? Guess. But you'd never guess. It's only Cléo de Mérode, whom I've never been able to fit into the pattern. She has never changed.

Changed. . . . I finish writing this word and raise my eyes. Was it a magical word? Everything is new. The new, the springtime, arrive as I write. The Palais-Royal stirs at once under the influence of humidity, of light filtered through soft clouds, of warmth. The green mist hanging over the elms is no longer a mist, it is tomorrow's foliage. So soon! Yes, once again it is the sudden season. Let's continue to write; next time I lift my head it may be summer.

If I want some frank enjoyment, I arrange the photographs

bequeathed to me by my dumb career as a mime. In everything
to do with the music-hall I encounter a genuine naïvety. Acro-
bats and dancers, experienced in strength and grace, become
wooden in front of the lens. There's not much difference between
their portraits and the 'animated' scenes filmed by the late
Méliès. I reserve my keenest pleasure for a photograph where
my good friend Georges Wague threatens my breast with a knife
which is, at the very least, Catalan. I drop my eyes, I half open
my mouth for a (silent) cry, but I don't forget, despite the
urgency, to bring my left leg forward, knee slightly bent, in the
manner of a *diseuse à voix*; Georges Wague, in profile, reveals
that he has a gold ring in the lobe of his ear, a false 'rabbit's foot'
between ear and cheek, and an unparalleled ferocity of gaze. He's
going to stab this proffered breast — this pretty breast. . . . But
because the field is so narrow, he has more the air of intending
to tattoo his touching victim with the point of the dagger. . . .

And what do you make of this wild girl, shyly ensconced
beneath the skin of a newly-killed lion? You might think it rare,
in the jungle, for the skin of a newly-killed lion to boast a fringe
of cloth festooned with small teeth, and you would be right. But
I, I caress with my gaze this dentate cloth, rival of the dancing
shoes with Louis XV heels with which are shod, in egalitarian
fashion, the Olympian goddesses, the beggar-maids and the
ondines, of the music-hall. And then, let's face it, one had to
restore, intact, the tawny bedside rug which had been supplied,
on loan, by a furrier's.

And this one, and that one! Oh, that beautiful blue one! I'm
standing on one foot, Paul Franck supports my waist without
having to kneel more than half-way, my other foot steadies me
as best it can and the whole forms a strangely polypod grouping.
It is apparent from the picture that my role is that of a (very)
ragged vagabond, for the hem of my skirt is suitably slashed
with scissor-cuts.

And this one, with a knife between my teeth! And this one,
dressed as a man, with long trousers! Can I believe my eyes? . . .
This one (I shall destroy it, it's too ugly) commemorates a spell
at the Théâtre Royal — 6, rue Royale — which, despite its name,

held only some sixty seats. I was playing there in a little comedy, *Aux Innocents les Mains pleines*, what's called a really Parisian piece. As Parisian as my Burgundian accent, as the honest author from the Midi who did not sign it, and as the tailor who made up for me a striped maroon lounge-suit, a worthy Belgian named Van Coppenolle. As proof that I'm not lying, I got thirty francs an evening, matinées included, and Yves Mirande played on the same stage in a piece by Yves Mirande, *La Bonne Hôtesse*. Only he acted well. His partner? A short slender beginner, a marvellous comedian, one. . . . Victor Boucher. . . .

I used to listen to them, both of them, behind a set, and I bore them envy because they enjoyed themselves so extravagantly. . . .

The section 'artistic photographs' isn't so bad, either. Draped poses. Aspirations to the Greek. A small pedestal, consisting of an old Bottin concealed under some drapery. Reutlinger would have preferred me to hold a dove perched on my head. I rejected the stuffed pigeon, though it wasn't more ridiculous than the Greek drapery.

And this one? More rags? Yes, more. Rags, an evil spell and blood scattered about gave a satisfactory result, The new materials were aged with the help of acids, if need be I roughened the silk myself with a brick, and rumpling my hair in all directions with both hands before coming on stage, I threaded it with wisps of straw to make believe that I slept in haystacks before setting fire to them. This one here is *Oiseau de nuit*. Rags here, rags there, and a great sweep of rags which I deployed with arms extended behind me like the wings of an owl. In the finale I was nailed against the wall of the farm with jabs of a pitchfork. . . .

Looking closely at this photograph, survivor of a thousand postcards, I find it rather too cheerful, this fatal Bird. An optimistic owl. . . . It was because, though it didn't show yet, I was carrying a child. It's impressive, the smile of a happy pregnancy.

I remember welcoming the certainty of this late child — I was forty — with a considered mistrust, and keeping quiet about it. It was myself that I mistrusted. It wasn't a matter of physical apprehension. I was worried about my maturity, my possible inaptitude for loving, understanding, absorption. Love — so I thought — had already served me ill in monopolizing me for twenty years in its exclusive servitude.

It is neither beautiful nor good to start a child so hesitantly. Not in the habit of probing my future, for the first time I planned for a definite contingency, when it would have been amply sufficient to think four weeks ahead. I considered, I made myself lucid and reasonable. Intelligent cats usually make bad mothers, sinning through excess of zeal or through distraction. They walk their children, seized by the scruff of the neck; the hollow of an armchair is a comfortable nest, though less so than beneath an eiderdown, but perhaps the peak of comfort resides in the second drawer of the chest of drawers. . . .

The first three months, anxious to act for the best, I divulged my burden to almost no one. Charles Sauerwein gave me his advice as a friend and father of a family. One phrase he used struck me : 'Do you know what you're doing? You're having a man's pregnancy. A pregnancy ought to be more amusing than that. Put your hat on and come and have a strawberry ice at Poirée-Blanche.'

Fortunately, I changed, though I wasn't aware of it at first. Those around me began to comment on my good appearance and good temper. An involuntary smirk was to be seen even on the optimistic owl — for I continued serenely to play in the *Oiseau de Nuit*, with its arranged fights, blows with a pitchfork, the hand-to-hands on the table, under the table. A male pregnancy? A champion's pregnancy, rather. . . . And the flat, muscled belly of a gymnast.

But it happened that, at the fourth month, my friend Georges Wague reminded me of the 'Geneva job'. The Geneva job would come up during the fifth and sixth months. . . . I confessed everything precipitately, leaving behind my two dismayed friends, my two partners, Wague and Christine Kerf, to contemplate the ruins of the Geneva job. . . .

Insidiously, unhurriedly, I was invaded by the beatitude of the woman great with child. I was no longer the prey of any malaise, any unhappiness. Euphoria, purring — what scientific or familiar name can one give to this saving grace? It must certainly have filled me to over-flowing, for I haven't forgotten it and I think of it whenever life no longer brings any satisfaction. . . .

One grows weary of suppressing what one has never said — such as the state of pride, of banal magnificence which I savoured in ripening my fruit. The recollection I have of it is linked with that of the 'Geneva job'. For, after the break-up I inflicted on our act, I called Wague and Christine Kerf back and, strong in my fine health and good humour, I re-established our trio and our plans for separating on a sound basis. Georges Wague, moved, pretended that he wasn't, treated me like a broody woodowl, and assured me that my child would be day-blind. On the appointed day we departed and I celebrated my new-found importance by choosing the best room at the hotel. The lake cradled the swans on their reflections, the alpine snows were melting wreathed in vapour, I greeted the Swiss bread, the Swiss honey and coffee, with a smile.

'Look out for the cravings,' said Wague. 'What do you have for breakfast, now you're in trouble?'

'The same as before the trouble, *café au lait.*'

'Good, shall I order it for you when I go down, for eight tomorrow morning?'

'At eight o'clock. . . .'

At eight o'clock the next day there was a knock at my door and a hideously affected little voice chirped:

'It's the maid!'

If you have never seen a sturdy lad, all black hair, lean and muscular, half-naked in a chemise borrowed from Kerf, a red ribbon binding his mane to his brow, and done up in a tailored skirt, you can't imagine how much a gay pregnant woman can laugh. Gravely, her banner of black hair — strange adornment for a transvestite! — over her shoulder, Kerf followed, carrying a small tin percolator and preceded by the aroma of fresh coffee.

Good companions! In order that I might have a breakfast that was not like the 'hotel piss', they percolated fresh coffee, boiled the half-litre of milk over an alcohol flame, bought soft rolls every evening, and left the cube of good butter on the window-ledge at night. I was touched, I was pleased, I essayed my thanks; but Wague responded to this gratitude by assuming his chilly Basque expression: 'It's not for you, it's to keep down expenses.' And Kerf added: 'It's not for you, it's for your little one.'

On stage, that night, during the well-managed combat, I felt a precautionary arm insinuate itself between my loins and the table, aiding my exertion which it appeared to paralyse. . . .

Every evening I said a small farewell to one of the good periods of my life. I was well aware that I should regret it. But the cheer-fulness, the purring, the euphoria submerged everything, and I was governed by the calm animality, the unconcern, with which I was charged by my increasing weight and the muffled call of the being I was forming. . . .

Sixth, seventh month. . . . Suitcases to fill, setting off for the Limousin, a lightheartedness that detested rest. . . . As I grew heavier, especially in the evenings, to ascend the road that spiralled round the hill on the way to my dwelling, I had recourse to my two shepherd dogs, Bagheera and Fils; they hauled me along at the ends of their two leashes. The first strawberries, the first roses. . . . Can I call pregnancy anything but a long holiday? One forgets the anguish of the term, one doesn't forget a unique long holiday; I've forgotten none of it. I particularly recall that sleep used to overwhelm me at capricious hours, and that I would be seized, as in my childhood, by the desire to sleep on the ground, on the grass, on warm straw. Unique 'craving', healthy craving. . . .

Towards the end I had the air of a rat that drags a stolen egg. Uncomfortable in myself, I would be too tired to go to bed and would exhaust the resources of a book or a newspaper in a com-fortable armchair before getting into bed. One evening, when I had exhausted a daily paper up to and including the racing fore-casts and the name of the editor, I sank as low as the serial. A high-class serial, all counts and marquises, carriage-horses that knew no other speed, noble beasts, than the triple gallop. . . .

'Feverishly the Count paced up and down his study. His black velvet indoor clothing accentuated even more the pallor of his face. He pressed a bell; a footman appeared.

"Ask Madame the Countess to join me here," ordered the Count sharply.

In a moment Yolande entered. She had lost none of her energy, but it could be seen that she was about to swoon. The Count held out the fatal letter, which quivered in his grasp.

"Madame," he said with teeth clenched, "have you decided to reveal the name of the author of this letter?"

Yolande did not reply directly. Straight and white as a lily, she took a step forward and articulated, heroically:

"Shit on Ernest." '

I re-read the last line to dispel the hallucination. . . . I had read correctly. The revenge of a dismissed typographer? A practical joke? The Countess's reply restored to me the strength to laugh and to get into my bed, on which the June wind, through the French window, scattered acacia flowers.

Even then, the weight and the tiredness did not interrupt my long holiday. I was borne on a shield of privilege and solicitude. 'Take this armchair! — No, it's too low, this one's better. I've made you a strawberry tart — Here's the pattern for the little bootees, you start by casting on fifteen stitches. . . .'

Neither fifteen nor ten. Neither embroidering a bib nor cutting out a vest nor dreaming of snowy wool. When I tried to picture my creature to myself, I imagined her naked and not bedizened. She was satisfied with a sober and practical English layette, without little lace flounces, without fancy patterns, and bought — from superstition — at the last moment.

The 'male pregnancy' did not lose all its rights; I worked on the last part of *L'Entrave*. The child and the novel drove me on, and the *Vie Parisienne*, which was publishing my unfinished novel as a serial, was catching up with me. The child indicated that it was going to arrive first and I screwed on the cap of my fountain-pen.

My long holiday came to an end on a cloudless day in July. The imperious child, on its way towards its second life, ill-treated a body, no less impatient than itself, which resisted. In my small garden, surrounded by gardens, shielded from the sun, furnished with books and magazines, I waited patiently. I heard my neighbour's cocks crowing and the accelerated beating of my heart. When no one was looking, I unhooked the hose from its stand and sprinkled the parched garden — which I should not be able to succour the next day and the days to follow — with some watering on account.

The outcome. . . . The outcome is of no importance, and I do not accord it a place here. The outcome is the prolonged cry that issues from every woman in childbirth. If I want, even today, to hear its echo, I've only to open the window on the Palais-Royal; from under the arcade there rises the modest clamour of a neighbour who is bringing her sixth son into the world. The outcome is sleep and appetite, selfish and restorative. But it's also, once, the attempt to creep towards me of my little swaddled larva which had been put down for a moment on my bed. Animal perfection! She divined, scented, the presence of my forbidden milk, strove towards my stopped-up source. Never have I wept with so rebellious a heart. What is the suffering of asking in vain compared with the pain of denial?

The outcome is the contemplation of a new person who has entered the house without coming in from outside. The outcome, strangely, is the haughty and final rejection by the austere Beauceronne bitch, who never again condescended to enter the nursery. I struggled for a long time to soften the heart of this abstracted enemy, who would brook no rival in my heart, even to offering her my daughter sleeping in my arms, one small hand dangling, with bare rose-coloured feet, even to telling her: 'Look at her, lick her, take her, I give her to you. . . .' The bitch condescended only to an embittered silence, a look of red-gold that soon turned away.

Did I devote enough love to my contemplation? I should not like to say so. True, I had the capacity — I still have — for wonder. I exercised it on that assembly of marvels which is the new-born. Her nails, resembling in their transparency the convex scale of the pink shrimp — the soles of her feet, which have reached us without touching the ground. . . . The light plumage of her lashes, lowered over her cheek, interposed between the scenes of earth and the bluish dream of her eye. . . . The small sex, a barely incised almond, a bivalve precisely closed, lip to lip. . . .

But the meticulous admiration I devoted to my daughter — I did not call it, I did not feel it as love. I waited. I studied the charming authority of my young nurse, who kneaded and powdered the small body with her clenched fists like dough, suspended it by the feet with one hand. I did not derive from these scenes, so long awaited in my life, the vigilance and emulation of besotted mothers. When, then, would be vouchsafed to me the sign that was to mark my second, more difficult, violation? I had to accept that an accumulation of warnings, of furtive, jealous outbursts, of false premonitions — and even of real ones — the pride in managing an existence of which I was the humble creditor, the somewhat perfidious awareness of giving the other love a lesson in modesty, would eventually change me into an ordinary mother. Yet I only regained my equanimity when intelligible speech blossomed on those ravishing lips, when recognition, malice and even tenderness turned a run-of-the-mill baby into a little girl, and a little girl into my daughter.

In the contest between book and childbirth it was the novel, thank God, that came off worse. Honourably, I had returned to the unfinished *L'Entrave*, which did not recover from the blows inflicted by the feeble and triumphant creature. Consider, hypothetical readers, consider the scamped ending, the inadequate corridor through which I desired my diminished heroes to pass. Consider the fine but empty tone of an ending in which they do not believe, and the modal chord, as a musician might say, so hurriedly sounded. . . .

I have, since, tried to rewrite the ending of *L'Entrave*. I have not succeeded. Between the drafting and the resumption I had performed the laborious delectation of procreation. My strain of virility saved me from the danger which threatens the writer, elevated to a happy and tender parent, of becoming a mediocre author, of preferring henceforward the advantages conferred by a visible and material growth : the worship of children, of plants, of breeding in its various forms. Beneath the still young woman that I was, an old boy of forty saw to the wellbeing of a possibly precious part of myself.

If, exceptionally, when I was young I busied myself with some needlework, Sido would shake her divinatory brow : 'You'll never look like anything but a boy sewing.' Had she not said to me : 'You'll never be more than a writer who has produced a child,'? She, at any rate, would not have been unaware of the fortuitous nature of my maternity.

Thirteen

A first flower, pink as a roofing-tile, appears before the leaves at the top of the chestnut-tree before my window. It is an annual exception. On the summit of this tree there is manifest the beginning of spring and the first rust of autumn. It does not fail to flower again, sparsely, in September. I have always found it faithful in its task. Does it think as much of me? For how many hours, how many days, how many years have I been in this place? The time doesn't seem very long; yet the underside of my right sleeve is visibly worn. I need another working jacket, as warm and soft as this one. Maybe it won't need to be very long-wearing. . . . It's curious, this shininess of the right sleeve, which looks as if it had been much licked by moths. The quite trivial to-and-fro of the forearm on the paper shears velvet, polished silk, wears out both wool and myself. We are a one-armed race. One of my mothers-in-law, the second, was practically ambidextrous. She used to sew with her left hand, wrote with her right, painted and dealt cards with the left. She rediscovered Martin's varnish, was the first to hang her walls with 'chocolate paper', anticipated Iribe and Poiret in their essays towards an art of furnishing. Should one conclude from this that ambidexterity indicates a greater imaginativeness in intelligence and performance than we righthanded ones may possess?

The weather's fine. The lawn absorbs the recent rain. The business of the gardener about the flower-beds promises us that, after five years deprived of flowers, we shall once again have the red, pink and violet harmony which distinguishes the Palais-Royal in September. The weather is that of a premature May. I suffer in very bearable fashion, in a rhythm of twinges and waves that I can capitalize musically, as one does the pistons of a train. One of my medical friends has arrived to try out a new and unpublished treatment: injections of a thermal water brought from the source. That's something new, something entertaining. So long as the cure won't have gone out of fashion next summer. . . .

Mme Odehowska's tame nightingale has paid me a visit, with its mistress. It has drunk from my thimble and slept on my shoulder, clothed in the sombre livery, brown streaked with black, of a Polish nightingale. When its beloved mistress summoned it to depart, it betrayed her momentarily by refusing to follow her and whispered something in my ear, then, seeing her go out of the door, uttered a cry and rejoined her. Snug in her corsage, between silk and skin, it went off to take the Métro. One day when it flew off and got lost in the Métro, Pouli had the good sense and composure to stay still on the ground, almost black and very conspicuous against the white stoneware of the wall, waiting, hoping. It saw the arrival of her who sought it, threw itself into her arms. . . . Haven't I anything better to write today? I doubt it. What is it that prevents me from putting a final full-stop here? No part of this miscellany is intended towards a peroration or an apotheosis. 'When will you decide to let us have your memoirs?' Dear publisher, I shan't write them any more, any better, any less than today.

My publishers are all younger than I am. On the evidence of their elders who witnessed my beginnings — their names were Paul Ollendorff, Alfred Vallette, Arthème Fayard, the elder Flammarions, Ferenczi the father and Albin Michel the father-in-law — I believe that their juniors have formed a confused but highly-coloured impression of my life. God forgive them, do they expect a sort of *journal secret*, in the style of the Goncourts? But 'where there is nothing, the king loses his rights'. The publisher too.

It's taken me a long time to scribble some forty volumes. So many hours stolen from travelling, idleness, reading, even from healthy feminine stylishness! How the devil did George Sand manage? That sturdy woman of letters found it possible to finish one novel and start another in the same hour. And she did not thereby lose either a lover or a puff of the narghile, not to mention a *Story of my Life* in twenty volumes, and I am overcome by astonishment. Forcefully, she managed her work, her recoverable sorrows, and her limited pleasures. I couldn't have done as much, and where she thought in terms of the stacked barn, I have lingered to contemplate the green flower of the corn. Mauriac consoles me with the biting praise: 'Where hasn't she foraged, this great bee?'

At the moment she is making a very little honey from the two flowers — they are two now — on the pink chestnut-tree. The day turns towards evening. Is not everything evening, vespers, for me? The days not so much miserly as rapid. Is not the sixth boy who was born this week under my window beginning to walk? The oldest of the six, shepherd of this male flock, leads it to the garden, where it scatters. To get them back again he collects them together, carrying one of his lambs under each arm. They grow like chickens, the one who was crawling begins to run, the one who had his hair done in fat ringlets is cropped like a man, and I get mixed up among them. Everything alters the moment I take my eyes off it. The life of a virtually immobilized being is a vortex of hurry and variety.

What used to make me proud for so long — my competence as a handyman, my acquaintance with hammer and nails, rake and dibber — must be replaced by mere show.

At the age I've reached, didn't Sido wrestle hand-to-hand with the enormous 'Prussian wardrobe', pierced by a bullet in 1870? It's all over for me now, my pride as plumber and cabinet-maker. I pretend to no usefulness other than my existence, and even this utility I confine to those who love me. And having, for half a century, written in black on white, I've written in colours on canvas for the last years.

The blunt needle in my fingers, I guide the wool caught in its oblong eye. My women friends say that I amuse myself thereby, my best friend knows that I find it restful. Simply, I've found my aim therein and have decided that the foliage shall be blue, the marguerite varicoloured, the cherry enormous and marked, at its equator, by four white stitches.

My talent for tapestry-work, as you see, is not recent. This primitive stitchwork, the childhood of the art as it were, I did not dare to make the art of my childhood. The 'boy who sews' thereby unburdens himself of a secret, assumes a satisfying occupation, endorses a virtue nourished by tradition. It was one tactfully adopted by you shadowy young girls of the nineteenth century, stifled in the maternal gloom and drawing the needle. . . . Balzac has an eye on you. 'What are you thinking about, Philomène? You're overstepping the pattern. . . .' Three stitches too many on the tracing of the slipper meant for her father, and Philomène de Watteville will reveal her deep and criminal preoccupation. . . . But she undoes the three stitches that overstep the pattern and begins again, invisibly and perilously, to weave the ruin of Albert Savarus.

The parallelogram of the cross-stitch is so arranged as to give us the illusion of curves. Four stitches outline the round pupil of an eye and sixteen its iris, two hundred constitute a plump strutting dove. A frenzy of ingenuity bewitches the patterns of the cross-stitch. What other art makes use of so many hearts and turtle-doves, forget-me-nots, sheep, umbilicated roses, cushions that say *Papa*, medallions that swear *Friendship*? On a tombstone — is it not so, dear Dignimont — there prays a dog in little squares, while around the mausoleum there flutter cabalistic words such as ABC, DEF, GHIJK, QRSTU. . . . But, leaving on one side the stammerings and the emetic emblems, we find in the best periods of cross-stitch those impetuous flowerings, those colours, which electrify the 'elect'. Either I'm mistaken, or it really seems to me — from the canvas sails, the woollen rigging, the convolvulus flowers which nurse empurpled starfish in their azure funnels — it seems to me that I'm entering harbour.

Some years ago Christian Bérard was attracted by tapestry-work. He was bound to succeed where others had failed, and he filled aristocratic ladies with enthusiasm for the work. These are known not to be the soul of constancy. There remains, I think, of their fine fervour some heavenly blue armchair sewn with ermine tails, some little teneriffe figure with a Sevigné hair-do on a pink background. Then affectation and zeal saw to it that cross-stitch joined macramé and the netting embroidered with darning-stitch in oblivion. To my knowledge, only Mme Lanvin now does tapestry-work because of a desire to do tapestry-work, that is, to project on to canvas the surplus of her raging creative faculties.

It's not for me to say whether my exertions in cross-stitch embroidery are in any way supererogatory. I pierce, I pierce again. The eel of a needle shines between two threads, tows its woollen tail. My memories are written in blue foliage, in pink lilac, in varicoloured marguerites. I shall begin from nature the portrait of my evening star. My thousandfold repeated movement knows all the tunes by heart. 'We scribblers,' Carco used to say, 'we are the only ones who can't sing while we work.' My new work sings. It sings *Boléro* like everyone else. It sings: '*Croyant trouver de la bécasse au bas des prés. . . .*' It sings: '*Quand j'étais chez mon père — Petite camuson. . . .*'

To unlearn how to write, that shouldn't take much time. I can always try. I shall be able to say: 'I'm not concerned with anything here, except this rectangular forget-me-not, this rose shaped like a jam-puff, this silence when the sound of excavation produced by the search for a word has been suppressed.'

Before reaching my goal, I continue to work. I don't know when I shall succeed in not writing; the obsession, the compulsion date back half a century. The little finger of my right hand is somewhat bent because, when writing, the right hand supports itself on it like the kangaroo on its tail. Within me a tired mind continues with its gourmet's search, looks for a better word, and better than better. Fortunately, the idea is less demanding, and well-behaved provided she is well decked out. She is used to waiting, half asleep, for her fresh verbal fodder.

All my life I have taken a good deal of trouble over strangers. Reading me, they fell in love with me and sometimes told me so. Clearly, I can't expect a piece of tapestry-work to win them over in future. . . . How hard it is to set a limit for oneself. . . . If it is necessary only to try, all right, I'll try.

On a resonant road the trotting of two horses harnessed as a pair harmonizes, then falls out of rhythm to harmonize anew. Guided by the same hand, pen and needle, the habit of work and the commonsense desire to bring it to an end become friends, separate, come together again. . . . Try to travel as a team, slow chargers of mine : from here I can see the end of the road.